The Red Book
Eat Well in Wales
Y Llyfr Coch

Intro

Welcome to the first edition of *The Red Book*.
I hope this guide will help you to eat well in Wales.
A decade ago Wales was described as a gastronomic desert! – a hard comment to swallow for those who were already working hard to raise food standards in Wales. However, in the past ten years this industry of sourcing, preparing and presenting good food has come a long way.

The Red Book bears testament to the energies and aspirations of those in the hospitality industry in Wales who today are able to provide the public with top-quality eating experiences. It is the first independent guide to recognise and highlight those cooks who work with such commitment to achieve their goals.

The Red Book is no ordinary guide. It encompasses the whole sector of "Eating Well in Wales" from youth hostels to pubs, the small cafes to the grandest hotels. It promotes good cooking created from the best of local fresh ingredients. All are welcome to apply to *The Red Book* for the necessary inspection which must be passed in order to qualify for inclusion.

Criteria for entry to the guide are simple. The requirement for every entry is the same, whether large or small. The team of six inspectors is looking for cooks who follow that one golden rule, "DO WHAT YOU DO WELL". Whatever the size of establishment, it must achieve its aspirations. The energy and enthusiasm of the staff is always a good sign, and our inspectors take time to talk through the aspirations of each place they visit. We are looking for good scones and jam for tea, the very best home-cooked food in the pub, and top-quality cooking with the best of local ingredients when paying for an expensive meal.

That said, please note one proviso: clearly a farmhouse with three bedrooms cannot offer the same breadth of cuisine as a restaurant run by a team of chefs. The price of the meal should reflect the skills in the kitchen as well as the overheads of the establishment. On inspection, we have taken this into account, and we ask our readers to do the same.

The Red Book is much more than a guide. It offers readers information on every aspect of eating and shopping for local produce. It examines the geography of Wales to show which flavours mark out one region from another, the history which has influenced the food of today, and suggests which regional ingredients to expect on the menu. *The Red Book* also provides a guide to shopping for the best Welsh ingredients. Welsh cheeses and wines are listed, and there is a selection of recipes from some of the establishments listed.

Compiling this first edition of the guide has been a challenge, and at times I wondered why I put my head above the parapet; yet there were always friends to offer a tin hat! I wish to thank my team, all of whom have kept their sense of humour; we hope it shows throughout *The Red Book*, along with our enthusiasm for the rapidly improving prospects for diners throughout Wales.

Published by Western Mail Books

Editorial
Gilli Davies, editor in chief
Martin Greaves, gazetteer entries
Manisha Harkins, contributing writer and researcher
© Gilli Davies Ltd 1997

Design and Typesetting
Andrew Jones, Carol Williams, Karen Avery, Rosemary Dymond-Ward,
Special Publications, Western Mail & Echo Ltd
© Western Mail Books

Advertising
Ceri Richards, Western Mail

Cover Design
Peter Gill Associates

Photography
Wales Tourist Board Photolibrary

Printed by
Stephens & George Ltd, Goat Mill Road, Merthyr Tydfil, Mid Glamorgan.

With special thanks to Ann Boston, Ken Goody, Chris Chown, Meic Watts, Rhian Nest James, Harry Williams, Allan Fletcher John Cosslett and Gren Jones, and to the Wales Tourist Board for their support with the launch.

Entries in The Red Book represent the views of our inspectors at the time of their visit. The details quoted in this guide are as supplied to The Red Book and to the best of the company's knowledge are correct on going to press.

All rights reserved. No part of this publication may be reproduced, stored in a retrieval system, or transmitted in any form or by any means, electronic, mechanical or otherwise, without the prior permission of the copyright holder.

The Red Book
Gilli Davies Limited
Glebe Farm, St. Andrew's Major. CF64 4HD
Tel: 01222 514141   Fax: 01222 514142   E.mail: 100755.3423@Compuserve.com

ISBN: 1-900477-03-3

The Red Book
Eat Well in Wales
Y Llyfr Coch

Sponsors and Partners

British Gas L P Gas

Cegin Cymru - Antur Teifi

Midland Bank plc

Palser Grossman Solicitors

Terry Platt Wines and Spirits Co

Vin Sullivan Foods Limited

Wales Tourist Board

Welsh Quality Meats

Contents

Introduction	1
Acknowledgements	2
How to use the Guide	4
The Red Book Awards	8
Regional Flavours and Shopping Lists	10
The Red Book Entries	
North Wales region	47
Mid Wales region	81
South & West Wales region	103
Youth Hostels	157
A Welsh Wine List	159
A Welsh Cheeseboard	161
A Selection of Recipes	163
Tidbits...Memorable Quotes	174
The Gastronomic Desert	176
A Chief Inspector's Cry	177
Application Form for 1999	185
Readers Recommendations & Red Book 1999 order form	186
Maps of the regions	
North Wales map	188
Mid Wales map	189
South & West Wales map	190
Index	191

How to use The Red Book

Quality is the main priority of The Red Book, with great emphasis given to the sourcing of the ingredients, the standard of cooking, the service and the general ambience of the establishment.

Where there is accommodation, this is noted with a description of the type and number of rooms and their cost. Where possible, we list the price of special breaks – based on a two-night stay for one person sharing a double room.

Additional discounts often apply for stays of three nights or more, while in many cases there may be a supplement for single occupancy.

Once you have decided where you wish to stay – or dine – book ahead if you can to avoid disappointment. Many of the smaller establishments are busy all year, and find it difficult to cater for those who turn up unannounced.

All establishments listed in The Red Book, have passed a demanding inspection by one of our team. Those establishments who failed to gain entry this time have been offered advice and will be encouraged to re-apply.

The Red Book has divided Wales into North, Mid and South and West, and all entries are listed alphabetically under the nearest town or village which can be found easily on road maps.

Since this is the first edition of The Red Book we will particularly welcome your comments. Perhaps you would like to recommend some other excellent establishments and help us to improve our next edition. Or you may feel that an establishment fails to meet the standards we have set. In this case, please first discuss the problem with the proprietors before contacting us. Good or bad, we are keen to know. Forms for your comments may be found at the back of the book.

■ *This symbol appears beside entries where our inspectors found excellent use of local ingredients.*

Key to Symbols

 Chef proprietor (i.e. one of proprietors or their family personally cooks or supervises all of the cooking).

Cogydd berchennog (h.y. un o'r perchnogion, neu'r teulu, sydd naill ai'n paratoi'r bwyd neu yn cadw llygad ar yr holl goginio).

 Wide choice of vegetarian dishes available: usually also cater for special diets.

Dewis helaeth o lysfwytawyr ac, fel arfer, darpariaeth hefyd ar gyfer anghenion arbennig.

 Good selection of Welsh cheeses available.

Cynigir amrywiaeth dda o Gaws Cymru.

 Children's portions or menus, usually with facilities for children, e.g. high chairs.

Plateidiau bach a bwydlen arbennig i blant, ynghyd â chyfleusterau, fel rheol, megis cadair uchel.

 Food is served and can be eaten outside.

Darperir bwyd ac mae modd bwyta y tu allan.

 Single cigarette symbol – No smoking in the dining room.

Un sigaret – dim ysmygu yn yr ystafell fwyta.

 Double cigarette symbol – No smoking at all, or in limited areas only.

Dwy sigaret – dim ysmygu o gwbl, neu, mewn llefydd cyfyngedig yn unig.

 Access to premises and accommodation suitable for wheelchairs.

Mynediad i'r adeilad a'r ystafelloedd yn addas ar gyfer cadair olwyn.

 Full range of beers, including real ales.

Dewis helaeth o gwrw, gan gynnwys cwrw go iawn.

 Wine list which offers especially good choice, quality and value for money.

Rhestr winoedd yn cynnig dewis ardderchog, safon uchel a gwerth am arian.

For Example

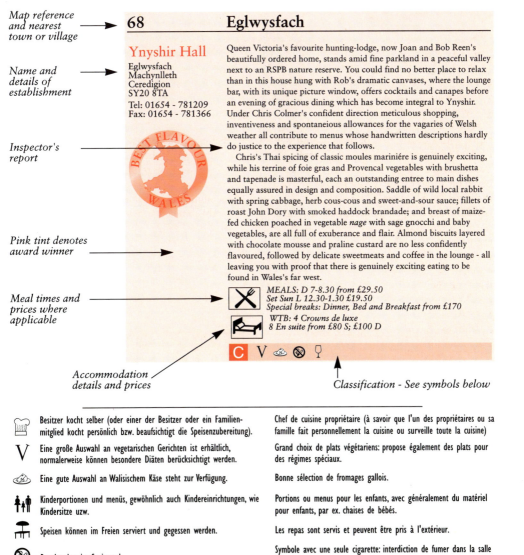

Map reference and nearest town or village → **68 Eglwysfach**

Name and details of establishment → **Ynyshir Hall**
Eglwysfach
Machynlleth
Ceredigion
SY20 8TA
Tel: 01654 - 781209
Fax: 01654 - 781366

Inspector's report → Queen Victoria's favourite hunting-lodge, now Joan and Bob Reen's beautifully ordered home, stands amid fine parkland in a peaceful valley next to an RSPB nature reserve. You could find no better place to relax than in this house hung with Rob's dramatic canvases, where the lounge bar, with its unique picture window, offers cocktails and canapes before an evening of gracious dining which has become integral to Ynyshir. Under Chris Colmer's confident direction meticulous shopping, inventiveness and spontaneous allowances for the vagaries of Welsh weather all contribute to menus whose handwritten descriptions hardly do justice to the experience that follows.

Chris's Thai spicing of classic moules mariniére is genuinely exciting, while his terrine of foie gras and Provencal vegetables with brushetta and tapenade is masterful, each an outstanding entree to main dishes equally assured in design and composition. Saddle of wild local rabbit with spring cabbage, herb cous-cous and sweet-and-sour sauce; fillets of roast John Dory with smoked haddock brandade; and breast of maize-fed chicken poached in vegetable *nage* with sage gnocchi and baby vegetables, are all full of exuberance and flair. Almond biscuits layered with chocolate mousse and praline custard are no less confidently flavoured, followed by delicate sweetmeats and coffee in the lounge - all leaving you with proof that there is genuinely exciting eating to be found in Wales's far west.

Pink tint denotes award winner →

Meal times and prices where applicable → MEALS: D 7-8.30 from £29.50
Set Sun L 12.30-1.30 £19.50
Special breaks: Dinner, Bed and Breakfast from £170

WTB: 4 Crowns de luxe
8 En suite from £80 S; £100 D

Accommodation details and prices →

Classification - See symbols below →

	Besitzer kocht selber (oder einer der Besitzer oder ein Familien-mitglied kocht persönlich bzw. beaufsichtigt die Speisenzubereitung).	Chef de cuisine propriétaire (à savoir que l'un des propriétaires ou sa famille fait personnellement la cuisine ou surveille toute la cuisine)
V	Eine große Auswahl an vegetarischen Gerichten ist erhältlich, normalerweise können besondere Diäten berücksichtigt werden.	Grand choix de plats végétariens: propose également des plats pour des régimes spéciaux.
	Eine gute Auswahl an Walisischem Käse steht zur Verfügung.	Bonne sélection de fromages gallois.
	Kinderportionen und menüs, gewöhnlich auch Kindereinrichtungen, wie Kindersitze usw.	Portions ou menus pour les enfants, avec généralement du matériel pour enfants, par ex. chaises de bébés.
	Speisen können im Freien serviert und gegessen werden.	Les repas sont servis et peuvent être pris à l'extérieur.
	Rauchverbot im Speisesaal.	Symbole avec une seule cigarette: interdiction de fumer dans la salle à manger.
	Vollkommenes Rauchverbot oder nur in bestimmten Bereichen.	Symbole avec deux cigarettes: interdiction de fumer partout, ou seulement dans des zones limitées.
	Zugang zu den Räumlichkeiten auch für Rollstuhlfahrer geeignet.	Les personnes en chaise roulante peuvent accéder au restaurant et à l'hôtel.
	Große Auswahl an Biersorten, einschließlich "real ales".	Grand choix de bières, y compris des ales.
	Weinkarte bietet besonders gute Auswahl, Qualität und Preis-Leistungs-Verhältnis.	Liste des vins qui offre un choix, une qualité et un rapport qualité-prix particulièrement bons.

The Welsh National Culinary Team has been formed from members of the Welsh Chefs Circle, with the aim of promoting Wales and its food to the world. The team represents a wide variety of specialist skills, and each member will be able to demonstrate his own strengths. All members give freely of their time and effort and are backed by the owners of their various establishments. The Team is affiliated to the newly formed Welsh Culinary Association.

WELSH
NATIONAL
CULINARY
TEAM

UNDER THE AUSPICES OF THE LLANDUDNO HOTELS AND RESTAURANTS ASSOCIATION

The National Chef of Wales 1998

Sponsored by

WELSH QUALITY MEATS LTD

Neyland - Pembrokeshire

1st Prize: £650 and Trophy
2nd Prize: £250
3rd Prize: £100

For rules and conditions please contact:
Mr John Retallick, Emlyn Arms Hotel, Newcastle Emlyn, Carmarthenshire.
Telephone - 01239 710317

WALES
Great Little Places

Find out about Great Little Places, a collection of 50 small hotels, guest houses, farmhouses and inns. Their blend of quality, individuality and value for money has made them famous. 'Great Little Places' include everything from luxury farms to coastal hideaways – you can even stay at a genuine castle, Welsh vineyard, historic mansion or lighthouse!

For your free brochure please contact:
**Great Little Places, Prince's Square, Montgomery SY15 6PZ, Wales, UK
Tel (01686) 668030   Fax (01686) 668029**

WELSH RAREBITS

Welsh Rarebits is an exclusive collection of Wales's top hotels. Welsh Rarebits members include luxurious country house hotels, historic inns, lakeside retreats and coastal properties. The emphasis is on quality, individuality. and value for money.

For your free copy of the brochure listing 40 personally selected places to stay, please contact:

**Welsh Rarebits,
Prince's Square,
Montgomery
SY15 6PZ,
Wales, UK.
Tel (01686) 668030
Fax (01686) 668029**

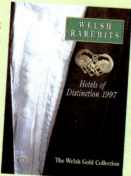

We're Cooking With Gas

advertising feature

Gas is the choice of top cooks, chefs and consumers everywhere and Gilli Davies is no exception. She chooses to cook with gas because she thinks there's nothing to beat it for controllability, speed and convenience.

Unlike electricity, when you turn the gas down it reacts immediately making it far easier for sauces and other recipes that require slow steady heat. However, many people who live beyond the mains gas supply believe they can only cook with electricity.

British Gas can solve this problem. It helps more and more people enjoy the benefits of gas by extending its services to include delivery and installation of liquefied petroleum gas (LPG). This means that turning to British Gas LP Gas could make dinner party disasters a thing of the past.

There are a wide range of cookers that run on British Gas LP Gas available at your nearest Energy Centre or independent stockist. For example, the Leisure Rangemaster 110 is a stunning double-oven free-standing range-style cooker with two automatic ovens, a non-stick griddle and a separate waist-level grill. It is available in Racing Green, Regal Blue and Claret with the distinctive contrast of non-tarnishing brass-effect control knobs and door handles.

Its more compact sister the Leisure Rangemaster 55 gas cooker is a family-sized oven that offers all the features you need to help your meals turn out like the picture in the recipe book.

Other leading manufacturers such as New World, Parkinson Cowan, Cannon and Stoves also have a wide choice of cookers that run on LPG.

In addition to using gas for your cooking it is also available for your heating and hot water requirements, with a wide variety of boilers for central heating and hot water, as well as fires and tumble dryers that run on LP Gas.

The LP Gas tank can be installed either above or below ground. If you decide to bury your tank underground, British Gas LP Gas can give advice on companies who can carry out the excavation work or you can handle it yourself. British Gas LP Gas will also check the new installation to ensure that it is safe, and carry out regular inspections when the fuel is delivered direct to your home.

Once the system is installed, British Gas LP Gas keeps track of how much gas has been used so that the gas is delivered regularly and reliably without you having to worry about it. In fact, British Gas LP Gas is so confident about its delivery service that it offers compensation if you should ever run out of fuel.

In addition to the installation and delivery, British Gas LP Gas can also arrange expert advice on systems and appliances. For example, British Gas LP Gas offers advice as to which appliances are available and will direct you to your nearest Energy Centre or independent stockist. British Gas LP Gas also provides a 24-hour emergency back-up service.

British Gas LP Gas covers most of the country. Simply call the Sales Centre on **FREEPHONE 0800 574 574** to receive free advice, further information and bring an end to those dinner party nightmares. A no obligation visit can be arranged free of charge.

← *Leisure Rangemaster 110-LPG Model*

The Red Book Awards

Test of Time

This award is given to Franco and Ann Taruschio, of the Walnut Tree Inn, Llandewi Skirrid, near Abergavenny, for the enduring quality of the food they serve. Franco and Ann share a determination to use only the finest ingredients, and this award is a token of our appreciation for a couple who lit the gastronomic torch in Wales 35 years ago, and have ever since led the way in producing some of our best cooking.

Three Inspirational Chefs

In the eyes of our inspection team, three exceptionally-gifted young chefs are cooking to a standard that is lifting the image of culinary Wales. They each display great skills, creativity and flair and a confident resolve to put Wales on the map in terms of good eating.

We applaud

Chris Colmer, Ynyshir Hall, Eglwysfach, Machynlleth.
Jason Hornbuckle, Tyddyn Llan, Llandrillo, near Corwen.
Shaun Mitchell, Plas Bodegroes, Pwllheli.

Tip Top Tea

For those who appreciate top-quality home cooking, Liz Hainsworth has created a mecca at Bramleys Tearoom, Plough Penny Field, St Florence, near Tenby. With a menu of two dozen home-baked cakes, magnificent pastry and gutsy soups and snacks, Liz has set a high standard and amply deserves the award.

Hospitality Off The Beaten Track

At Llanerchyndda Farm, Cynghordy, Llandovery, Nick and Irene Boynton's welcome is surpassed only by their genuine hospitality and desire to please their guests. Nick's enthusiasm for local wildlife is infectious, and Irene has the perfect refreshment after a day out – whether tea and crumpets or a bowl of steaming soup.

Best Bistro

Deborah and Martyn Peters have set a hard-to-match standard at Woods Bistro in Talbot Green over the past three years, with consistently adventurous, innovative and imaginative cooking. Their growing clientele particularly enjoy the good-value lunch from a versatile kitchen.

A Unique Welsh Gift......

For that special someone!
A special gift, from a special place!

Whether it's to celebrate a special personal event such as a birthday or anniversary, or to recognise an outstanding achievement at work.
Our unique gifts will commemorate the occasion in a unique and memorable way.

Traditional wicker hampers and elegant baskets filled with the finest Welsh wine and foods.
A unique quality gift for a true friend or just a fine reward for a colleague or member of staff.
Whatever the occasion
          - whatever the budget.

Call now for our new free catalogue:
Cegin Cymru Cardiff on 01222 577018
Cegin Cymru Aberaeron on 01545 570460
Cegin Cymru Llandovery on 01550 721452

Bwydydd Cymreig o safon
Quality Welsh Foods

Flavours of North Wales

By Manisha Gambhir Harkins

North Wales is for many the essence of Wales, distinguished by the lofty heights of Snowdonia and the sea-girt Isle of Anglesey across the Menai Strait. Although mostly a mountainous region, it is easily accessible via the A55 which links England to all of North Wales. The region has a long and varied coastline which stretches from the solitary Lleyn Peninsula, whose outstretched arm separates Cardigan and Caernarfon Bays, to the Dee estuary along the English border, and boasts plenty of fish and shellfish all around. In the centre of the region is the fertile Conwy Valley, while a good coastal stretch and pretty Victorian piers lie further north.

To the east are the borderlands of Denbighshire, Flintshire and Wrexham where agriculture and commercialism happily coexist. With Merseyside and Cheshire so close by, the combined influences of the Welsh and English are prevalent in this corner of the North in terms of both culture and food.

North Wales is shrouded in mountains, myth and a turbulent past with Celtic tribes, valiant princes and castles having left their lasting imprints. Beaumaris on the Isle of Anglesey, Caernarfon and Conwy, amongst others, were medieval castles built by Edward I during his conquest of Wales. Named after its highest peak, Snowdonia – or Eryri – is the largest national park in Wales and is a magnet for mountaineers and tourists. Traveller George Borrow wrote in *Wild Wales* in 1862, "Perhaps in the whole world there is no region more picturesquely beautiful than Snowdon." Despite the rugged terrain of Snowdonia, North Wales has plenty of arable land and excellent grazing.

Hidden between mountains, lakes and sea is a rich industrial heritage. Copper was mined under Great Orme's Head in Llandudno around 4,000 years ago and on Anglesey, while in Flintshire, native Celts mined lead for the Romans. Slate mining, however, has been termed "the most Welsh of Welsh industries", and Welsh slate once covered the roofs of the world.

The oldest living European language, Welsh is a source of great pride in the north, where it is spoken by much of the population. Recognisable by their multiple double consonants, Welsh words have a way of provoking consternation in novices who attempt to pronounce them! North Wales even holds the village with the longest name in Britain: Llanfairpwllgwyngyllgogerychwyrndrobwllllantysiliogogogoch.

Music, too, plays a dominant role in the lives of North Walians, with the annual International Musical Eisteddfod in Llangollen, a colourful and competitive gathering of musicians from all over the world.

Thanks to an extensive coastline and the bounty of the Irish Sea, seafood is a strong suit in North Wales. The tasty summer delicacy of marsh samphire is collected from Lavan Sands, while crabs from the Great Orme, brown shrimps from Rhyl and lobsters from Anglesey are all available. Lobsters are being restocked in the Menai Strait, which separates the Isle of Anglesey from the mainland, and lobster-potting is still a favourite summer pastime among locals. King scallops are collected from November to May and petite, nutty queen scallops are fished all year round.

Anglesey sea salt is also being produced at the Anglesey Sea Zoo, and unlike commercially

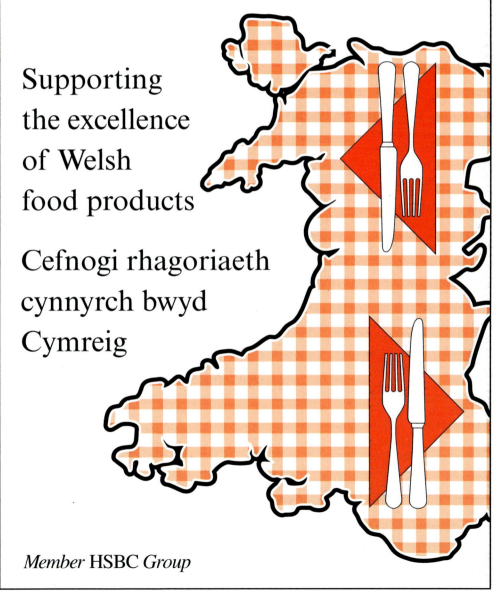

produced salt which contains up to 2 per cent additives, the flaking crystals are entirely pure and natural with their clean taste of the sea.

Native oyster beds were worked in the Menai Strait up until the turn of the century, when stocks were decimated. Now, gigas – or Pacific oysters are being successfully harvested instead. Mussels were hand-harvested at the month of the River Ogwen back into the last century; bottom cultivation began in the early 1960s to supplement hand-picking, and the molluscs are still abundant here today. Like all the shellfish in Wales, however, the great portion of the catch heads for the Continent, to an appreciative population.

Seas, rivers and even lakes are rich in fish. The north coast provides turbot, grey mullet, skate, brill, sea bass and mackerel direct from the Irish Sea. The rivers of the north are the best for sewin (the prized Welsh sea trout), of which 1,236 were caught in the River Dwyfor in 1994 alone. Salmon and sea trout are caught in the Mawddach, which reaches the Sea at Barmouth, and the Dovey, which rises in southern Snowdonia, is an excellent source of salmon. The River Conwy and its tributaries hold brown trout as well as salmon and sewin, and many other rivers and streams are fished by ardent anglers.

The most unusual and fascinating fish to be found dwells in the deep, cold lakes of the north which were formed during the Ice Age. The rare "torgoch" or Arctic char, with its pink belly, is only caught by rod and line during the summertime.

The Isle of Anglesey is affectionately known as "Môn Mam Cymru", or the Mother of Wales, because it fed the Welsh population with liberal amounts of grain. It was said that the Welsh princes who held control over Anglesey during battle could last substantially longer than those without its supplies. A few corn mills have been restored in recent times and wheat, barley and stoneground flours continue to be produced. Good arable land and a kind climate are features of the island, with soft fruit, herbs, potatoes and brassicas produced for sale at the gate or at market.

Market gardens seem to thrive in the east as well, with roadside stalls full of maincrop vegetables around the lowland area of Wrexham, as well as pick-your-own fruit farms and a few organic fruit and veg producers. Soft fruit is used for the freshly-baked cakes and breads produced from east to west, and even the younger generation has shown interest in traditional baking, setting up a number of small businesses in Llanwrst and beyond. Llandrillo College, as others in the north, has encouraged its graduates to stay on the local culinary scene and so North Wales has managed what many rural areas have not – to keep its young talent at home.

Traditional breeds thrive in the north, where the slopes of Snowdonia are natural havens for Welsh mountain sheep. "Oen y Glasdraeth" – or salt-marsh lamb – feed on the grasslands found along the Flintshire coast and around the Glaslyn estuary, while the Denbigh moors and lush Conwy Valley provide good grazing as well.

Lamb, however, is not the only meat on the menu. The uplands are home to Welsh Black cattle, naturally reared to produce tender, marbled beef. These rugged, ebony cows have been native to Wales since pre-Roman times, and can be seen grazing near Llanwrst, Bala, the Lleyn Peninsula and Dolgellau.

Traditional bacon and cured meats are produced in Lleyn, where naturally reared rosé beef (free-range veal) can also be found. A young farmer is now rearing free-range pigs near Conwy, and game including pheasant, mallard, widgeon and teal is also available in North Wales. Venison, too, comes from the estates of Llandudno, Conwy and the Lleyn Peninsula.

Well-established co-operative creameries in the north are making good mature Cheddars, and in terms of drinks spring water, beer and Welsh mead are produced. Even a vineyard has been planted. From east to west, local food companies are thriving along the A55, producing everything from hand-made patés to wholefoods – a veritable feast of flavours from an industrious region.

IMPECCABLE
PROFESSIONAL
SERVICE

Whether dining out, or dealing with legal problems, quality of service is vital. We offer a varied menu of five-star expertise. Our in-house specialities are personal injury and commercial litigation, company and commercial matters, employment issues, commercial and domestic property transactions.

For further information on how we can serve you, make a reservation by calling Chris Nott in Cardiff, Julian Lewis in Bristol or Jane Garland-Thomas in our Swansea office.

PALSER GROSSMAN
SOLICITORS

Discovery House, Scott Harbour, Cardiff Bay CF1 5PJ Tel 01222 452770 Fax 01222 452328
One Bridewell Street, Bristol BS1 2AA Tel 0117 927 9889 Fax 0117 927 9811
Clipper House, Quay West, Quay Parade, Swansea SA1 8AB Tel 01792 653336 Fax 01792 649004

Food List
North Wales

(food producers/retail outlets -- may be seasonal or have special hours)
S = shop; W = visitors accepted; R = ring ahead or for information; P = production site

Aberdovey

S   David Roberts, Copper Hill St (butcher) 01654 767911

Anglesey

S   E T Jones Sons & Daughter, Bodedern, Holyhead (butcher)   01407 740257
W, S   Strawberry Farm, Pentraeth (traditional handmade cakes)   01248 450922
S, R   Llangefni Market (livestock, stalls of local produce)   01248 723332
S   The Whole Thing, Llangefni (wholefoods)   01248 724832
W   Gwydryn Hir, Brynsiencyn (PYO fruit) 01248 430322
W   Peacock Herbs, Carmel   01248 470231
P   Wilsons of Holyhead (King and Queen scallops)   01407 763933

Bangor

R   Menai Oysters, Ger y Mynydd 01248 361313 & 430878
S   Dimensions, Holyhead Rd (wholefoods) 01248 351562
S   The Fridge, Port Penrhyn (fishmongers) 01248 351814
P   Myti Mussels, Port Penrhyn 01248 354878

Barmouth

S   Goodies, High St (deli)   01341 281162
S   Kith 'n Kin, King Edward St (bakery) 01341 281071

Caernarfon

S   Just Natural, Pool St (deli) 01286 674748

Colwyn Bay

S   Speronis Delicatessen, Conwy Rd 01492 533101

Conwy

S   I G Edwards, High St (Q Guild butcher) 01492 592443
R   Oakwood Park Farm, Sychnant Pass Rd (free range/welfare assured pork & pork prods.)   0370 547075 & 01492 596328

Corwen

P   Meridian Foods, I.E. (wholefoods) 01490 413151
P   Wholebake, Tyn y Llidiarth (cereal bars, snacks)   01490 412297

Denbigh

S   Ty Newydd Farmshop, Rhyl Rd (organic)   01745 812882
S   Alwyn Thomas Bakery, Vale St 01745 812068
R,W   Bragdy Dyffryn Clwyd, Chapel Place (brewery)   01745 815007
S   Broadleys Farmshop, A543 (local produce)   01745 812991

TERRY PLATT
WINE MERCHANT

An award winning, family owned, wine merchant, supplying quality minded restaurants and hotels throughout the Principality.

Alsace	California	Liqueurs	Rhone Valley
Arbois	Canada	Loire Valley	Roussillon
Argentina	Chablis	Maconnais	Sake
Australia	Champagne	Madeira	Sherry
Beaujolais	Chile	Marsala	South Africa
Bordeaux - Red	Germany	Mexico	Spain
Bordeaux - White	Half Bottles	New Zealand	Sparkling Wine
Brandy	Hungary	Olive Oil	Spirits
Burgundy	Italy	Oregon	Vin de Table
	Languedoc	Port	Wales
	Lebanon	Portugal	Washington State

Please telephone or fax if you would like a copy of our 1998 Wine List.

Ferndale Road, Llandudno Junction, Conwy. LL31 9NT
Telephone: 01492 592971
Fax: 01492 592196

Dolgellau Area

S Popty'r Dref, Upper Smithfield St (deli & bakery)　01341 422507
P Cambrian Brewery, Dolgellau　01341 421000
W Pentre Bach, Llwyngwril (all natural fruit & veg)　01341 250294

Harlech

W Welsh Mountain Garden, Maes Y Neuadd, Talsarnau (handmade flavoured oils, preserves, etc)　01766 780319
S Bwtri Bach Delicatessen, High St　01766 780373

Kinmel Bay

P Decantae Mineral Water, Tirllwyd I.E.　01745 343504

Llanberis

S Snowdon Honey Farm, High St　01286 870218

Llandudno

S The Fish Shop, Builder St　01492 870430

Llangollen

S Megan's Kitchen, Bishop Trevor (bakery)　01978 860063

Llanwrst

S Sigwr a Sbeis (bakery)　01492 641775
S Blas ar Fwyd, Heol yr Orsaf (local foods, homemade preserves, deli)　01492 640215

Mold

P, R Robinford (handmade pates)　01352 731652
S Fresh & Fancy Delicatessen, Daniel Owen Precinct　01352 757486

S Roberts Bakery, Wrexham St　01352 753119
S Roberts Deli, Wrexham St　01352 755339

Porthmadog

S Joe Lewis, High St (fish, organic vegetables)　01766 512229
S Cadwalladers Ice Cream, High St　01766 514235

Prestatyn

S Cahills Delicatessen, High Street　01745 853199

Pwllheli

S Tony Page, Jail St (butcher)　01758 612136
P Cig Moch Pen Llyn, Penrhos (bacon, cured meat)　01758 701737
P South Caernarfon Creameries, Chwilog (cheddar)　01766 810251
W Rhosfawr Nurseries, Rhosfawr (organic produce)　01766 810545
P, R Cig Rosé Llyn, Mynytho (rosé beef)　01758 730282 & 730597

Ruthin

S Maguire's Delicatessen, Well St　01824 702670
P Patchwork Traditional Food Co, Lon Parcwr (handmade pates)　01824 705832

Twywn

S Halo Foods, Pendre (honey shop, reduced calorie choc bars)　01654 711171

Wrexham

P Knolton Farmhouse Cheeses, Overton on Dee　01978 710221
S Bellis Country Market, Holt (fruit & veg)　01829 270304

Bringing a taste of the World to Wales

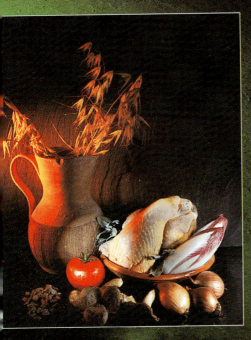

Purveyors of fine fresh fish, game, poultry, couverture, fresh exotic fruit and vegetables, baking products and dry goods for the discerning caterer.

Vin Sullivan Foods Ltd.

Gilchrist Thomas. Blaenavon NP4 9RL
Tel 01495 792792
Fax 01495 792277
E.Mail – finefood@sprynet.co.uk

Flavours of Mid Wales

By Manisha Gambhir Harkins

Mid Wales, the lush midriff of Wales, extends from the Brecon Beacons in the south to Snowdonia and the Berwyn Mountains in the north. Offa's Dyke forms the eastern boundary and Cardigan Bay the west. The broadest expanse of the region is known as Powys, once divided into the old counties of Brecknockshire, Radnorshire and Montgomeryshire. Ceredigion borders the coast with sandy beaches and rocky shores on which seaside resorts such as Aberystwyth developed. The largest natural resource of Mid Wales is water, and the Plynlimon range sources both the Severn, Britain's longest river, and the Wye, while lakes and reservoirs such as the Elan Valley supply the denizens of Birmingham.

A glorious green envelops Mid Wales, with plentiful rain producing healthy grass for its huge population of sheep. The undulating hills of the Brecon Beacons and rolling countryside throughout the region attract walkers and outdoor enthusiasts. Rural life is at the core of an area which relies upon agricultural revenue, and this is reflected in its past.

During the last century, livestock reared in upland areas was driven "on the hoof" by drovers to English lowlands to be fattened for market. Sheep, cattle, even pigs and geese were prepared for the long journey and "driven" at a steady pace of two miles per hour.

Upon the drovers' return, rural communities would eagerly await gossip from across the border, along with supplies of salt and cloth. Drovers' routes are still visible today; look out for a clump of three scotch pine trees, which indicate that food, accommodation and pasture were once provided at a particular location.

In the past, Mid Wales boasted some mineral wealth. The Romans initially mined gold near Llandovery, in a mine which was still in use as late as 1938, and there was a significant discovery of Welsh gold in 1862. Montgomeryshire was the centre of the Welsh flannel industry during the 1800s, and Radnorshire gained a reputation for its healing waters during the Victorian age. Llandrindod Wells, Builth Wells and Llanwrtyd Wells were all popular spa towns, as well as Llangammarch Wells, where many flocked to partake of the rare barium chloride springs. Today the essence of Mid Wales is felt in its bustling market towns, with the local economy enjoying annual events such as the Brecon Jazz festival and the Hay Literary Festival in the curious border town of Hay-on-Wye which has become the second-hand book capital of the world.

Fish lovers will note that Hay sits on the River Wye, the premier salmon river of Wales. Major tributaries of the Wye such as the Irfon and Ithon are good brown trout and grayling rivers with better salmon catches late in the season, and the Elan Valley affords opportunities to catch trout, as does the Severn in the north. To the west in Ceredigion the Dovey is known for salmon and sewin, the Clarach for its wild brown trout; the Rheidol is one of the best sewin rivers in Wales, and the Teifi, which was historically known for its salmon, is now an excellent mixed-game river offering trout and sewin as well.

The Ceredigion coastline provides excellent seafood, from small and sweet crabs, local lobsters and prawns to turbot and brill. The pretty harbour towns of Aberystwyth, Aberaeron and New Quay were key herring ports in the 1800s until over-fishing took its toll. Enjoying summer mackerel is a tradition around here and during the war years people from all over the

Welsh countryside would queue for the oily fish. Alas, prized Cardigan Bay scallops were mostly fished out during the 1970s, but they are slowly being reseeded. Today much of the lobster catch goes to France but there is a move to conserve stocks through an association set up by 15 local lobster fishermen.

With a healthy mixture of lowlands and uplands, the rolling countryside of Mid Wales is ideally suited to grazing sheep. Indeed it houses more sheep than humans, which is why Wales is the largest supplier of lamb to Europe. What makes Welsh lamb so good? Is it the breed or the feed? During the last century, the traditional breed of Welsh mountain lamb was the winning combination for Hamers Butchers of Llanidloes, who achieved royal patronage for their Plynlimon mutton, sent by train daily to London.

Hardy, pure Welsh mountain sheep graze in high upland pastures where they feed on indigenous herbage and natural grasses, producing distinctively sweet lamb. Today, the lamb industry must suit a more modern consumer who demands larger, leaner, butchers' cuts. Throughout Wales, lamb is produced to a top-quality specification in the most natural surroundings, and few chant Thomas Love Peacock's ditty:

> *The mountain sheep are sweeter,*
> *But the valley sheep are fatter,*
> *We therefore deemed it meeter*
> *To carry off the latter!*

From east to west, Mid Wales has attracted a number of organic producers. Lamb and beef, both raised organically, are available in the region, and in particular, Radnorshire supplies organic pork, wild boar, goat, mutton and chicken. Soft ewes' milk cheese, too, is produced in the area, while organic cider is produced further east. Organic dairy produce comes straight from the farm in Ceredigion, where cream, hand-churned butter, Greek-style and bio-yoghurts, cheese and buttermilk are made according to time-honoured methods. Vegetables are grown organically, health food shops stock a good range of organic dry goods, and the organic gardens at The Centre of Alternative Technology in Machynlleth are worth a visit.

There is a wild side to food in Mid Wales. Look out for honey made from heather, wild flowers or late-summer pollen. Gather whinberries (Welsh bilberries) on the uplands in August, taste fresh spring waters and, of course, there is local cider – sparkling, dry and medium sweet. In Radnorshire, the border country offers such delicacies as freshwater crayfish, exotic lettuces, herbs straight from the nursery and even tasty chicken-of-the-woods mushrooms which, so they say, thrive around local yew trees. In Brecknockshire a herd of red deer is reared naturally to produce tender farmed venison.

In July, Builth Wells is the place to catch the Royal Welsh Show, the largest annual agricultural show in Wales, and traditional markets are also a must in Mid Wales. Historic market towns still hold weekly livestock and general markets. Newtown's market dates back to 1279 whilst Welshpool's livestock market also goes back seven centuries. The general markets are held either indoors or on the streets and provide a taste of Welsh country life.

Here are some Mid Wales market days:
- Newtown - Tuesday
- Welshpool - Monday
- Knighton - Thursday and Friday
- Machynlleth - Wednesday
- Aberystwyth - Monday
- Llanidloes - Saturday

The Best Meals Start long before the chef starts preparing it...

Long before the chef draws his or her knife or even turns on the oven... a great deal of care has already gone into making your meal a meal to remember...

We have searched the Principality to ensure that we have provided the chef with only the best quality meats that Wales can provide.

Whether it's succulent Welsh Lamb, grazed on upland slopes or the taste of traditional beef, you can be sure that with Welsh Quality Meats ... you're getting quality.

Suppliers of natuarally reared Welsh Black beef & premium quality Welsh lamb

GOLD MEDAL - AWARD WINNING WHOLESALE CATERING BUTCHERS

GOLD MEDAL - AWARD WINNING WHOLESALE CATERING BUTCHERS Welsh National Championships "CATERING BUTCHER OF THE YEAR" for three consecutive years.

Ty Sir Benfro, Sir Benfro House, Brunel Quay, Neyland, Pembrokeshire.
Telephone: 01646 601816 Fax: 01646 601664

Food List Mid Wales

(food producers/retail outlets -- may be seasonal or have special hours)
S = shop; W = visitors accepted; R = ring ahead or for information; P = production site

Crickhowell and Brecon

S   Black Mountain Smokery, Crickhowell   01873 811566

R   Elgin Truffles, Talybont on Usk (handmade luxury choc truffles)   01874 676498

S   Top Drawer, Brecon (deli, wholefoods)   01874 622601

W   Welsh Distillers, Brecon (single malt, blended whisky)   01874 622926

R   Welsh Venison Centre, Bwlch, Brecon   01874 730929

Hay on Wye

S   Hay Wholefoods, Lion Street   01497 820708

P, R   Wyecliff Wine, A.J. Gibson Watt   01497 820317

Llanwrtyd & Builth Wells

S   Bernards Bakery, Irfon Crescent, Llanwrtyd Wells   01591 610391

S   Cheese and Chives, High St, Builth Wells (deli)   01982 551171

P, R   Netherbourne Fine Foods, Irfon Bus. Community (speciality teas)   01982 552012

R   Pencerrig Home Farm, Llanelwedd (goats' cheese)   01982 553177

Llandrindod Wells & Nearby

S   Grosvenor Stores, Wellington Rd (butcher + baker)   01597 824369

S   Van's Good Food Shop, Middleton St   01597 823074

R   Yan Tan Tethera, Llanbister Road (yoghurt, cheese)   01547 550641

S   Graig Farm, Dolau (organic/additive-free meat)   01597 851655

W   Whimble Nursery, Kinnerton (herbs)   01547 560413

W, R   Ralph Owen, Kinnerton (cider)   01544 350304

W, R   Apicius Sauces Limited, Knucklas, Knighton (original Roman recipe sauces)   01547 528376

Newtown

S   MacBeans, High St (wholefoods)   01686 627002

P, R   Zest Foods Ltd, Mochdre I.E. (natural savoury sauces)   01686 622058

P, R   Boynes Chocolates Limited (handmade fudge, sugar mice)   01686 625794

Montgomery & Nearby

S   Castle Kitchen, Broad St (wholefoods)   01686 668795

R   Little Cefn Smokehouse, Hyssington   01588 620603

S   Montgomery Natural Spring Water - Harry Tuffin Ltd, Church Stoke   01588 620226

Savour the pleasure of a holiday break in South & West Wales

Select a break from distinguished country house hotels, charming inns, cosy guest houses, traditional farmhouses or choose from a selection of self catering accommodation.

Most of the accommodation on offer boast excellent restaurants some of which have gained international acclaim, winning several awards for their cuisine.

Telephone
Haverfordwest
01437 766330
(quoting RB)

Wherever you decide to stay in South and West Wales you can be assured of receiving a wonderful welcome - book a holiday break and enjoy yourself!.

Ring before Friday 27 February 1998 and find out how to win a short break in South and West Wales to the value of £250

The South Wales Borderers and Monmouthshire Regimental Museum of the Royal Regiment of Wales,

The Barracks, Brecon, Powys LD3 7EB

Zulu War Room;

Guns, Uniforms, Equipment, Paintings and War Mementoes spanning 300 years of service; Large Medal Collection with 16 Victoria Crosses won by officers and soldiers of the Regiment. Gift counter. Facilities for the disabled.

Rorke's Drift 1879

Opening Times:
9am to 1pm and 2pm to 5pm
1st April to 30th September every day;
1st October to 31st March week days only.

Tel: 01874 613310

The National Coracle Centre and 17th Century Flour Mill

Cenarth Falls, Carmarthenshire SA38 9JL
Tel: 01239 710980 or 01239 710507

The Coracle Centre is situated beside the beautiful Cenarth Falls, and houses a unique collection of Coracles from all over Wales and many parts of the world, including Tibet, India, Vietnam, Iraq and north America.

Coracles date back to the Ice Age, and these once skin covered boats are still made and used for salmon fishing in West Wales today.

- Access for disabled
- Guided tours available
- Nature trail
- Picnic area
- Wonderful views of the salmon leap and falls
- Tea garden

**Open Sun-Fri
10.30 - 17.30 from
Easter to End October**

All other times by appointment.

E Mail Address:
http://www.west
wales.co/ukcoracle.htm

Welshpool & Llanfyllin

S   John Langfords, Severn St, Welshpool
    (butcher)   01938 552331
S   Down To Earth, Narrow St, Llanfyllin
    (deli, wholefoods)   01691 648841

Llanidloes

S   Edward Hamer Ltd, Plynlimon House
    Longbridge St, (butchers) 01686 412209
S   Meredith Bakery, Great Oak St
                                 01686 412628

Machynlleth Area

W   Felin Crewi Watermill (flour)
                                 01654 703113
W   Centre for Alternative
    Technology (organic gardens)
                                 01654 702400

Aberystwyth & Nearby

S   The Welsh Cellar, Pier St (deli)
                                 01970 617332
S   The Tree House, Pier St (organic
    produce)   01970 615791
W   Rachel's Dairy, Dolybont, Borth
    (organic dairy produce)   01970 625805
W, R   Merlin Cheeses, Ystrad Meurig
                                 01974 282636
P,R   Ty Nant, Bethania (spring water)
                                 01974 272111

Aberaeron

S   Fish on the Quay   01545 571294
S   Cegin Cymru, Market St, (Welsh
    speciality products)   01545 570460

Tregaron

S   Huw Evans, Castle House (butcher)
                                 01974 298229

Cardigan & Nearby

S   Go Mango, High St   01239 614727
W   Penbryn Organic Farmhouse Cheese,
    Sarnau (Gouda type)   01239 810347

Lampeter

P,   Organic Farm Foods, Llanbedr Ind. Est.
     (Wholesale Fruit,Veg)   01570 423099
R   Welsh Organic Foods Ltd, Llanbedr
     Ind. Est. (Pencarreg cheese) 01570 422772
R   Gorwydd Caerffili   01570 493516

Llandysul & Nearby

S   Popty Bach, Llandysul (bakery)
                                 01559 362335
S   Quail World, Penrhiwllan
    (quail eggs, pickled eggs)
                                 01559 370105
R   Tregroes Waffles, Tregroes
                                 01559 363468
W   Rhydlewis Trout Farm, Rhydlewis
                                 01239 851224
W, R   Teifi Farmhouse Cheese, Ffostrasol
                                 01239 851528

The Borders

S   Georges, Kington (deli, health foods)
                                 01544 231400
S   The Grapevine, Kington (fish)
                                 01544 231202
S   Hussey's, Kington (food store)
                                 01544 230381
R   Dunkerton's organic cider, Pembridge
                                 01544 388653
W   Wroxeter Roman Vineyard, Shrewsbury
                                 01743 761888
S   Embreys, Bishops Castle (butcher,
    cheese)   01588 638584
S   Morray & Son, Bishops Castle (bakery)
                                 01588 638458

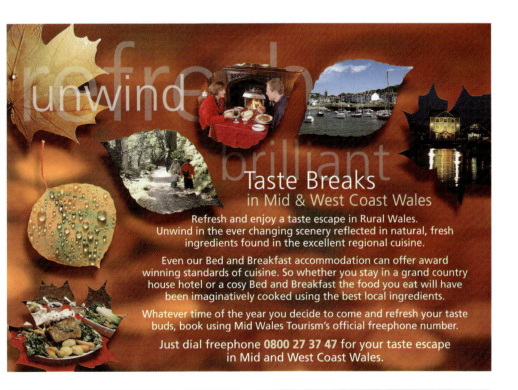

Taste Breaks
in Mid & West Coast Wales

Refresh and enjoy a taste escape in Rural Wales. Unwind in the ever changing scenery reflected in natural, fresh ingredients found in the excellent regional cuisine.

Even our Bed and Breakfast accommodation can offer award winning standards of cuisine. So whether you stay in a grand country house hotel or a cosy Bed and Breakfast the food you eat will have been imaginatively cooked using the best local ingredients.

Whatever time of the year you decide to come and refresh your taste buds, book using Mid Wales Tourism's official freephone number.

Just dial freephone **0800 27 37 47** for your taste escape in Mid and West Coast Wales.

Welsh Royal Crystal
The Welsh Masters Of Fire & Glass
Meistrolwyr Tan â Gwydr Yng Nghymru

The Welsh Royal Crystal Visitor Centre

The Principality's foremost maker of fine hand-crafted crystalware including trophies and gifts for presentational, celebratory & commemorative purposes.

Workshop tours, cafeteria and well stocked crystal and gift shop.

Sales enquiries to Aurwen Mills

5 Brynberth, Rhayader,
Powys. LD6 5EN
Telephone 01597 811005
Fax 01597 811129

CENTRE FOR ALTERNATIVE TECHNOLOGY

- Water-powered Cliff Railway
- Solar Power
- Hands-on displays
- Beautiful Gardens
- Plenty for all ages

Open every day from 10am.
Find us 3 miles north of Machynlleth,
on the A487, Powys, SY20 9AZ

☎ **01654 702400**

Flavours of South Wales

By Manisha Gambhir Harkins

South Wales successfully combines the peace of the countryside with bustling towns and cities. The warmth provided by the Gulf Stream, lands which lend themselves to good arable and dairy farming, city centres full of shops and markets and convenient access to the M4, are all reasons why the majority of residents in Wales settle in this region.

The winding Usk and Wye valleys in the east are today mostly green and unspoilt, stretching through border counties where mixed cultures prevail. With its temperate climate, the area is best known for fine river fishing and vineyards which are found along gentle south-facing slopes once planted by Romans. Nearby, the industrial South Wales valleys were carved out for their coal and iron more than a hundred years ago.

The industrial revolution in South Wales fuelled the capital city of Cardiff, a commercial port where numerous ethnic minorities integrated smoothly with the indigenous population and engendered a multicultural outlook and cuisine. An hour west of Cardiff is the maritime city of Swansea, once a major port, which was heavily bombed during The World War II. Now, Swansea is a pleasant harbour-side city with a bustling marina and traditional market. Further west are the well grazed pastures of Carmarthenshire, an agricultural county with livestock sales taking place throughout the region, and temperate Pembrokeshire, surrounded by water on three sides, is a county with an abundance of fresh seafood. Both counties have a strong dairy-farming tradition, and milk provided a generous income for many farmers, much of their production being sent by train to London. With the introduction of milk quotas in the 1980s, however, many farmers have turned instead to traditional farmhouse dairy products made from their excess milk.

A cornucopia of flavours awaits the visitor of South Wales. One favourite pastime for keen fishermen in the southeast includes fishing for elvers (young eels) at the tidal reaches of the River Wye – though with their value now reaching around £160 per kilo, it is not surprising that elver eating contests are relegated to the past.

The Rivers Usk and Wye are famous for their salmon, while trout and grayling from their tributaries are also in demand. Around Bridgend those who fish on the winding River Ogmore will tell you about their plentiful catches of brown and rainbow trout, and a celebration is due when they catch a sewin. The canny water bailiff sticks by the saying, "The time is right for sewin when the foxgloves are out."

In Carmarthenshire, coracle fishing is an ancient craft with the few coracle fishermen rowing along the Rivers Teifi and Towy in their circular willow, hazel and tarred-canvas boats. Although Milford Haven is no longer the thriving port it once was, fresh fish is still available on the harbour and throughout bountiful Pembrokeshire.

Mackerel, sea bass and lobster are featured on local menus, and anglers can be spotted along the Cleddau estuary patiently waiting for trout and salmon. Fish farms also stock healthy rainbow or brown trout for visitors.

There are more than a dozen vineyards operating in the south, where the weather is generally kinder to the vines. In the Welsh marches cider is a drink that has been enjoyed for centuries by country folk, and locally brewed beer has satisfied the thirst of the workers. Do

Getaway to beautiful North Wales

Explore the varied North Wales Coast, boasting miles of golden sands, dunes and craggy headlands as well as lively seaside resorts.

Dominating the North Wales landscape are the majestic mountains of Snowdonia, a magnet for walkers and outdoor enthusiasts. Yet on the fringe of this wild and beautiful countryside you can visit an exciting range of family attractions or soak up the atmosphere at one of our many Castles, Historic Stately Homes and gardens - Something For Everyone.

Whether you choose to stay in an Elegant Country House Hotel, Guest House or Farm House renowned for their good food and warm welcome, or sample the freedom of Self Catering - North Wales has the accommodation to suit your taste.

For that Great Break in North Wales Call FREEPHONE 0800 834820
or write for a FREE copy of the Great Breaks Brochure (RB) 77 Conwy Road, LL29 7LN

CAREW
CASTLE & TIDAL MILL

A **MAGNIFICENT NORMAN CASTLE**, which later became an Elizabethan residence. Royal links with Henry Tudor and setting for the Great Tournament of 1507. Archaeological evidence of much earlier settlement.

ONLY RESTORED TIDAL MILL in Wales. The fine four storey building contains an introductory slide-tape programme, automatic 'talking points' and a special exhibition, 'The Story of Milling'.

Situated on the banks of the Carew River, the castle and mill are linked by a round house. Close by is the 13 foot tall Carew Cross, one of the finest in Wales (CADW guardianship). Signposted off the A 477 Kilgetty to Pembroke Dock. Open every day April to end of October 10am to 5pm.
Telephone Carew Castle (01646) 651782.

FREE PARKING ● PICNIC SITE ● GUIDED TOURS ● SHOPS

Site managed by the Pembrokeshire Coast National Park

Rock Mill
(Woollen & Water Mill)
Tel: 01559 362356
Capel-Dewi, Llandysul SA44 4PH

Visit a listed Woollen Mill dating from 1890

Manufacturers of pure new wool tapestry bedspreads, blankets, throws, rugs, table mats etc.

Open: Mon - Fri 10am - 5pm
April to October

Sat 10am - 1pm
May to September

Telephone for Winter Opening Times

The mill is on the B4459 at Capel Dewi, just off the A475 Lampeter-Newcastle Emlyn road at Rhydowen or off the A485 Lampeter-Carmarthen road at Alltwalis, or follow Rock-Mill signs from Llandysul.

be tempted also by fruit cordials, spring water or a refreshing lemon-scented elderflower spritz.

Farm-gate sales of organic or free-range produce are a regular affair, with meat and poultry produced from east to west as well as vegetables, herbs and dairy produce. Do take a jaunt to Pembrokeshire for its famous early potatoes, along with calabrese and unusual lettuces. South Wales in particular is a hive of organic activity where even wheat is being produced organically and sold to working mills. Free-range poultry breeders rear Muscovy and Gressingham ducks, geese and quail, and many a butcher will regale you with tales of the superiority of the region's Welsh Black beef. Hunting is an age-old tradition throughout the principality with shoots for pheasant, rabbit and even grouse; and along the marches, deer have been hunted for centuries.

Milk production once made up the bulk of many a farmer's wages, especially in the west, where placid dairy cows pepper the green grass of Carmarthenshire and Pembrokeshire. Unsurprisingly, a number of farmhouse cheeses are sold locally and abroad. Visitors can sample the cheeses and even view cheese-making at many farms. Farmhouse butter, yoghurt, clotted cream and ice cream are also produced. Baking is another home-grown skill which can be seen at work in the Museum of Welsh Life at St Fagans, and a proper Welsh tea should not be missed.

The Italian immigrants who came in droves to South Wales a hundred years ago set up milk bars throughout the valleys to feed the mining communities. Today their resilience is evident in busy cafes where traditional ice cream and coffee are sold. In the Tawe Valley, one enterprising Italian produces a fine pecorino, and near Cardiff another runs a charcuterie where prosciutto, pepperoni and all manner of traditional Italian sausages are hand-made.

Cardiff, without a doubt, is a hub of activity. The capital city has myriad speciality food shops catering for its diverse population, and spices and exotic ingredients can be easily procured. The towns of South Wales are well known for their indoor markets, which stem from humble beginnings – medieval street markets which provided a focal point for social gatherings. At the far end of Cardiff Central Market is a gleaming counter full of fresh seafood, from squat lobsters to sea bass. It is here, at Ashton's, that you will witness the various ethnic groups queuing for the catch of the day.

Swansea Market is a traditional indoor market where one can have Welsh cakes or bara planc (griddle bread) hot off the griddle. At Coakley Green's stall, local sewin and lobster mingle with exotic fish, with plenty of seafood being landed at Swansea docks. In one corner of the market are the casuals – a group of vegetable growers from the Gower Peninsula with their freshly-picked beetroot and cauliflower or potatoes and parsley.

And at the centre of it all is what Swansea and the Gower Peninsula are all about: laverbread and cockles sold at a large rotunda, indicating the importance of this cottage industry which ekes out its livelihood from the sea. Laverbread is the beloved Welsh seaweed, boiled and pulped into a dark mass which is traditionally fried with oatmeal and bacon for breakfast. Cockles have a long association with this area. These tasty little molluscs are gathered by hand at Penclawdd sands on the Gower by licensed gatherers, after which they are washed and cooked and prized, for their delicious slightly-sweet flavour of the sea. Cockle-gathering was once the exclusive preserve of women.

Carmarthen Market is the heart of all that is good in the south-west, with stalls showing off the home-baked bread and cheeses of West Wales, freshly-caught sewin from the Towy, and Carmarthen Ham – a salt-cured ham sold thinly sliced.

And to complete your visit, why not take home some thick cut slabs of good old-fashioned bacon from the Carmarthenshire countryside – a natural accompaniment to scrambled eggs, with cockles or fried laverbread?

BONTDDU HALL HOTEL

BONTDDU, Nr BARMOUTH, GWYNEDD, LL40 2UF.
Telephone: Bontddu (01341) 430661. Facsimile No: 01341 430284

*The views from this restaurant are said to be among the finest in Wales.
The cuisine matches this accolade.*

A devoted team of chefs prepare classic cusine using the best of fresh local produce - Welsh Mountain Lamb, Mawddach Salmon, Barmouth Bay Lobster, and many more delicacies.

Our country house evening dinner offers half a dozen choices on each of the three courses (always with a vegetarian dish, and 1 or 2 fish choices).

The carefully prepared wine list gives an informative choice from a world-wide selection.

Bontddu Hall is an historic house with elegant reception rooms, original fireplaces, marble columns, wood panelling, and a timeless ambience. Twenty bedrooms en-suite, individually designed and decorated, with all the amenities you would expect from a three star country house hotel.

AA★★★ RAC★★★
AA ☸ ☸ For Cuisine,
RAC Merit for restaurant,
comfort and hospitality.
AA 'Courtesy & Care Award' 1997

Tre-Ysgawen Hall
Country House Hotel

*Award winning in both Accommodation
& Restaurant, proudly present their*
Brasserie Restaurant
*and for the more intimate occasion,
candlelight dining in our*
Capel Coch Restaurant.

A La Carte & Table d'Hôte

**Capel Coch, Llangefni,
Isle of Anglesey LL77 7UR**

Tel: 01248 750750 Fax: 01248 750035

Dolmelynllyn Hall
Country Hotel

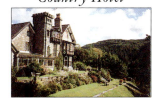

QUOTED BY THE BEST GUIDES
Johansens Country Houses & Which Hotel Guide
Wales Tourist Board ☸☸☸☸ Highly Commended
AA ★★★ ☸

*Dolmelynllyn Hall is a small manor house dating
from the 16thC. set in large terraced gardens
overlooking the Mawddach Valley.*

Dine in elegant surroundings in the
mahogany panelled Dining-room
from a varied menu accompanied by
a large range of medium
priced wines.

Ganllwyd, Dolgellau,
Gwynedd LL40 2HP.

Telephone: (01341) 440273
Fax: (01341) 440640

Food List
South Wales

(food producers/retail outlets -- may be seasonal or have special hours)
S = shop; W = visitors accepted; R = ring ahead or for information; P = production site

Abergavenny & Nearby

S	Vin Sullivans, Frogmore St (deli)	01873 856989
S	Thimbles, St John's St (Welsh fudge, wildflower honey, Belgian choc)	01873 853134
S	H J Edwards, Flannel St (butcher)	01873 853110
P	Abergavenny Fine Foods, Castle Meadows Park (cheese)	01873 850001
W	Brecon Court, Llansoy, Usk (wine, venison)	01291 650366
W	Sugar Loaf Vineyard, Llwyndu (wine)	01873 858675
W	Crucorney Trout Farm, Llanfihangel Crucorney (fishery)	01873 890545
R	Upper Pant Farm, Llanddewi Rhydderch (organic meat)	01873 858091

Monmouth Area

S	Hancocks, Monnow St (speciality sausages, butcher)	01600 712015
S	Irma Fingal-Rock, Monnow St (deli)	01600 712372
W	Offas Vineyard, Llanivangel-Ystern-Llegwern	01600 780241
S, R	Monnow Valley Wine, Osbaston	01600 716209
P	Usk Valley Poultry, Glascoed (poultry)	01495 762295
W	Great Tyrmynach Farm, Raglan (PYO)	01291 690470

Newport Area

S	Graham Palfrey, Church Rd (Q Guild butcher)	01633 259385
S	William Baldock's Deli, Market Hall	01633 257312
W	Berryhill Fruit Farm, Coedkernew (PYO/shop)	01633 680938

The Valleys

W	Minoli's of Machen, Machen (ice cream)	01633 440551
P	Welsh Hills Bakery, Hirwaun, Aberdare	01685 813545

Cardiff & Nearby

S	The Old Brewery Shop, S.A. Brains, St Mary Street	01222 395828
S	Beanfreaks, St Mary Street (health foods)	01222 251671
S	E. Ashton, Cardiff Central Market (fishmonger)	01222 229201
S	J.T. Morgan, Cardiff Central Market (butcher)	01222 388434
S	The Cheese Stall, Cardiff Central Market	01222 383796
S	Wally's Deli, Royal Arcade	01222 229265
S	Keith the Fish, Outdoor Market (traditional fishmonger)	01222 220575
S	Shelly's Deli, Cathedral Rd	01222 227180
S	Howells Food Hall, St Mary St	01222 231055
S	Madhav's, Lower Cathedral Rd (Indian grocer)	01222 372947
S	Jim's Eastern Chinese Supermarket, Tudor Street	01222 397148
W	Gorno's Speciality Foods, Taffs Well (Italian meat/deli)	01222 811225

LLANGOED HALL

*A Magnificent Country House Hotel in Wales
On the Banks of the River Wye*

Set in glorious countryside at the foot of the Black Mountains Llangoed Hall has built an enviable reputation for fine food and wines.

Exciting and innovative menus reflect the season, ensuring that a summer dish is full of sunshine and a winter dish is full of warmth, with great emphasis placed on local produce from nearby villages and farms, and of course the River Wye itself.

Head Chef Ben Davies is a Master Chef of Great Britain and is proud to have achieved a Michelin Star for Llangoed Hall and 3AA Rosettes.

For further details and reservations call Llangoed Hall on 01874 754525

Guidfa House

This stylish Georgian Guest House has earned an enviable reputation for its comfort, good food and service.
It offers superior en-suite accommodation including a ground floor room.
Enjoy the imaginative meals prepared by Cordon Bleu trained Anne accompanied by an excellent wine list.

For a brochure please telephone or write to:
**Guidfa House, Crossgates,
Llandrindod Wells, Powys, LD1 6RF**

Telephone: (01597) 851241
Fax: (01597) 851875

LOWER HAYTHOG

A warm Welsh welcome awaits you "down on the farm" at Lower Haythog.

Set in 250 secluded acres of picturesque, unspoilt countryside.
All our well appointed bedrooms are en-suite, have tray facilities and central heating.
And for the children, we have a play area on the lawn, or they can ride a pony or watch the cows being milked.

"Not so much a B&B, more like staying with friends"

Taste of Wales Farmhouse Food Award Winner 1996.

Spittal, Haverfordwest, Pembrokeshire
Telephone 01437 731279

W	Derwen Bakehouse, Museum of Welsh Life, St Fagans	01222 573500
S	Gwalia Stores, Museum of Welsh Life, St Fagans (speciality foods)	01222 577018
S	David Lush, Glebe Street, Penarth (butcher)	01222 707007
S	Williams of Penarth, Glebe Street, Penarth (bakery)	01222 709349
S	Charles Saddler, Victoria Rd, Penarth (poultry & game)	01222 709100
W	Ices from the Fruit Garden, Peterston-Super-Ely (PYO, ice cream)	01446 760358
R	Pant Teg Wine, Lisvane	01222 753834

Cowbridge & Nearby

S	Glyn T Jenkins, High St, Cowbridge (deli)	01446 773545
P	Glyndwr Vineyard, Folly Farm, Llanblethian	01222 220587
S, R	Croffta Wines, Groesfaen, Llantrisant	01443 223876
W	Llanerch Vineyard, Pendoylan	01443 225877
R	Pencoed Organic Growers, Pencoed (organic produce)	01656 861956
W	Ton Fruit Farm, Merthyr Mawr, Bridgend (PYO/shop)	01656 650090
S	Holland & Barrett, Bridgend (health foods)	01656 653748

Swansea, The Gower & Nearby

S	Swansea Fishermen Ltd, Fish Market (fish from the docks)	01792 655800
S	Swansea Market (market info)	01792 654296
S	Coakley Green, Swansea Market (fishmonger)	01792 653416
S	Goodies, Swansea Market (cheese)	01792 456250
S	Mavis Davies, Swansea Market (Welshcakes)	01792 641088
S	Karen Evans, Swansea Market (Welshcakes)	01792 646846
R	Cwm Tawe Cheese, Glais (Pecorino cheese)	01792 844637
P	Lynch Cockle Factory/Selwyn's Penclawdd Seafoods, Llanmorlais (cockles/laverbread)	01792 850033
S	H. Howell & Son, Caefolland, Penclawdd (butcher)	01792 850371
S	Wendy's Hot Bread Shop, Killay Shopping Precinct	01792 208663
S	Colin Davies, Killay Shopping Precinct, Killay (butcher)	01792 290114
P	Gower Spring Mineral Water, Upper Killay	01792 204818
S	Colin Jones, Gower Rd, Sketty (fruit & veg)	01792 206962
P, R	Felinfoel Brewery, Llanelli	01554 773356

Carmarthen & Nearby

S	Carmarthen Market (market info)	01267 228841
S	Albert Rees, Carmarthen Market (Carmarthen ham)	01267 231204
S	The Farmhouse Cheese Shop, Carmarthen Market	01239 851528
S	Raymond Rees, Carmarthen Market (fishmonger)	01267 234144
S	Sue Rees, Carmarthen Market (baker; call market info)	01267 228841
W	Nantybwla Farmhouse Cheese, College Rd	01267 237905
S	Peppercorn, Llandeilo (cookware shop)	01558 822410
S	A Case of Wine, Llanwrda (wines & dry goods)	01558 650671
S	Eynon's Family Butchers, St Clears	01994 230226
W	Caws Ffermdy Cenarth, Newcastle Emlyn, (cheese)	01239 710432
P	Llanboidy Cheese, Login, Whitland	01994 448303
W	Pemberton's Victorian Chocolates, Llanboidy	01994 448768

Fishguard & Nearby

S	PM & B Hughes, High St (meat and fish)	01348 872394

Belle Vue Royal Hotel

A combination of Victorian architecture and modern sophistication makes The Belle Vue Royal Hotel a very elegant, spacious and comfortable place to stay.

Set in an enviable position on the Aberystwyth sea front, the hotel offers a magnificent view of Cardigan Bay with its spectacular sunsets.

The hotel serves a wide selection of wines and local produce from succulent steaks to fresh fish for lunch and dinner. Both Table d'Hôte and á la carte menus are on offer.

The Belle Vue is the ideal venue for your Conference or Wedding Reception and whether you require a professional or personal approach we will cater for the occasion.

The perfect base for sightseeing, golf with discount rates, walking - in fact, just about everything.

AA ★★★ AA
RAC ★★★
WTB
Highly Commended

The Promenade, Aberystwyth, SY23 2BA.
Tel: 01970 617558 Fax: 01970 612190

Cyfie Farm

Only minutes away from the fairy tale landscape of Lake Vyrnwy.

De Luxe farmhouse in magnificent setting, its prized feature of spacious barn and stable suites offer the comforts of a top hotel.

Cosy log fired lounges, peace, tranquillity, a real "Taste of Wales" in hospitality and cuisine. Working farm.

We are proud to be nominated for the Best Small Tourism Business Award.
Open 1-12 B&B pp £20.50 - £26.50 Weekly, D, B&B pp £201-£237, 2 Nights Break, D, B&B pp (Weekend & Midweek(£66 - £74
Breaks available 31.5.97 & 1.10.97 - 23.12.97
Including Bank Holidays

Llanflhangel-yng-Ngwynfa, Llanfyllin SY22 5JE
Tel: 01691 648451 Fax: 01691 648451
Central Res: 01691 870346

The Empire Hotel

An elegant family run hotel - beautifully furnished with antiques and fine paintings.

Our stylish and traditional

Watkins Restaurant

offers an extensive daily changing table d'hôte menu with interesting dishes made from local produce complemented by an impressive wine list

Churchwalks, Llandudno
Telephone 01492 860555

❖ Wales Tourist Board - Five crown de-luxe
❖ AA-Rosette for Food - '92, 93, 94, 95, 96
❖ RAC 3 star, Merit Award for Restauarant, Hospitality and Comfort

W, S Llangloffan Farmhouse Cheese, Castle Morris   01348 891241

Newport (Pembrokeshire)

S Fountain House Foods, Market St (deli/take-away meals)   01239 820151
S Bwydydd Cyflawn, East St (health foods, organic wines)   01239 820773
S Yr Hen Bopty, East St (grocer/deli)   01239 820199
R Cilgwyn Herb Garden, Cilgwyn   01239 820398

Crymych & Nearby

S Bwyd y Byd, Prospect Place (health foods)   01239 831537
S JK Lewis & Sons, Preseli Stores (bakery)   01239 831288
S The Farm Shop, Brolas, Crymych (fruit & veg)   01239 831687
R Mary's Farmhouse Ice Cream, Crymych   01239 831440
S Pencrugiau Organic Farm Shop, Felindre Farchog   01239 881265
R Pant Mawr Farm, Rosebush (cheese)   01437 532627
W, S Wendy Brandon, Boncath (handmade speciality preserves)   01239 841568
R Nag's Head Brewery, Abercych (traditional ales)   01239 841200

St Dogmaels

W Y Felin Mill, St Dogmaels (stoneground flour, bread)   01239 613999
R Priory Poultry, St Dogmaels   01239 881312

Tenby & Nearby

S J V Rowe & Sons, High St (butchers)   01834 842465
S The Caldey Shop, Quay Hill (Caldey Island produce)   01834 842296
W Pembrokeshire Fish Farm, Vicars Mill, Llandissilio   01437 563553

S Pobyddion Beca, Efailwen (bakery)   01994 419339
S The Old Moat House, Narberth (deli)   01834 861491
R Drim Farm, Narberth (clotted cream)   01437 541295
R, W Green Meadow Mushrooms, Kilgetty (button, flat)   01834 813190
W Cwm Deri Vineyard, Martletwy   01834 891274
S White's Golden Crust Bakery, Lamphey   01646 672102
W Springfields Fresh Produce, Manorbier (PYO/shop)   01834 871746
R Upton Farm Ice Cream, Pembroke Dock   01646 685777

Milford Haven & Haverfordwest

S The Fish Plaice, the docks, Milford Haven   01646 692331
S Wine Shop on the Green, St Thomas Green, Haverfordwest   01437 766864
W New Creamson Farm, Creamston Rd Haverfordwest (PYO)   01437 763732
R Growing Concern, Camrose (organic produce)   01437 710384
P Welsh Quality Meats, Neyland (catering butcher)   01646 601816
R Oneida Fish, Neyland   01646 600220
R Meat Centre, Welsh Hook (organic meat)   01348 840466

St Davids Area

S St David's Food & Wine, High St, St Davids (deli)   01437 721948
S, R Caerfai Farm (organic cheese/produce)   01437 720548
R The Pumpkin Shed (organic produce)   01437 721949
P Carn-Nwchwn Farm (Gressingham duck)   01437 720288
S Keith Thomas, Solva (butcher & bakery)   01437 720997

Sir Rocco Forte's new company, RF Hotels, is building the first hotel of five-star standard in Wales, due to open in Cardiff Bay in June 1998.

The hotel's restaurant will offer informal dining in a chic and cosmopolitan setting with an outside terrace and stunning views over the bay.

Affordable menus will include a range of colourful and unique dishes with both classical and eclectic styles, catering for 120 covers.

RF HOTELS
Rocco Forte's new Hotel Group

RF Hotels was established in 1996 to manage luxury hotels, initially in Europe, and is already managing the five-star Balmoral Hotel, in Edinburgh.

Other plans include a chain of executive hotels in the former Soviet Union and the creation of a small, high quality restaurant business in London.

Work commenced in May 1997 on the first hotel in the executive chain in Nizhny Novgorod, and Les Saveurs, one of London's top restaurants in Mayfair, was purchased in April 1997.

Other facilities will include:

- ❖ 104 bedrooms with balconies and views over the bay
- ❖ 12 one-bedroom suites and 4 junior suites with terraces overlooking the sea
- ❖ 1 lounge catering for 50-60 covers
- ❖ Private garden and terrace for guests
- ❖ 7 meeting rooms
- ❖ One large reception room, seating 140 banquet style, 210 theatre style
- ❖ Business centre incorporating the latest technology
- ❖ Health spa, offering the latest thalassotherapy treatments, gym and exercise pool
- ❖ Discussions are also under way for the addition of a marina to the development.

Penally ABBEY

Country House Hotel & Restaurant,
Penally Nr Tenby, Pembrokeshire SA70 7PY, Wales, UK.
Tel (01834) 843033 Fax: (01834) 844714

Penally Abbey is a gem, commanding spectacular views across Carmarthen Bay, the hotel, a dignified Grade II listed mansion offers the rare experience of true country house accommodation by the sea.
Genial hosts Steve and Elleen Warren and their welcoming staff are renowned for their hospitality and have awards to prove it.

The food - delicious but unpretentious, mirroring the style of the hotel - has also won praises. Dinner is an intimate candlelit affair with tempting seasonal delicacies, completing the picture of pure romance.
Penally Abbey - The Perfect Place to unwind.

Ramsey House

St David's

Catering exclusively for adults in our high class, non smoking establishment, we offer a unique combination of professional hotel standards of accommodation with traditional Welsh cooking using only the finest, fresh, local ingredients

- ❖ **Ideal location for Pembrokeshire Coast Path, St David's Cathedral, beaches and attractions.**
- ❖ **Dogs welcome** ❖ **Private parking**
- ❖ **Restaurant for residents only**

WTB 3 Crowns Highly Commended
RAC Highly Acclaimed AA QQQQ Selected
Les Routiers Casserole and Wine Awards

Lower Moor, St David's,
Pembrokeshire SA62 6RP

Tel: 01437 720321 Fax: 01437 720025

Italian Restaurants

As Seen On TV
Family Run Est. 1982

™ *Originally Givovanni's*

FRESHLY PREPARED ITALIAN FOOD

★ Private Functions ★ Weddings
★ Office Parties ★ Birthdays

Tel: 01222 220077	Tel: 01222 645000/665500
38 The Hayes, Cardiff, CF1 2AJ	Cardiff's Café Quarter
Specialists in Celebrations	11 Mill Lane CF1 1FL
Dine with the Stars	*Cabaret & Dancing. Dine 'Al Fresco'*

Now Open Our Presidents Lounge and Function Suites
(Acquired from the Welsh Rugby Union - Cardiff Arms Park)

WINE BAR & RESTAURANT

The Ideal Venue For Your Business Lunch

Open 11am - 7pm
Mon - Fri

The ideal venue for your business lunch or for that special occasion or private party, we are available evenings and weekends

**8 Mount Stuart Square,
Cardiff Bay
Tel 01222 464628**

Kath and Steve welcome you to

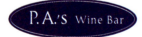

Mumbles • Swansea

Great Chefs, Friendly Atmosphere and
Fine Wines From Around The World.

For reservations please ring
Swansea (01792) 367723

95 Newton Road,
Mumbles, Swansea.

NEW INTERNATIONAL HOTEL
KINGSWAY, CARDIFF • OPENING CHRISTMAS 1998

Located adjacent to the Castle, City Hall and the National Museum, this exclusive development by TBI is perfectly situated in the centre of Cardiff. Part of an internationally renowned group the hotel offers: an exclusive leisure club; banqueting for 350; a business centre; 200 rooms boasting the latest technology in communications and entertainment; two restaurants in a Grand Conservatory with a world class chef and spectacular views over the castle grounds; a unique VIP suite on the 7th floor.

A new flagship facility for the capital city.

TBI plc, Conway House, St Mellons Business Park, Cardiff, CF3 0LT. Tel: 01222 360700

Restaurant Castell

*Where dining is an experience to remember
Superb food.... beautifully served*

Here at the Angel Hotel we ensure that a meal out is an occasion to remember. We offer a fabulous menu selection devised by our head chef Vivien Marshall, from light meals to a four course extravaganza!

So why not treat yourself or a loved one?

Sample great food served in an intimate atmosphere and service second to none.

We look forward to hearing from you.

For Reservations call 01222 232633
Castle Street, Cardiff, CF1 2QZ

Benedicto's

Gourmet Evenings
4-Course Candlelit Dinner for Two -
FOR THE PRICE OF ONE
Patron's Special Menu

Example
STARTERS
Baked Eggs with Smoked Salmon & Asparagus
Avocado Prawns & Crab Salad
MAIN COURSES
Hake with Clams in White Wine,
Asparagus & Parsley Sauce
Veal with Pineapple & Prawns
Paupiettes of Sole, stuffed with Crab meat
& Ginger sauce
Choice of Desserts & Coffee

Sunday Lunch Special
Make Sundays special and take time to enjoy the company of friends & family, with excellent food, fine wines and elegant surroundings.

SUNDAY LUNCHEON MENU
Example: **STARTERS**
Fresh Mussels with Chilli & Mint Sauce
Grilled Goats Cheese with Salad
& Raspberry Vinaigrette
MAIN COURSES
Rack of Lamb in Red Wine & Mint Sauce
Supreme of Guinea Fowl in Orange Sauce
with Chestnuts
Breast of Chicken with Spinach stuffing in Filo Pastry
& Wild Mushroom Sauce
Choice of DESSERTS & COFFEE

For Reservations &
further details...

Benedicto's
4 Windsor Place, Cardiff.
☎ **(01222) 371130/226337**

Yesterdays
Restaurant & Rooms

De-Luxe En-suite rooms
Delightful cosy restaurant
Simple country cooking using
the best local ingredients
Completely non-smoking

Located in the beautiful upper Severn valley, ideally situated to visit the castles, rivers, lakes and mountains of Mid Wales.

Severn Square, Newtown, Powys, SY16 2AG

Tel: 01686 622644

The Dylan Thomas Centre

Somerset Place, Swansea

Weddings all year round

Themed Dinners

Sunday Lunches £7.95

Teas & Coffees Tues - Sun
10.30am - 3.00pm

Lunches Served until 2.30pm

Conferences
Day Delegate Rate Available
Tel 01792 463980
Fax: 01792 463993

CITY AND COUNTY OF SWANSEA
DINAS A SIR ABERTAWE

DECANTAE
The Prince of Natural Waters

Decantae is one of the purest waters you'll ever drink, as it bubbles to the surface through miles of rock strata laid down more than 400 million years ago. Analysis has shown it to be particularly low in the heavy metals and salts which nowadays are regarded as health hazards when consumed in quantity.

Many centuries ago our water was a well kept secret enjoyed by the privileged few. Now Decantae is bottled at its source in the beautiful Snowdonia foothills, once inhabited by the ancient Celtic tribe from which it takes its name.

Whenever you want one of the purest drinks available, use Decantae to enhance gourmet food or to preserve and enhance the character of high quality spirits.

DECANTAE, A UNIQUELY PURE PLEASURE – DRINK YOUR HEALTH WITH IT.

JUNCTION 28

Out of Town & Out of Hassle!

The venue for that all important luncheon meeting

JUNCTION 28

provides an exciting variety of quality food in a relaxed and friendly atmosphere.

Ideally located off Junction 28 of the M4 for easy access from Cardiff (15 mins), Caerphilly (10 mins).

The surrounding business communities are offered an easy, direct route with secure parking facilities.

The extensive choice of excellent food and personal service includes an outstanding á la carte menu perfect for both luncheon and dinner.

'FULLY AIR-CONDITIONED'

- ❖ Á la carte menu available Evenings & Lunchtimes
- ❖ Special Early Evening Flyer (5.30 - 7.00pm)
- ❖ 3 course - £11.95, extensive selection
- ❖ Great choice - Lunchtime menu

SUNDAY LUNCH -
Excellent value Set Menu
2 course £8.95
3 course £10.95

Wide selection of Traditional & Modern dishes

Open: Mon-Sat Evenings 5.30-9.30pm (last orders)
Mon-Sun Lunchtimes 12.00-2.00pm
(Sunday lunch last orders 4.00pm)

Station Approach, Bassaleg, Newport
☎ (01633) 891891

Just a few examples from our Menu...

STARTERS	
Roast Double Pigeon Breast on green French lentils with garlic & bacon, game sauce	£3.95
Deep Fried Cambozola with tomatoe and herb chutney	£3.95
King Prawns baked in Filo pastry with spring onions, ginger & sweet and sour sauce	£4.95
Puff pastry case of Smoked Haddock, mushrooms & poached egg, glazed with lightly curried hollandaise	£3.95
MAIN COURSE	
Fillet of Beef Wellington with Madeira sauce	£8.95
French style casserole of Goose Breast, Duck joints & local sausage	£7.95
Fillet of Red Mullet, Black Pasta, light cream of shellfish & tarragon	£10.45
Paupiette of Brill filled with Lobster Mousse on a bisque style sauce	£11.50
A selection of Delicious Desserts	

Prices correct at time of going to print

Robert, Sheila & Timothy
extend a very warm

Welcome to Town
Bistro Tavern
at Llanrhidian, Gower

*Enjoy your Wining and Dining...
in the heart of the glorious Gower...
or just pop in for a drink*

Open for lunch & Evening Meals
Tues to Saturday
Full menu on Thurs, Fri & Saturday

'Light Bites' available Tuesday & Wednesday Lunch & Evenings

Reservations advisable
Tel: 01792 390015

HERBS cookshop

307-309 High Street, Bangor
Tel: 351249

For a fast, efficient take out service or a meal in our informal, friendly restaurant, Herbs provides delicious home cooked vegetarian fare, using only the best quality local Welsh produce.

Our wide range of freshly prepared foods includes soups, pastries, hot dishes, salads, breads and patisseries, whilst we also stock a high quality range of ground coffees, teas, cheeses and preserves.

In addition to this we also offer an outside catering service for any occasion.

Cariad 'Flights' to Fancy

In international wine competitions wines are scrutinised 'blind' by two panels of experts. If 'commended' they are further judged for colour, bouquet, flavour, complexity, fullness, sweetness and lingering flavour by a second panel of most experienced experts.

Normally only 15% of the wines tasted are proposed for medals, which are resampled and judged.

In the recent announcement of the results of the 1997 International Wines and Spirits Competition at Vinexpo, in Bordeaux, Cariad Wines won 4 medals, one in each of the categories it entered.

Judged against the best wines in the world, **Cariad** won a silver award for the **Cariad** Blush Vintage Quality Sparkling Wine 1995, while the **Cariad** Dry White, **Cariad** Medium Dry White and **Cariad** Rosé all took bronze awards.

Insist on the internationally acclaimed Welsh wines to compliment the best Welsh cuisine and order **Cariad**

Llanerch Vineyard

Cariad Wines Ltd., Llanerch Vineyard, Hensol, Pendoylan, Vale of Glamorgan CF72 8JU. Tel: 01443 225877 Fax: 01443 225546

Photograph - Richard Bosworth

Brecon Court Vineyard

Largest Planted Vineyard in Wales

Nestling in the heart of the Usk Valley, Brecon Court Vineyard, set in 8 acres of the most spectacular and tranquil countryside is planted with a wide variety of vines.

Our farm shop, wine tasting and summer tours are open to the public from May to September.

Come and visit our Red Deer Herd - a magical sight to see

Llansoy Nr, Usk, South Wales NP5 1DT
Tel 01291 650366 & Fax: 01291 640555

The SugarLoaf Vineyards

Welsh Wine

Visit the only Vineyard in the Brecon Beacons National Park. The Sugar Loaf Vineyards are a mile from the centre of Abergavenny - Tour the vineyards, taste the wine.

M. & I.B. Hofayz
Dummar Farm,
Pentre Lane,
Abergavenny,
NP7 7LA
Tel/Fax:
(01873) 858675

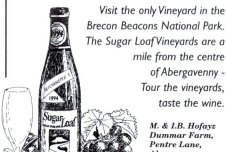

St Davids Food & Wine
High Street, St Davids

We have a well stocked cheese display with a large choice of local Welsh varieties.

Locally Smoked Salmon & Trout, Cooked Meats, Salami, Paté, Quiche & Pies.

An extensive range of quality preserves, pickles, chutneys etc, from Elsenham, Epicure, Patak and Cottage Delight.

Chocolates from Lindt and Bendicks of Mayfair.

A wide choice of Wholefoods.

A selection of Welsh Wines and Spritzers from Cwm Deri Vineyard and Cariad.

Please Telephone
01437 721948 & 720816

EVAN REES (BUTTER) LTD

Directors: R.P. Carman   D.M. CARMAN

BUTTER PACKERS & EXPORTERS

*Suppliers of quality butter nationally to the multiples and catering trade.
Specialist in packet butter for the export market.*

HOLLYBUSH BUTTER

a taste of luxury, at a price you can afford.

2 Viking Way, Winch Wen,
Swansea SA1 7DA

Tel **01792 310567**
Facsimile
01792 700345

OFFA'S VINEYARD

A taste of the Mediterranean from

The Heart of Monmouth

Grown on the southerly facing slopes, our ranges of beautiful red and white wines are a delight to enjoy - either on their own or as a complement to that special meal

Offa's Vineyard
Old Rectory, Llanvihangel-Y-Llewern,
Monmouth NP5 4HL

Tel 01600 780241

MARY'S FARMHOUSE
Crymych, Pembs.
Tel 01239 831440

Real Dairy Ice Cream & Sorbet

Carefully made in the Preseli Hills of West Wales using only natural ingredients

Mary's Farmhouse Ice Cream gives you a taste that is pure, fresh and unspoilt.

Meringue's are also baked on the premises to the same high standard.

For Lovers of Good Wine as well as the language

A free taste of Wales!

The vineyard was planted in 1986 on a South facing field of Pant Teg farm below Graig Llysfaen in Morgannwg.

The planting of the vineyard followed an old tradition that took root in Cymru at the time of the Romans and was kept alive through the Dark and Middle Ages by the monasteries.

In recent years, new varieties of vines have been developed which can yield superb wines in today's climate, and we can now participate in what must have been one of the more enjoyable of the worldly pursuits of the mediaeval monks.

When drinking Pant Teg wine, if you share no more than a fraction of the pleasure and hwyl experienced by those who have laboured in this agreeable vineyard to produce it, we for our part will be more than content.

Gwir Flâs o Gymru!

Plannwyd y Winllan ym 1986 ar oleddf heulog o dir Pant Teg dan gysgod Craig Llysfaen. Aed ati i blannu gan adfer hen draddodiad a ddaeth i Gymru gyda'r Rhufeiniaid ac a gadwyd yn fyw drwy'r canrifoedd gan y mynachlogydd.

Heddiw, mae mathau newydd o winwydd sy'n cynhyrchu gwinoedd rhagorol yn yr hinsawdd Cymreig. Cawn felly gyfranogi yn un o weithgareddau bydol mwyaf dibryder yr hen fynachod.

Wrth brofi Gwin Pant Teg, os y profwch chwithau ond rhan fechan o'r mwynhâd a'r hwyl a ddaeth i ran y rhai a fu'n llafurio yn y Winllan ddedwydd hon, yna byddwn ninnau o'n rhan ni yn fwy na bodlion.

Award winning wines of Wales

PANT TEG
Gwin Cain Cymreig, Llysfaen,
Sir Gaerdydd, Cymru
Tel 01222 753834 Fax 01222 763284

Our latest summit

Innovative 'Spoon in the Lid' impulse tubs join our extensive ranges of Real Dairy Ice Creams made for our customers over 50 Golden Years

THAYER'S is a Division of The Premium Ice Cream Company Limited

Thayer's Dairy Ice Creamery, Wentloog Road, Rumney, Cardiff. CF3 8ED U.K. ☎ 01222 778808 Fax 01222 777872

With our produce we've captured a taste of the Welsh Countryside

Elm Dairy is set in the heart of West Wales. We bottle milk from our own and other local farms that meet our high standards so that you are assured of the freshest taste of the Welsh countryside available.

Try our delicious Elm Fresh Milkshakes
Available in three flavours ● Strawberry, ● Chocolate ● and Banana

Butter as butter should taste ...
The rich, creamy taste of butter made from fresh local milk

ELM DAIRY

Gilfach, Llanboidy, Whitland Carmarthenshire SA34 0DN

Llanboidy (01994) 448206
Fax (01994) 448734 - Accounts
Fax (01994) 448633 - Orders

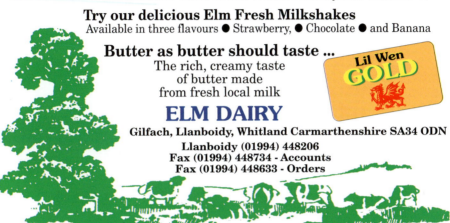

Caws Ffermdy
NANTYBWLA
Farmhouse Cheese

❖ Awarded Gold Medal at the International Food and Drink Exhibition 1997

❖ Winner of Regional Flavours of Europe Cup Award 1995

❖ Best Caerffili Royal Welsh Show on numerous occasions

The cheese at Nantybwla is made with vegetarian rennet and is available in 10lb wheels and 14oz waxed minis in plain and with garlic, chives and smoked varieties.

Directions: Approx. 2 miles from Carmarthen town on the Trevaughan Road.
Open: 10.30am - 5.00pm Monday to Saturday. Cheese making days vary - please telephone to check. Evening visits can be arranged for parties.
Facilities: Viewing windows to cheese making room; museum and shop with disabled access. Video of cheese making.
Admission Charges: £2.00 adults; £1.00 children.

Eiddwen and Edward Morgan
Nantybwla, College Road,
Carmarthen, SA31 3QS
Telephone: (01267) 237905

This premium quality **Welsh Butter** is produced at the BS5750 accredited Llangadog creamery, situated on the bank of the River Towy, Dyfed in West Wales.

Llangadog has an enviable reputation within the industry with its awards for butter at major dairy shows.

In 1995 it was the proud holder of the Supreme Butter Trophy at the Royal Welsh Show.

Available in 250g packs and 7g Portion Packs.

To place an order for this product please contact:
Justine Morgan on
Tel: 01550 777765   Fax: 01550 777647

The Creamery, Llangadog,
Dyfed, West Wales, SA19 9LY

Rachel's Dairy
delicious organic yogurts from Wales... naturally!

RACHEL'S DAIRY LTD
Unit 63, Glanyrafon Industrial Estate,
Aberystwyth, Ceredigion, Wales SY23 3JQ

Tel: 01970 625805 Fax: 01970 626591
Email: rachelsdairy@netwales.co.uk
Web: www.webaware.co.uk/bestofwales/rachdry

NORTH WALES ENTRIES

1   Abersoch

Porth Tocyn Hotel

Bwlch Tocyn
Abersoch
Gwynedd
LL53 7BU
Tel: 01758 - 713303
Fax: 01758 - 713538

The Fletcher-Brewer family's extremely comfortable summer resort is renowned for the warmth of its welcome, full of good humour and enthusiasm. Standing by its heated swimming pool in fine gardens the hotel enjoys stunning views across Cardigan Bay to the mountains of Snowdonia and the Rhinogs.

    Dinner runs to an inventive five-course menu changed daily by Louise and her team, though those with smaller appetites are not obliged to order more than two. Starters include baked fillet of smoked haddock glazed with Welsh rarebit over braised fennel, or pan-fried scallops on a cucumber and garlic sauce with deep-fried leeks; then some equally interesting soups such as carrot, honey and ginger or leek, sherry and potato precede main courses like grilled halibut on braised red cabbage with caramelised mango and mustard hollandaise, or possibly a simple grill of turbot, sea bass and salmon with a prawn sauce. First-class lamb, beef and duck also come with well-judged sauces, or plain on request. Hot and cold sweets, Queen of Puddings and sticky toffee are among the favourites, followed by Welsh and continental cheeses, after which you can sit back comfortably with coffee and petits fours. An exceptional value Sunday Spectacular is perhaps Porth Tocyn's greatest gastronomic contribution; guests help themselves from the vast hot and cold buffet, the only apparent restriction being "no dirty plates or doggy bags"!

*MEALS: D 7.30-9.30 from £21;
Set Sun L 12.30-2 £16
Special breaks: Dinner, Bed and Breakfast from £125*

*WTB: 4 Crowns highly commended
17 En suite from £55 S; £85 D
Closed: mid-Nov-Easter*

2   Abersoch

Riverside Hotel

Abersoch,
Gwynedd
LL53 7HW
Tel: 01758 - 712419
Fax: 01758 - 712671

John and Wendy Bakewell have just marked 30 summer seasons at their unpretentious and relaxing harbour-side hotel where they have been honest pioneers of fresh, unfussy cooking. Non-residents are welcome to enjoy morning coffee, bar lunches or afternoon tea in the garden, and to take a swim in the covered heated swimming pool, in a comfortable haven where the welcome is warmly informal.

    The daily three-course, fixed-price menu finishes with excellent coffee and offers very good value. Starters will perhaps include smoked salmon, a grilled goats cheese salad, an enterprising soup such as parsnip and apple or a light crab tart with deliciously lemon-scented mayonnaise. Main dishes generally feature Welsh sirloin steak in various guises and fresh local fish – perhaps red mullet poached in a chive and cream sauce – and maybe a mildly-spiced chicken and coconut casserole, served with rice and some simple, nicely-done vegetables. The Riverside's home-made ice creams, chocolate meringues and brandysnap baskets stacked with local soft fruits are a Wendy Bakewell speciality; alternatively toffee and banana pie or a well-nigh perfect creme caramel will easily erase the last traces of appetite.

MEALS: D 7.30-9 from £22
Special breaks: Dinner, Bed and Breakfast from £108

WTB: 4 Crowns highly commended
12 En suite from £32 S; £64 D
Closed: Nov-Mar

3   Bala

Pale Hall

Llandderfel
Bala
Gwynedd
LL23 7PS
Tel: 01678 - 530285
Fax: 01678 - 530220

Approaching Llandderfel from Bala and dropping down to the beautiful River Dee below the Berwyn mountains, you catch your first glimpse of this great Victorian house's rooftops and tall chimneys above the trees; then as you turn and cross the river Pale Hall appears grandly and romantically before you. There can be few more splendid country houses in Wales – even Queen Victoria was impressed – and Saul Nahed and his wife have spared little expense in restoring the house and grounds to their former glory.

Staff are welcoming and eager to please, while the kitchen offers a commendably short dinner menu, neither too complicated in its concept nor over-ambitious in execution. Among the simple but tasty starters you might find a salad of avocado, crispy bacon and unspecified blue cheese, and warm smoked salmon with poached egg and chervil cream sauce; then pass on to a medley of four fish – salmon, red mullet, sewin and smoked haddock – with a mild curry sauce, or Welsh Black rib-eye steak for which there is a supplement. Follow a dessert of assorted home-made ice creams in a brandysnap basket or treacle and walnut tart with Chantilly cream with coffee and chocolates in one of the handsome lounges that look out over mature parkland to the valley below.

MEALS: L 12-2; D 7-9 from £23.95
Set Sun L £15.95

WTB: 4 Crowns highly commended
17 En suite from £69 S; £95 D
Special breaks: Dinner, Bed and Breakfast from £125

4   Bangor

Goetre Isaf Farmhouse

Caernarfon Road
Bangor
Gwynedd
LL57 4BD
Tel/Fax: 01248 - 364541

Fred and Alison Whowell's idiosyncratically-run farmhouse stands high above the intersection of the A5 and A4087 just south of the Britannia Bridge and about two miles from Bangor. The site of the present 18th century house has been in constant occupation for four centuries and much original slate, stone and old materials have been incorporated.

Alison's evening meals, the focus of a stay, are chosen over a pot of tea in the conservatory. Eating preferences are tailored to suit: some returning guests have even arrived bearing their own herbs and spices!

Soups on offer might be mushroom, cauliflower or Armenian, the latter made with lentils and dried apricots, and main course choices may well include fresh Penrhyn fish, Welsh lamb or Welsh Black beef collected from a local organic butcher and prepared to individual taste. There's no obligation, but among various accompaniments on offer we went for garden nettles, collected by Fred in the rain and pureed with nutmeg (interesting), and finished with rhubarb and ginger Charlotte and a cheeseboard of locally-procured cheeses to nibble over a communal chat.

The three bedrooms (one with bathroom) – without TV, radio or telephones but boasting exceedingly comfortable beds – all have a fair share of views up towards the looming Snowdon foothills or down the long valley to Caernarfon Bay.

 MEALS: D 7.30 from £11
Special breaks: Dinner, Bed and Breakfast from £44
No credit cards

 WTB: 1 Crown
3 Rooms, 1 En suite from £15.50 S; £37 D

5   Bangor

Herbs Cookshop

307-309 High Street
Bangor
Gwynedd
LL57 1UL
Tel: 01248 - 351249

A new location just two years ago has much expanded the catering arm of Pam Marchant's cookshop, so that the larger section of her two interlinked properties now provides comfortable surroundings in which to enjoy arguably the best vegetarian food in town.

Besides the popular takeaway in the wholefoods section, a half-dozen or more new cafe tables facing the display counters attract a young office and university crowd drawn to vegetarian food that is both unusual and full of flavour.

From early morning there's a steady trade in breakfast muffins, bara brith and chocolate Florentines to accompany coffee or cappuccino, and by mid-morning the baked jacket potatoes and filled baguettes are supplemented by a couple of soups, perhaps tomato and lentil and

cream of potato and artichoke, plus hot daily specials like broccoli and potato Korma with a punchy Brinjal pickle. Lunchtime starters such as garlic mushrooms, and apricot and cashew-nut pate are quite filling for a quick snack at give-away prices, while tacos with chilli and cheese or Glamorgan sausages with a Greek salad will scarcely break the bank at well under a fiver.

For a treat, finish with carrot and syrup pudding with marmalade sauce, strawberry and apple crumble or raspberry and mango torte. Welsh and cream teas, locally-made dairy ice creams and first-rate freshly-squeezed orange juice are further indicative of the care taken in every department of Pam's commendable cafe.

 MEALS: All day 8.30-4.30
No credit cards. Unlicensed
Closed: Sundays; 25 & 26 Dec

6 Bangor

Penrhyn Castle

The National Trust
Bangor
Gwynedd
LL57 4HN
Tel: 01248 - 353084

The magnificent parkland which surrounds this fantasy neo-Norman castle, looking out across Lavan Sands and Conwy Bay, carries an admission charge to non-members, but there's plenty to see and do in the grounds, from the Victorian walled garden to the adventure playground.

You get a measure of the scale of the place if you follow a trail from the courtyard past the former scullery and pantries and then climb up to a present-day refectory overlooked by the battlements.

At lunchtime, daily blackboards offer variously-filled hot jacket potatoes and salad selections which include a Dairymaid's Platter of assorted Welsh cheeses. Penrhyn's specialities include pea and mint soup and rum plum cake, both made from local recipes (the latter recently discovered at the castle), and some imaginative hot dishes dreamed up by a keen catering team. As well as the popular Lobscaws (thick Welsh cawl with red cabbage) and St David's cheese and red onion savoury tart, they've launched – to instant acclaim – Cottage Pie with Leeky Roof, this favourite dish given a Welsh touch by its creamy leek and potato topping with a crust of Welsh Cheddar.

From 2pm the fare switches to Penrhyn and Welsh Garden teas, but there are simpler snacks for youngsters, who can pass the time poring over puzzles and colouring sheets which are always available.

 MEALS: All day 11-5
Closed: Tues; Nov-end Mar

7 Beaumaris

Bulkeley Hotel

Castle Street
Beaumaris
Isle of Anglesey
LL58 8AW
Tel: 01248 - 810415
Fax: 01248 - 810416

With its commanding position overlooking the Conwy coastline from the shore of the Menai Strait and with Snowdonia forming a moody backdrop, the Bulkeley is something of an Anglesey institution, and to a point this applies to its Mona restaurant too. The stylish room dominated by crystal chandeliers, carved sideboards and well-stocked dessert and cheese trolleys is essentially traditional and enjoys a clientele who won't expect food at the cutting edge of modernity.

Expect by contrast a kitchen which busies itself with prawn and crab cocktail, pork liver pate, and egg and asparagus salad among starters with traditional accompaniments such as sauce Marie Rose, Melba toast and lemon mayonnaise; melon and Parma ham or smoked salmon with prawns will attract supplements at dinner. More extravagant main courses such as grilled brill fillets with herb and lemon butter, beef fillet with Bordelaise sauce and rack of Welsh lamb with honey and rosemary glaze, will also be supplementary to the nightly table d'hôte, which always includes a daily roast and both salad and vegetarian alternatives, with generous selections of potatoes and vegetables. For diners overwhelmed by the desserts ranging from chocolate profiteroles and sherry trifle to raspberry Pavlova there's a deservedly popular Welsh cheeseboard featuring Pencarreg, Hen Sir and St Illtyd, though it would help perhaps if staff were better schooled as to their origin!

MEALS: D 7-9.30 from £16.50;
Set Sun L 12-2 £9.25
Special breaks: Dinner, Bed and Breakfast from £92

WTB: 4 Crowns highly commended
41 En suite from £55 S; £85 D

North Wales

8 Beaumaris

Plas Cichle

Beaumaris
Isle of Anglesey
LL58 8PS
Tel: 01248 - 810488

Plas Cichle is a working 200-acre farm rearing sheep and cattle in a wooded vale near Llanfaes and close to Anglesey's south-easterly tip at Penmaen Point. Spick and span throughout, the farmhouse has three letting bedrooms equipped with TVs and tea-trays: all have private bathrooms of which two are en suite. With its spacious lounge where the grand piano takes pride of place and a bright breakfast-room with closely-spaced tables, it's a place for making friends both with fellow guests and with hostess Eirwen Roberts, for whom nothing seems too much trouble.

For a splendid start to the day there'll likely be a compote of rhubarb and fresh yoghurt along with the usual cereals, warm home-made muffins and perhaps a hot potato and onion pancake to accompany home-cured bacon, locally-produced sausages, free-range eggs and, of course, the ever-present home-made jams and marmalade. Though evening meals are not available, you can find plenty of choice a few minutes' drive away in Beaumaris and evening trips are assiduously planned.

Plas Cichle is one of a small group of farms on the island which together offer similarly high standards of accommodation and a traditional Anglesey welcome: further details can be obtained from Mrs Roberts. No children under six can be accommodated here, and dogs are discouraged as the new season's lambs may be grazing unprotected within feet of the front door.

WTB: 3 Crowns highly commended
3 Rooms - 2 En suite from £45 D
Breakfast only. No credit cards

9 Beaumaris

Ye Olde Bull's Head

Castle Street
Beaumaris
Isle of Anglesey
LL58 8AP
Tel: 01248 - 810329
Fax: 01248 - 811294

With its cobbled rear courtyard and massive 17th Century single-hinged gate, the original coaching inn dates from 1472; the bedrooms have been modernised to a Victorian theme, named after characters from Dickens to commemorate the author's stay in 1859. The old pub, hung with local memorabilia, is still the heart of the place; from here stairs and passageways lead up to the atmospheric dining room among the hammer-beamed rafters.

Despite venerable surroundings, Keith Rothwell displays a confident contempoary touch in his re-workings of classics from around the world. Start with home-cured bresaola with black olives and parmesan, Bury black pudding grilled with a Conwy mustard sauce, Arbroath smokies, or roulade of locally-smoked salmon with cucumber tartare. Colourfully presented main courses are accompanied by vegetables commendable for their quality and variety; roast breast of Hereford duck on a pink grapefruit, honey and cardomom juice; pan-fried fillet of Welsh beef with Lleyn bacon and wild chanterelles; or roast sea bass fillet with marinated potatoes and warm tomato and herb vinaigrette. An aubergine mille feuille with roast Mediterranean vegetables, pine nut crust and pesto cream sauce could tempt all but the most hardened carnivore, and the sweet-toothed might end with a classic creme brulée and local raspberries.

MEALS: Set Sun L 12.30-2 £14.95
D 7.30-9.30 (9 Sun) from £20
Special breaks: Dinner, Bed and Breakfast from £117

WTB: 4 Crowns highly commended
15 En suite from £47 S; £77 D

10 Betws-y-Coed

Tan-y-Foel Country House

Capel Garmon
Nr Betws-y-Coed
Gwynedd
LL26 0RE
Tel: 01690 - 710507
Fax: 01690 - 710681

Living proof of the "small is beautiful" principle, Tan-y-Foel bursts with enthusiasm and good hotelkeeping. Central to Peter and Janet Pitman's philosophy is the cosseting attention to detail extended to both new and returning guests. Their luxurious, peaceful country hotel is a dreamland set in five acres high on a wooded hillside with unparalleled views down over Llanrwst (4 miles) and the Conwy Valley: the turn to Tan-y-Foel is off the A470 a mile or so north of Betws-y-Coed.

The distinctive, not to say surreal, setting is in a newly-added conservatory surrounded by a futuristic rock-garden of gargantuan proportions.

Despite the limited number of evening dishes, you'll be spoilt for choice between, typically, steamed fillet of sea-bass with smoked trout mousse and lobster nero sauces and Mediterranean-style Melyn-y-Coed goats' cheese with black olive, tomato and anchovy dressing to start, and main dishes like loin of Welsh lamb with pea puree, seasonal vegetables and a lemon and garlic mint sauce or red snapper fillet set on warm gazpacho sauce with brunoise of vegetables. Each dish is a self-sufficient combination of textures and flavours executed with proficiency and an artist's eye for detail. To follow there's always fresh fruit and Welsh cheese, with home-made piccalilli perhaps, alongside creme brulee dressed with cherries and rolled tuiles or rhubarb Charlotte with ginger coulis.

Small wonder that so many devotees take advantage of two- and three-day bargain breaks which offer such feasts, a warm homely welcome and formidable breakfasts to set you on your way.

 MEALS: D 7.45-8.30 from £24
Special breaks: Dinner, Bed and Breakfast from £135

 WTB: 4 Crowns de luxe
7 En suite from £55 S; £80 D

11 Blaenau Ffestiniog

The Miners Arms

Llechwedd Slate
Caverns
Blaenau Ffestiniog
Gwynedd
LL41 3NB
Tel: 01766 - 830523

The Slate Caverns, a major tourist attraction since 1977, are well on their way to recording their six millionth visitor. In addition to two superb underground rides into the hillside and vertically down into the Deep Mine, history is reincarnated in the former miners' workshops and cottages whose last inhabitants moved out in the 1970s. At the Old Bank museum visitors exchange their decimal currency for re-minted Victorian coins with which to buy a penn'orth of boiled sweets in the corner shop or lunch for a couple of bob at the Miners Arms.

Here, two tiny rooms have been recreated as a late Victorian pub where only the metric spirit optics look out of place. Glasses of Chwerw (bitter) or Mwin (mild) are sold over the bar along with a Miner's Lunch of pork or cheese. For five old pence – or £2 – the carrot and lentil soup is a hearty snack, while the potted home-made meals such as beef hot-pot, lamb and mint pie and Welsh chicken with honey and mustard will set you back about eleven pence ha'penny.

There's plenty of seating outside with pop, filled rolls and bara brith on sale and space for the youngsters to play overlooking the old village square: well worth a visit.

MEALS: All day 11-5.30
No credit cards

12 Bontddu

Bontddu Hall

Bontddu
Nr Barmouth
Gwynedd
LL40 2SU
Tel: 01341 - 430661
Fax: 01341 - 430284

With its beautifully appointed Victorian rooms and picture-windowed dining-room, Bontddu boasts one of the most magical views in Wales, and diners sit at immaculately set tables looking out through majestic Scots pines across the Mawddach estuary to the grandeur of Cader Idris. There's a pleasant air of informality amid the splendour, the welcome is friendly and assured and the food on offer is good and genuine.

Using local ingredients wherever possible, many courses have a distinct Welsh flavour, from the handsome grilled goats' cheese salad and prettily dressed local salmon terrine starters to main dishes using the freshest lobsters, Brecon venison and local poultry. Superb Meiriohnydd lamb is a speciality here, and can arrive as a perfectly roasted rack, crisp on the outside but well rested and pink within and flavoured with a redcurrant jus. Puddings, perhaps a trio of chocolate mousses, a frangipane tart with apricot glaze, shortbread biscuits sandwiched with fruit or the acclaimed bread-and-butter pudding, are nicely judged to end the meal, though prime Welsh cheeses and a Stilton are also on offer. In the best weather, cafetiere coffee served with chocolates may be taken out on the terrace – a perfect spot, too, for Bontddu's celebrated afternoon teas – or indoors with a share of the same magnificent view overlooking the estuary from the comfort of the high gothic Green Room.

MEALS: Set D 7.30-9.30 from £23.50;
Sun L 12-2 from £12.96

WTB: 4 Crowns de luxe
15 En suite from £53 S; £90 D
Closed: Nov-Mar

13 Brynsiencyn

Anglesey Sea Zoo

Brynsiencyn
Isle of Anglesey
LL61 6TQ
Tel: 01248 - 430411
Fax: 01248 - 430213

Follow the "lobster" signs to the award-winning Sea Zoo, some six miles from the A5 Britannia Bridge: look out, though, for the sharp left turn in that village with the long name! You can spend all day here exploring the ray pool, lobsters' lair and seahorse garden (family tickets from £10), and entry to the coffee shop is free of charge and a useful watering hole after a stroll along the Menai shoreline opposite.

For lunch, the new self-service counter between 11.30am and 2.00pm promises fresh soup and a daily hot dish such as beef and Guinness casserole, plus various snacks – broccoli, sweetcorn and cheese pasties filled rolls such as ham, tuna or cheese, and various summer salads. Cream teas are served after 2.30pm, with a tempting selection of home-made bara brith, date and walnut cake, fish-shaped shortbread and chocolate fudge slices. Younger children can play with paper and crayons in between "snappy bites" with potato and beans, and fudge sundae. With plenty of well-spaced tables and high chairs inside, picnic tables on the patios and level access to gift shop and toilets, family requirements are well catered for: all that remains on the way out is to buy some home-made fudge for the trip home.

MEALS: All day 10-5 (3 in winter); L 11.30-2
Closed: Mon-Fri during winter

14 Caernarfon

Ty'n Rhos Country House

Seion
Llanddeiniolen
Caernarfon
Gwynedd
LL55 3AE
Tel: 01248 - 670489
Fax: 01248 - 670079

Lynda and Nigel Kettle's comfortable and homely hotel has evolved over the years out of a working farm which was once home to their own dairy herd. These days a neighbour's cattle graze the 72 acres of pastureland while Ty'n Rhos's droves of returning guests now sleep soundly in the byres. With her farming background and instinctive feel for country produce, Lynda is a meticulous shopper in at least three local butchers, hand-picking the freshest fish at Port Penrhyn and whenever possible using her own vegetables, fresh herbs and soft fruit from the kitchen garden.

Nightly set dinner, written up beforehand for residents, might be terrine of chicken, hazelnut and apricots served with pickled honeyed vegetables; then salmon with wine and chervil butter sauce on home-made noodles, followed by a pear clafoutis tart, Nantybwla cheese with home-made oatmeal biscuits and delectable petit fours with a cafetiere of fresh ground coffee. Seasonal alternatives a la carte offer three courses priced according to the main course: venison collops with asparagus spears and juniper berry sauce, locally-caught sea-bass on fennel and Pernod with deep-fried vegetables, or mushroom, leek and Stilton crumble with herb butter sauce typify the range. Dinner is not available to non-residents on Sunday or Monday nights.

Freshly-squeezed orange juice and home-made bread and preserves contribute to an excellent breakfast, adding a memorable conclusion to the shortest of stays.

*MEALS: Set D 7-8.30 from £23.50;
Set Sun L 12.30-1.30 £14.95
Special breaks: Dinner, Bed and Breakfast from £105*

*WTB: 4 Crowns de luxe
14 En suite from £45 S; £60 D
Closed: 24-30 Dec; Sun-Mon D non-residents*

15 Chirk

Chirk Castle Tearoom

The National Trust
Chirk
Denbighshire
LL14 5AF
Tel: 01691 - 777701
Fax: 01691 - 774706

A mile-and-a-half of driveway meanders through wooded parkland before visitors park and take the free bus or climb the final 200 metres to the castle keep, imposing in its hilltop splendour and master of all it surveys. The admission fee to the gardens entitles visitors to access to the tea-room which occupies the castle's former kitchens facing the courtyard. "Jack Fire", on which the household's meats were roasted right up to the 1940s, takes pride of place in the main cafe, and there's more seating in the fascinating 13th century Distil Tower.

The standard mid-morning fare of coffee and cakes leads into lunch which always offers a hearty vegetarian soup, Welsh-style gammon steak with laverbread cakes, fried egg and tomatoes, a tart of tomatoes with Melyn-y-Coed goats' cheese and spiced spinach tart from an original 1699 recipe. Home-made pancakes (served until 3.30pm) are a speciality of the dessert menu, after which a Welsh cream tea with bara brith and home-made scones, jam and cream, or the Woodman's savoury tea – with Welsh cheese, butter and onion relish – are the preferred options.

*MEALS: L 11-2.15; T 2.30-5 from £2.95
Closed: Mon-Tues; Mon-Fri (Oct); Nov-end Mar*

16 Colwyn Bay

Cafe Nicoise

124 Abergele Road
Colwyn Bay
Conwy
LL29 7PS
Tel: 01492 - 531555

Cooking reminiscent of the Cote d'Azur on the North Wales coast is scarcely the norm, and it's a tribute to Lynn and Carl Swift's patience and persistence that they have in no way compromised their principles since starting out here eight years ago.

From Tuesday to Saturday at lunchtime, and Monday to Thursday nights, Carl cooks a regularly-changing Menu Touristique which represents the best value for miles around, yet neither fine ingredients nor cooking skills are in any way overlooked. No one could ask for a better-balanced three-course lunch than a starter of tomato salad with fresh mussels and pesto dressing, followed by navarin of lamb dressed with spring vegetables, ending with a fresh strawberry vacherin.

For those who seek still more, the monthly carte offers smoked goose with seed mustard mayonnaise, warm scallop salad with basil and tomato or roast red-pepper salad with garlic croutons, as curtain raisers to such accomplished main dishes as canon of Welsh lamb with aubergine confit, and grilled sea-bass with pan-fried cucumber and asparagus bouillon.

Creme brulee with fresh raspberries, perhaps, white chocolate parfait, or mango tart with creme chantilly, can be ordered separately or combined in an assiette du chef, while the cheese assiette promises a selection of French and Welsh varieties to suit all tastes. Friendly, relaxing surroundings and service, as well as carefully chosen French house wines, translate Nicoise into a thoroughly enjoyable experience.

MEALS: L 12-2 from £10.95;
D 7-10 from £12.95
Closed: L Mon-Tues; Sun; 1 week Jan; 1 week June

  V

17 Conwy

Berthlwyd Hall Hotel

Llechwedd
Conwy
LL32 8DQ
Tel: 01492 - 592409
Fax: 01492 - 572290

Standing on the lower slopes of Sychnant with views back down towards Conwy, Berthlwyd is an elegantly-proportioned Victorian mansion run by Brian and Joanna Griffin. Bedrooms are few enough to engender a family feeling among guests, and occasional house parties with dinner served around a communal table have been voted a great success. Joanna is an accomplished cook herself, but this year has installed a full-time chef to leave her with more time for renovating the day rooms and for her house guests. So far results have lived up to expectations and her long experience here ensures that the finest produce reaches her table: certificated Welsh Black beef, pork and bacon from the Freedom Herd at neighbouring Oakwood Farm, locally reared venison and Anglesey monkfish all appearing on the menu.

A seasonal a la carte list might start with roasted Mediterranean vegetable soup, fresh salmon mousse with Thai dressing, or four-cheese terrine, moving on to roast monkfish wrapped in home-cured bacon with tomato and basil sauce or venison mignons with savoury stuffing and a port and redcurrant sauce; finishing with local strawberries as a high-summer alternative to some decadent sugared pancakes filled with orange mousse on a bitter-orange and Grand Marnier sauce. The Truffles Restaurant itself opens on to the south-facing sun terrace where an antique wine-press takes pride of place – several wines on the varied list are of Brian's personal choosing on his frequent trips to Provence.

MEALS: Set Sun L 12-2 £10.95;
D 7-9.30 from £23
Special breaks: Dinner, Bed and Breakfast from £107

WTB: 4 Crowns highly commended
8 En suite from £58 S; £62 D

18 Conwy

The Old Rectory

Llansanffraid
Glan Conwy,
Colwyn Bay
Conwy
LL28 5LF
Tel: 01492 - 580611
Fax: 01492 - 584555

Hoteliers of long standing and high repute, Michael and Wendy Vaughan run a sophisticated house of elegance and charm commanding breathtaking views down the tidal reaches of the Conwy estuary from above the A470 at Llansanffraid.

Carefully avoiding regular restaurant conventions, Michael invites guests to arrive from 7.15pm for dinner served at 8, gathering first for a drink and appetisers in the lounge where there's generally a live musical interlude on Welsh harp or piano before the main event.

A description of a typical dinner perhaps best illustrates the style of the set evening meal created by Wendy Vaughan (special food preferences are solicited well in advance).

A platter of fresh and smoked salmon is presented in seven different ways with embellishments which include grey shrimp and caviar and a garnish of black potatoes, seaweed and tomato vinaigrette. Roast rack of Welsh lamb, dressed with a mint and green peppercorn crust, is served with a tian of aubergine and miniature vegetable decorations. Each dish consists of up to a dozen constituent parts, a creative and complex composition for the diner. After an optional interlude of Welsh and Celtic farm cheeses (or perhaps a grilled goats' cheese alternative) a choice of two puddings might offer chocolate pear tart with a trio of sauces, or creme brulee with a brandysnap basket of strawberries Chantilly and home-made strawberry ice cream.

 MEALS: D @ 7.15 for 8
from £25

 WTB: 4 Crowns de luxe
6 En suite from £79 S; £99 D
Closed: Dec; Jan

19 Deganwy

Paysanne North Wales

Station Road
Deganwy
Conwy
LL31 9EJ
Tel/Fax: 01492 - 582079

Standing by the road into Deganwy from Llandudno Junction, Paysanne is separated only by rail tracks from the shore of the Conwy estuary. During nearly ten years in operation as we publish, it has established a loyal following locally and from the accessible Cheshire borderlands for its French-style country food. The Rosses' studied informality alternates Bob's as genial host and inveterate wine buff with Barbara's frequent forays from the kitchen.

Alternatively-priced menus offer up to a half-dozen choices at each stage: at "150 francs" are potage du jour, tarte Alsacienne and crepe aux asperges to start, and main courses such as carbonnade de boeuf and pintade chasseur. For "175 francs" diners are offered chevre chaud baked on olive bread with tomato and olive salad and filet de boeuf dijonnaise cooked to order and served with a creamy mushroom and Dijon mustard sauce. The same dessert choices for both price ranges are listed on a portable blackboard, combining profiteroles with chocolate sauce and a thoroughly British Summer Pudding alongside a platter of Welsh fromages. Irrespective of fluctuating exchange rates Paysanne retains the standard pound sterling for ten francs' worth of food, so the price you'll pay stays as reasonable as ever.

MEALS: D 7-9.30 from £15 (Sat 6.30-10)
Closed: Sun-Mon

North Wales

20 Dolgellau

Dolmelynllyn Hall

Ganllwyd
Dolgellau
Gwynedd
LL40 2HP
Tel/Fax: 01341 - 440273

Inside the grounds of this 16th-century house you enter into a rare peace and stillness. Victorian in atmosphere, it was once the home of the Maddocks family of Porthmadog and Tremadog fame, and has wonderful views down the Ganllwyd valley towards Cader Idris. Jon Barkwith now welcomes you into his home of unpretentious comfort, and his daughter Joanna Redcliffe cooks with a vibrance and enthusiasm which are both admirable and surprising amid all this stillness.

The four-course dinner offer good value, Joanna's innovative starters including warm salads, risottos and salsas or perhaps a light crab tart with rich red pepper vinaigrette and a salad of fennel and dill. Main courses are strong on high-quality local lamb and beef and the freshest of local fish with unusual and well-judged sauces like the sherry, vinegar, and mint sauce which is served with a watercress kasha to accompany the lamb, and ragout of mushrooms and parsley couscous with peppered fillet of beef. There's also a superb dish of baked monkfish wrapped in parma ham in a pastry lattice on a white wine and orange cream sauce. Varied and generous puddings include a light but still naughty toffee and brandy cheesecake with caramelised pecans and really fruity raspberry coulis. Good coffee and home-made sweetmeats are also included in the price of a memorable dinner.

MEALS: D 7.30-8.30 from £23.50
No children under 10
Special breaks: Dinner, Bed and Breakfast from £125

WTB: 4 Crowns highly commended
11 En suite from £50 S; £95 D
Closed: Dec-Mar

21   Dolgellau

Dylanwad Da

2 Ffos-y-Felin
Dolgellau
Gwynedd
LL40 1BS
Tel: 01341 - 422870

Dylan Rowlands's is an informal, unfussy place with a Welsh emphasis, simply but comfortably furnished with pine tables and chairs and interesting pictures on the walls. His monthly menus use local ingredients generously, with each course sensibly limited to about four dishes and cooked with a distinct and tempting flavour of Wales.

   Start perhaps with a Welsh vegetable broth, faggots served cold with apple sauce, chicken and mushrooms in light puff pastry or a terrific warm salad of pigeon breast slices and crisp smoked bacon with grapes and herby leaves. Main courses might offer lemon sole fillets with a smoked salmon and cream sauce or tender local lamb loin with a well-flavoured spring onion stuffing and mint-scented port gravy; varied vegetables in unusual guises come plentifully in a separate dish.

   With such large portions you needn't feel obliged to venture beyond one or two courses, but should you so choose, desserts are all of high quality, highlighted by white chocolate cheesecake, warm rhubarb, peach and orange pie, and Dylan's ultimate banana and honey ice cream. Settle alternatively for the platter of four or five Welsh cheeses in prime condition, colourfully presented with fresh fruit and perhaps accompanied by a glass of port from the sensible and reasonably-priced wine list.

 MEALS: D 7-9 from £12.75
Closed: All Feb; Sun-Wed (except Easter);
Whitsun & Jul-Sep

---

22   Dolgellau

Penmaenuchaf Hall

Penmaenpool
Dolgellau
Gwynedd
LL40 1YB
Tel/Fax: 01341 - 422129

Built in 1860 as a summer residence for cotton magnate James Leigh Taylor, this splendid mansion stands in mature wooded grounds looking down on the Mawddach estuary and across to Snowdonia beyond. Penmaenuchaf today provides country-house accommodation on a grand scale, with dinners in the oak-panelled dining-room to match.

   A nightly fixed table d'hôte, offering a vegetarian main course as the only area for choice, leads diners from warm salad of pigeon and duck, ham with a raspberry dressing through a melon and ginger sorbet to chicken supreme filled with langoustines and spinach or gateau of potato, garlic, aubergine and pesto, and finishes with steamed butterscotch pudding and a vanilla cream.

   More varied (and steeply priced) choices on a wordily-composed alternative carte proffer "rillettes of guinea fowl served with home-made brioche and rhubarb chutney" followed by "loin fillet of Brecon venison carved on to a rosti potato with broad beans, spring cabbage and a light Madeira jus": an additional selection of seasonal vegetables, shown as a supplement, proves superfluous. Follow perhaps with iced honey and whisky parfait with cappuccino sauce and almond biscuits or Celtic farmhouse cheeses with celery, grapes and soda bread.

Lunches, including Sunday's, are generally in lighter vein: duck egg en croute; salmon with chive butter sauce; baked lime caramel cream with strawberry sauce, priced inclusively for two or three courses.

MEALS: L 12-2.30; D 7-9.30 from £25;
Set Sun L £14.95
Special breaks: Dinner, Bed and Breakfast from £130

WTB: 4 Crowns de luxe
14 En suite from £75 S; £90 D

23 Glanwydden

The Queen's Head

Glanwydden
Llandudno
Conwy
LL31 9JP
Tel: 01492 - 546570
Fax: 01492 - 546487

From either the A470 or the A546 there are two easy approaches to Glanwydden, hidden in lush countryside just a mile or so inland from Penrhyn Bay. Either way you'll encounter this regal little pub where Robert and Sally Cureton have held sway for a decade and a half. Both are accomplished cooks whose long experience confirms the merit of meticulous shopping in creating imaginative pub food in modern style for a well-heeled and loyal clientele.

No one is obliged to lunch on more than an open prawn sandwich or smoked goose breast salad with kiwi fruit, while others dine equally regally on specials like queen scallops with samphire and smoked cheese sauce, or pork fillet with Teifi and nettle cheese on a leek and Welsh whisky cream sauce, accompanied by new potatoes and crisp, fresh vegetables.

Long-standing favourites at The Queen's Head include Glanwydden lamb cutlets with plum and raspberry sauce, and Welsh smoked mushrooms filled with fresh crab and topped with hollandaise and toasted almonds.

A Welsh dresser is loaded with trifles, Pavlovas and pies, cheeses include Pencarreg and smoked Caerphilly, and the range of real ales and personally selected wines is impressive. Reservations are taken only at night and on Sunday lunch for parties of six or more: no children under seven.

MEALS: L 12-2; D 6-9
Closed: 25 Dec

24   Harlech

Castle Cottage

Pen Llech
Harlech
Gwynedd
LL46 2YL
Tel/Fax: 01766 - 780479

Close by the great castle, this friendly old building – now very much a Harlech institution – houses the pretty pink-and-white restaurant where Glyn Roberts cooks to deserved acclaim, while his wife Jacquie presides with quiet charm out front. In the cosy beamed bar diners browse through the regularly changing menu over Glyn's special little spring rolls, marinated beef on a skewer and a subtle hot lamb and coconut curry tartlet. An agreeable torment in electing to forego the local crab with avocado, hearty, authentic minestrone and an apple, mango and goats' cheese croustade, is assuaged by the warm smoked haddock mousse dressed with marvellous leek and cockle sauce.

Main courses might be roast rack of Welsh lamb with lavender crust and red wine jus, grilled fillet of local sea bass on squid-ink pasta – a happy marriage this, consummated with a hearty mushroom and cream sauce – and rib-eye of prime Welsh beef sauced with whisky and grain mustard.

For pudding, the light banana sponge with banana ice cream and toffee nut sauce, and dark chocolate slice with white chocolate sauce are seductive alternatives to the home-made ice creams, fruit sorbets and impressive Welsh cheeses on offer, while from the short, comprehensive list a red and a white wine of the week are always available by the bottle or glass.

MEALS: D 7-9.30 (9 in winter)
Special breaks: Dinner, Bed and Breakfast from £88

WTB: 3 Crowns highly commended
6 Rooms 4 En suite from £38 S; £54 D
Closed: 3 weeks Jan

25   Harlech

Plas Cafe

High Street
Harlech
Gwynedd
LL96 2YA
Tel: 01766 - 780204

This beautifully-maintained old building is in many ways the focal point of Harlech, serving good plain food in generous quantities from breakfast to bedtime. An elegant dining-room, conservatory and terraced tea-garden all share what is proudly described as Harlech's finest view, a panorama of the castle, the mountains of Snowdonia, Cardigan Bay and the Lleyn Peninsula.

The Plas day starts with a selection of teas, cafetiere coffees and hearty breakfasts; thereafter snacks (hot and cold), sandwiches cut to order and home-made cakes – coffee and walnut, and date and apricot are two favourites – continue until lunch and beyond. Midday fare features pate and cheese ploughman's, baked potatoes with various fillings, salads and more hot dishes, while afternoon teas revolve around hot jam doughnuts, bara brith and scones with jam and cream. Service never stops until dinner time, when for starters there'll be large prawn cocktails, oak-smoked salmon and marinated herring. To follow, fresh local trout, good Welsh sirloin steaks and excellent cold baked ham are perennial favourites, while the evening's specials might be breast of duck or lamb casserole, served with fresh, wholesome vegetables and first-rate chips. This all makes a virtue of simplicity in an honest and straightforward establishment providing cheerful service and reasonable prices in an unrivalled setting.

MEALS: All day 9-9
Closed: Jan & Feb

North Wales

26 Llanaber

Llwyndu Farmhouse

Llanaber
Nr Barmouth
Gwynedd
LL42 1RR
Tel: 01341 - 280144
Fax: 01341 - 281236

Paula Thompson welcomes you in and waits on table at this lovely 400-year-old house standing above the sea by the road out of Barmouth bound for Harlech. Husband Peter's cooking is hearty and ebullient; the rustic, comfortable food befits the house and the evening's offerings beguilingly keep a weather eye on the elements. So, on a cold and wet July evening he welcomes travellers with a butter-bean and bacon soup, Welsh rarebit with whisky, chicken livers cooked in butter and sherry and his signature dish, Ham Llwyndu – a rich concoction of Welsh cheeses in garlic mayonnaise wrapped in ham and gently grilled.

Serious proof that you need to be hungry to eat here ensues with a main course of smoked haddock with a sauce of scallops, Gruyére and dill, spare rib pork chop in a treacle and pineapple marinade, or a generous helping of Welsh Black beef sirloin, stir-fried in black bean sauce, with roast red peppers and crisp potato cakes flavoured with Chinese five-spice – accompanied withal by such a dish of fresh vegetables as to ensure that only the most heroic can proceed to a pudding. This might consist of banana-and-cream filled pancakes or a fresh apple and raspberry crumble accompanied by jugs of thick double cream; though lesser fry may stick with a selection of home-made ice creams. This is hearty, honest fresh fare which along with the self-service coffee at the end and some good, inexpensive bottles on a carefully compiled wine list, represents great value – but do bring an appetite!

MEALS: D 7.30 from £13.50
No credit cards
Special breaks: Dinner, Bed and Breakfast from £80

WTB: 3 Crowns highly commended
7 En suite from £28 S; £50 D
Closed: D Sun

27 Llanberis

Y Bistro

43-45 High Street
Llanberis
Gwynedd
LL55 4EU
Tel: 01286 - 871278

For 18 years a pioneer of real food in this part of Wales, the Robertses' unobtrusive bistro is a real Welsh treasure. While Nerys runs the kitchen virtually single-handed, producing outstandingly fresh and vivid food throughout the year, Danny and their daughter Rhian welcome and wait on table with unfailing good nature.

Canapes are served with drinks in the comfortable Welsh-style sitting-room, and on being shown to your table you find a basket of home-made bread and a bowl of salad with a choice of four dressings. The menu, in Welsh with English translations, offers perhaps a rich crab bisque to start, wild mushroom tart or Nyth Iau Cyw Iar a Chig Moch – perfectly grilled chicken livers wrapped in smoked bacon with chilled roast pepper sauce.

Main courses usually include local Welsh lamb (perhaps roast best end with redcurrant and lavender sauce), and maybe marinated roast duck breast in ginger served with a spinach and potato rosti. Pysgod a Chenin combines generous portions of the freshest salmon and haddock, masked with a creamy leek and wild mushroom sauce and crisply baked with breadcrumbs – a real winner in any language. "Pwdins" range from Tarten Eirin Wlannog (caramelised peach tarte Tatin) to Ffrwythau 'di Sychu – dried fruits poached in sparkling wine and rose-water. With Welsh cheeses to follow, and coffee and home-made sweets included, guests may sensibly choose from two, three or four courses at fixed prices.

 MEALS: D 7.30-9.30 from £19
Closed: Sun

28 Llandegla

Bodidris Hall Hotel

Llandegla
Nr Wrexham
Denbighshire
LL11 3AL
Tel: 01978 - 790434
Fax: 01978 - 790335

An ancient timbered house with huge fireplaces, beams and oak panelling – once the hunting lodge of Robert Dudley, Earl of Leicester – Bodidris is a stylish and comfortable hotel with bountiful cuisine to match its warm and gentle Welsh welcome. Within easy reach of Chester, Wrexham and Llangollen and open all year to those seeking a peaceful stay amid this beautiful countryside, it boasts a baronial dining-room overlooking the hotel's lake towards Llandegla Moor and produces food of real accomplishment.

The set-price three-course dinner menu changes daily and is adorned with extras that include a complimentary appetiser on arrival at table, a choice of sorbets after the starter course and an impressive selection of home-made breads and jams, chutneys and chocolates.

These all constitute fine accompaniments to a dinner which might start with succulent terrine of langoustines and monkfish dressed with seared scallops on a gazpacho sauce, and include among a choice of five main dishes rack of local lamb with wild mushroom sauce, ratatouille timbale and glazed garlic, and the best fresh fish such as halibut cooked on sweet peppers and served with asparagus mousse. A second "appetiser", chocolate parfait on a raspberry coulis perhaps, appears before a classically traditional dessert of cherries Jubilee with honey and walnut ice cream. The kitchen's aspirations for such food are ambitious, and its execution was one of the summer's most agreeable surprises.

MEALS: L 12-2; D 7-9.30 from £27.50;
Set Sun L £15
Special breaks: Dinner, Bed and Breakfast from £125

WTB: 4 Crowns highly commended
9 En suite from £55 S; £70 D

29 Llandrillo

Tyddyn Llan

Llandrillo
Nr Corwen
Denbighshire
LL21 0ST
Tel: 01490 - 440264
Fax: 01490 - 440414

This jewel of a small hotel in a lovely wooded river valley is the creation of Peter and Bridget Kindred, who welcome you with relaxed warmth. Arriving at their elegant, comfortable home furnished with antiques and Peter's modern paintings, you'll immediately want to stay for a long time. The kitchen, under Jason Hornbuckle, has recently become the hotel's crowning glory, for this willing refugee from London's West End is a young man of formidable talent who cooks vigorously and with clear and vibrant flavours to match the finest in Wales.

Jason produces a seasonal carte alongside his daily dinner menu from which you might start with a glorious pressed-tongue terrine or a warm salad of seared chunky smoked salmon, and proceed to a tantalising soup epitomised by his definitive French onion and accompanied by excellent home-made breads. Main dishes featuring local Welsh Black beef, lamb and fish are integrated with their vegetable components, as in tender rib-eye beef steak served with fondant potatoes topped with oxtail, carrots, crisp beans and mushroom and fennel beignets on a beetroot jus.

To follow can come a towering souffle or fruit-flavoured brioche-and-butter pudding either of which, together with a strong Welsh cheeseboard and Peter's fine wine list, is worthy of an accomplished young kitchen which is definitely moving on and up.

MEALS: L 12.30-2; D 7-9 from £25;
Set Sun L £15
Special breaks: Dinner, Bed and Breakfast from £120

WTB: 4 Crowns de luxe
10 En suite from £64 S; £97 D

30 Llandudno

Bodysgallen Hall

Llandudno
Conwy
LL30 1RS
Tel: 01492 - 584466
Fax: 01492 - 582519

Two miles from the busy resort town, Bodysgallen is a quiet haven, standing in two hundred acres of parkland where guests can wander in the great walled garden and sit out on its secluded terraces. Inside the Hall, with its beautifully proportioned oak-panelled rooms, graceful furnishings, antiques and oil paintings, guests are pampered with every modern comfort.

Good food has long been central to the hotel's appeal, offering a nightly three-course table d'hôte alongside a more complex Gourmet Menu of five courses, served in these elegant surroundings by long-serving staff who are unfailingly charming and helpful. Predictably, fresh fish features strongly on both menus; hake perhaps on a bed of risotto, and fillet of turbot with pan-fried queen scallops. However, after starters of asparagus and smoked bacon soup and smoked duck and pork rillettes with apricots, main courses were uninspiring, the lack of finesse (particularly at these prices) scarcely doing justice to the setting and the service. It would be churlish to conclude from one such experience that Bodysgallen's cooking pots have somehow gone off the boil yet it is, we hope, incumbent on a kitchen for so long at the cutting edge to retain its sharpness.

MEALS: L 12.30-2 from £11.50; D 7.30-9.30 from £27.50; Set Sun L £15
Special breaks: Dinner, Bed and Breakfast from £180

WTB: 5 Crowns de luxe
35 En suite from £95 S; £160 D

31 Llandudno

Empire Hotel

Church Walks
Llandudno
Conwy
LL30 4HE
Tel: 01492 - 860555
Fax: 01492 - 860791

Under personal family management now for 51 years, the Empire certainly has an enviable track record and thrives today as a comfortable, eminently lived-in hotel of charm, character and elegance lent by its collection of priceless antiques. A third generation is represented by son-in-law Michael Waddy as executive chef. The format of his menus adheres wisely to a longstanding formula that assembles each evening's five-course meal around daily home-made soups, traditional roasts and nursery puddings.

The best available Welsh Black beef fillets are bought locally, dressed perhaps with creamy mushrooms and a soft peppercorn sauce, and Conwy fishermen contribute, in season, sewin supremes (served with prawns and ginger) and haddock fillets which might be oven-roasted with a herb crumb crust. More inquiring palates might be enticed by locally smoked chicken with honey mustard dressing, a char-grilled vegetable platter with balsamic vinegar, calves' liver with pork and chive sausage, and medallions of sea-bass and rainbow trout with saffron beurre blanc. Elyse Waddy and her mother, Elizabeth Maddocks, organise their housekeeping with a homely eye for detail often overlooked by male counterparts, while Len Maddocks keeps an eye on the decor, adding ever more treasures for his guests to admire.

 MEALS: L (Sat & Sun only) 12.30-2; D 6.45-9.30 from £19.50
Set Sun L £11.50
Special breaks: Dinner, Bed and Breakfast from £90

 WTB: 5 Crowns de luxe
58 En suite from £45 S; £70 D

32 Llandudno

Epperstone Hotel
15 Abbey Road
Llandudno
Conwy
LL30 2EE
Tel: 01492 - 878746
Fax: 01492 - 871233

In a resort town like Llandudno, which aims to appeal to all comers, it's impossible to ignore the Drew family – father and son – whose remarkable, immaculate hotel on Abbey Road is handily placed between the North and West Shores and only minutes' walk from the seafront. With just eight bedrooms and the same number of dining tables, it's unlikely you'll eat here unless you are staying; so you share the non-smoking lounge and spotless dining-room with fellow residents, most of whom take advantage of full-board rates which, including the four-course dinner and coffee, give generous value for money.

  Stephen Drew changes his menu nightly, appeasing his more senior clientele's plainer tastes while adding such challenges to daring as grilled peaches with Stilton and fillet of haddock Caprice, accompanied by excellent new potatoes grown by Mr Drew Snr at his home in the Conwy Valley.

  Alternatively, there'll be prawn and egg mayonnaise, asparagus soup or a refreshing blackcurrant sorbet, and roast leg of lamb with mint sauce and redcurrant jelly; crisp, peppery white cabbage and chunkily-mashed carrots and parsnips contributing fully to the taste experience. Trifle and cheesecake complete the meal – or Welsh Cheddar with cherries, grapes, gooseberries and celery; coffee is taken communally in the conservatory. If you've reached the stage of wanting your food good, plain and plentiful at a cost of around £7 per head, you'll travel far from here to find better.

 MEALS: D 6.30-8
Special breaks: Dinner, Bed and Breakfast from £64

 WTB: 4 Crowns de luxe
8 En suite from £28 S; £50 D
Closed: 3 weeks Jan

33 Llandudno

Martin's Restaurant

11 Mostyn Avenue
Craig-y-Don
Llandudno
Conwy
LL30 1YS
Tel: 01492 - 870070
Fax: 01492 - 876661

Definitely a cut above the average neighbourhood restaurant, Martin James's residential townhouse stands a block back from the East Shore and a mile along the seafront from the Great Orme and Pier.

The bill of fare at once indicates the sound classical background of a world-travelled and accomplished chef (formerly of nearby Bodysgallen Hall), and Martin's dedication to home production of everything from first-rate breads to last-gasp sweetmeats quickly confirms a class act.

To start, a trio of sauces may accompany marinated fillets of lemon sole; oyster mushrooms, crispy bacon and herb croutons enliven a warm duck salad laid on crispy leaves, and fresh local crab basks in avocado mousse and watercress mayonnaise.

Among ten or more equally accomplished main courses look for Anglesey hare served with Madeira and bilberry sauce, marinated monkfish medallions on a white wine and mustard-seed sauce, and a puff-pastry pillow of wild mushrooms and braised leeks served with grilled tomatoes and lemon butter.

Finish with hot almond gateau, iced mandarin and Cointreau parfait or Welsh rarebit as a savoury alternative to cheese. Pre- and post-theatre set-price suppers, occasional musical entertainments and regular summer barbecues add variety, and the addition this year of four smartly-decorated bedrooms with bathrooms allows you to digest in comfort overnight.

MEALS: D 7-9.30
(Pre-theatre from 5.30 by arrangement)
Closed: Sun; Mon

WTB: 3 Crowns highly commended
4 En suite from £25 S; £40 D
Closed: 2 weeks Jan

34 Llandudno

Richard's Bistro

7 Church Walks
Llandudno
Conwy
LL30 2ND
Tel: 01492 - 877924

In his atmospheric basement bistro, Richard Hendey cooks with enthusiasm and gusto in full view of his public, orchestrating both kitchen and restaurant, with frequent gymnastic forays to check that his customers are happy. This they surely are in a comfortable room of stone walls, terracotta tiled floor and chunky pews and tables served by well-trained and watchful young staff, clad in long white aprons.

The menu tends towards solid trencherman helpings strong on chicken and steaks with hefty stuffings and rich sauces, with more innovative cooking being saved for daily blackboard specials which major in fresh local fish.

Start, then, with a Thai-style salad of stir-fried queen scallops or Anglesey oysters with smoked salmon, and follow with a splendid fresh dish of tangerine-sized king scallops straight from the sea, lightly sauteed with a sauce of shallots, garlic, brandy and cream, representing the best of Richard's cooking. For carnivores, the day's specials might include grilled black pudding with apples and grapes, followed by sauteed lambs' kidneys in red wine sauce.

The rich seam of desserts includes a winning chocolate and praline terrine, to be sampled on its own or as part of the house special "chocaholics' platter". The wine list represents formidable value.

MEALS: D 6-10 from £17.50
Closed: 25 & 26 Dec

35 Llandudno

St Tudno Hotel

The Promenade
Llandudno
Conwy
LL30 2HD
Tel: 01492 - 874411
Fax: 01492 - 860407

Janette and Martin Bland clearly inspire an infectious warmth and enthusiasm in their staff, whose faultless service instils confident anticipation of an enjoyable stay and memorable eating. Meticulous attention to detail is evident everywhere, from a first-rate wine list to their 1997 award as "Tea Place of the Year". The garden-themed dining-room is air-conditioned, comfortable and stylishly appointed, offering daily choices of two, three or four courses and a monthly Gourmet Menu where starters and puddings are particularly innovative. After seductive appetisers of hot smoked duck in batter and praiseworthy home-made breads, you might launch into crab risotto with saffron sauce, marinated sea bass or a perfect warm asparagus and Cashel Blue tart on rich tomato sauce.

A soup or water ice precedes main courses of confidently-sauced poultry and red meats, fresh local fish simply poached or grilled, and perhaps a more traditional fillet of Welsh Black beef Wellington with a precise Madeira sauce.

The commendably light desserts are a delight to the eye and the tastebuds – iced blackcurrant parfait, perhaps with a perfectly-matched quenelle of Drambuie cream, or the highly popular light vanilla-scented mousse with a compote of summer berries. Finally, a proud array of Welsh cheeses before you settle sated in the lounge over coffee and home-made sweetmeats.

MEALS: L 12.30-1.45 from £16.50;
D 7-9.30 from £22;
Special breaks: Dinner, Bed and Breakfast from £90

WTB: 4 Crowns de luxe
21 En suite from £73 S; £85 D

36 Llanfairpwll

Plas Newydd Tearoom

Nr Llanfairpwll
Isle of Anglesey
LL61 6DQ
Tel: 01248 - 714795

The traditional home of the Marquess of Anglesey, built by James Wyatt, stands on the banks of the Menai Strait with magnificent views across to Snowdonia. Visitors must pass the shop and tearoom to pay their admission, then take a leisurely 10 minute walk through delightful grounds to the main house. There may be time for coffee and bara brith before setting out, but if the walk is enough to work up an appetite, so much the better, for a tempting display of main meals is available from midday.

Home-made cheese and onion or broccoli, ham and mushroom flans are served with mixed salad or vegetables, and home-made hot dishes with a Welsh flavour include savoury minced pork, mushroom and onion pie, fish cakes with parsley sauce and Welsh cheese and ham pasta bake. For dessert you might find citrus fruits bread-and-butter pudding, syrup tart or summer fruits pie, and ice cream made locally on Anglesey includes the National Trust in Wales's orchard and hedgerow classic. Afternoons offer Welsh cream and garden teas for grown-ups and Marmite soldiers for the kids, who can crayon indoors with the kits provided or clamber over the climbing frames and tree houses in the garden.

MEALS: All day 10-5; L 12-2;
T 2-5 from £2.95
Closed: Sat; Mon-Thur during Oct; Nov-Mar

37 Llangefni

Tre Ysgawen Hall

Capel Coch
Llangefni
Isle of Anglesey
Tel: 01248 - 750750
Fax: 01248 - 750035

The Rowlands family took over this magnificent country pile, built in 1882, in February 1996: notwithstanding its grandly decorated and furnished splendour the house is comfortably warm and the welcome friendly and unstuffy.

In the stately dining-room you can choose from ambitious a la carte and three-course table d'hôte menus focusing on fresh local produce. Starters feature perhaps a brandade of cod with saffron potatoes or mille-feuille of asparagus and wild mushrooms with a piquant hollandaise, while main courses feature poultry such as roast guinea fowl with chervil stuffing, wild salmon with crayfish ravioli and watercress sauce, and similarly challenging variations on classically-based beef and lamb dishes.

Desserts range from warm chocolate pie and home-made ice creams to a brilliant summer pudding with "kirsch froth" – so welcome a change from dollops of cream – and a proudly Welsh cheeseboard. Diners may eat less expansively – and expensively – in the conservatory brasserie, where lunch is served daily: there's an extensive, if uninformative, wine list and good draught beers are available in the panelled bar, though bar meals are not usually offered.

MEALS: L 12-2 from £14;
D 7-9.30 from £19.95
Special breaks: Dinner, Bed and Breakfast from £130

WTB: 4 Crowns highly commended
20 En suite from £80 S; £110 D

38 Llangollen

Bryn Howel Hotel

Llangollen
Denbighshire
LL20 7UW
Tel: 01978 - 860331
Fax: 01978 - 860119

Family-run for more than thirty years and much extended from the Victorian red-brick original, this comfortable, relaxing hotel stands in mature and beautifully tended grounds streching down to the Llangollen Canal. The specially-angled windows in a modern bedroom extension afford each room its share of serene views towards the majestic hill slopes that surround the Vale of Llangollen.

The Cedar Tree Restaurant, with its suitably pastel decor, also has picture windows facing south to provide views beyond a vast cedar of Lebanon towards the old town just two miles away.

The setting demands a certain grandeur of style, which is reflected in the daily menus: at lunchtime chilled avocado guacamole, steamed delice of salmon with "dill fish cream" and warm apple strudel with an English sauce are as international as the annual Eisteddfod. The a la carte dinner adds more exotic combinations: asparagus spears and chicken fillet served on a "spiral of lemon-scented pasta", local pork fillet "perfumed with lemon grass and ginger" finished with a beansprout stir-fry, and a "delice of cheesecake", perfumed again with ginger, served on a puree of summer fruits. Each course is individually, and wordily, priced with a "minimum menu charge of twenty one pounds".

Head chef Dai Davies is an elder statesman of the Welsh tradition and a fine tutor whose protégés proliferate throughout the land – an accomplishment for which he doesn't always receive the credit he's rightly due.

MEALS: L 12-2 from £9; D 7-9 from £21
Set Sun L £13.50
Special breaks: Dinner, Bed and Breakfast from £120

WTB: 4 Crowns highly commended
36 En suite from £75 S; £99 D

39 Llwyngwril

Pentre Bach

Llwyngwril
Nr Dolgellau
Gwynedd
LL37 2JU
Tel: 01341 - 250294
Fax: 01341 - 250885

To sample one of Margaret Smyth's marvellous dinners you'll have to stay here – or in one of her self-catering cottages. This will prove no hardship: Pentre Bach was voted Britain's "Best Bed and Breakfast, 1996" by Radio 4's Food Programme, an accolade that she and husband Nick can rightly be proud of, so it doesn't get better than this.

Pentre Bach stands in a lovely spot by the sea with views across Cardigan Bay. All the vegetables and salads, along with much of the fruit, are organically grown in their own garden and wherever possible meats, poultry and fish are obtained locally and used in ways that allow their natural quality and flavours to speak for themselves.

In the compact but entirely comfortable dining-room Margaret serves food full of straight-forward goodness in totally unselfconscious fashion yet with a natural eye for presentation. You might begin with a salad of grilled goats' cheese and walnuts, a sunny vegetable soup or fresh salmon pate. A popular main dish of Margaret's is her special smoked duck with cranberry sauce: with it the vegetables picked just an hour before you sit down are a joy, redolent with flavours most of us have forgotten. Desserts are created with an equally loving touch – summer pudding full of rich berries, a crumble of soft garden fruit or chocolate parfait with a sharp coulis of fresh raspberries. Home-made sweetmeats then accompany a pot of rich coffee.

There is no licence here, though neither is there any corkage on the bottle should you care to bring your own.

 MEALS: D 7 to residents only from £13.95
Unlicensed

 WTB: 3 Crowns highly commended
3 En suite from £26-£40 S; £40-£52 D
Closed: D to non-residents

40 Marchwiel

Cross Lanes Country Hotel

Bangor Road
Marchwiel
Nr Wrexham
Denbighshire
Tel: 01978 - 780555
Fax: 01978 - 780568

Unpretentious and welcoming, the Cross Lanes stands in extensive, well-maintained grounds by the A525, conveniently placed for Wrexham, Llangollen and the North Wales Expressway.

In addition to its comfortable bedrooms, indoor pool and sauna there's a traditional hotel bar serving real ale and popular pub food, while the fairly unremarkable restaurant menus distance themselves from local competition with a keen eye for local produce – in particular the fish – and good value for money. A popular starter, for instance, is the platter of first-rate smoked halibut and smoked salmon with a dill and chilli mayonnaise; this is followed by daily-sourced fish dishes such as grilled marinated tuna with Provencal sauce, and baked sea trout in a buttered breadcrumb crust served with basil, shrimp and saffron cream.

There's general emphasis on fresh ingredients throughout: local lamb, poultry and prime steaks, imaginative vegetables like a mash of carrot and parsnip, crunchy asparagus tips and diced celeriac, all play significant roles.

To follow, you won't go far wrong with home-made treacle tart and tasty – proper – custard, or their "very own" strawberry cheesecake served over a pool of fresh, unsweetened strawberry coulis. Kept thus simple, the food we came across was good enough not only for us but also for a reporter from Liverpool and a very nice man from Basingstoke: all cooked by a confident second chef – he'd had a good day!

MEALS: L 12.15-2; D 7.30-9.30 from £14.50;
Set Sun L 12-2 from £9.75

WTB: 4 Crowns highly commended
16 En suite from £60 S; £86 D

41 Nant Gwynant

Pen y Gwryd Hotel

Nant Gwynant
Llanberis
Gwynedd
LL53 4NT
Tel: 01286 - 870211

For decades the headquarters of Snowdon Mountain Rescue, and decades ago a training base for Sir John Hunt's Everest-scaling heroes, Pen-y-Gwryd today lives in something of a time warp. Climbers who once left their boots in the hall may now find them suspended from the bar ceiling, in silent tribute to their former exploits.

Substantial soups, ploughman's lunches and sandwiches are much in demand to satisfy walkers' and climbers' appetites, as are lunch specials which might include steak and kidney pie with fresh vegetables or a bacon and cheese quiche accompanied by generous and interesting salads, with home-made apple pie to follow.

Gathering for five-course dinner, guests have a limited choice of main courses including traditional roast beef or breast of Barbary duck with plum sauce, followed by substantial puddings such as cherry clafoutis or steamed lemon sponge; the platter of Welsh cheeses to finish will surely conquer the heartiest mountaineer's appetite. The hotel's stunning location makes staying here a must for fans of Snowdonia's stark scenery with its vistas of mountain and deep, dark chasms. The legion of Danish staff will testify to the lure of the mountains and on days of inclement weather you can always help them with their Welsh!

MEALS: L 12-2;
D 7.30-8.15 from £15
Special breaks: Dinner, Bed and Breakfast from £70

WTB: 2 Crowns
16 En suite from £25 S; £50 D

42 Northop

Soughton Hall

Northop
Mold
Flintshire
CH7 6AB
Tel: 01352 - 840811
Fax: 01352 - 840382

North Wales

Approaching the hall along its stately tree-lined drive, it's hard to recall that just ten years ago the roof was about to collapse and the wonderful gardens were an overgrown jungle. On entry the beautifully proportioned day rooms' stately appearance is mellowed by a lived-in warmth reflecting the care and affection lavished upon them by John and Rosemary Rodenhurst. In a year-long celebration of the first ten years, the family's favourite dishes are collected in a three-course dinner menu at 1987 prices.

Unrecognisable from its humble beginnings, "The Hall's Posh Welsh Rarebit" is a peerless combination of Stilton and roast hazelnuts topped with smoked salmon and a poached egg, lightly dressed with pine nuts and vinaigrette. To follow, slow-roasted crispy duck with orange and Grand Marnier sauce is redolent of the early days, while the roast rack of Welsh lamb with Stilton and thyme crust and delicate port wine jus is bang up-to-date.

"Jim's gone to town" is a celebratory collection of the pastry chef's own favourite chocolate desserts with their complementary sauces. While this is grand country-house food to match the setting, the Rodenhursts' restrained approach skilfully avoids an overbearing service. As if to prove this, both hosts are on hand next morning in the servants' quarters, where residents are pampered with an old-fashioned country-house breakfast.

*MEALS: L 12-2;
D 7-10 from £19.95
Special breaks: Dinner, Bed and Breakfast from £140*

*WTB: 4 Crowns de luxe
13 En suite from £80 S; £110 D
Closed: 2 weeks Jan (Restaurant only)*

43 Northop

The Stables Restaurant

Soughton Hall
Northop
Mold
Flintshire
CH7 6AB
Tel: 01352 - 840577
Fax: 01352 - 840382

The atmospheric and highly-skilled conversion of former stables at the Rodenhursts' splendid country mansion has brought a fresh buzz to the scene – an informal and fun contrast to the grandeur of the main house, with its mien and menus to match (see preceding entry).

The Stables combines under one roof a busy real-ale bar, Racecourse Restaurant and Wine Shop for the in-crowd to mingle in and quaff at their leisure. This successful new departure has distinguished itself with some excellent food, for which young Simon Rodenhurst and his team deserve full credit.

Much of the food relies on the South Wales formula, whereby diners choose from refrigerated displays of butchers' meats and fish which are passed to the kitchen and cooked to order. But the "stewards of the racecourse" also take orders from the table for starters such as queen scallop tagliatelli with wholegrain mustard sauce, and "Simon's favourites" – braised shank of lamb with mashed tatties and rustic veg, battered cod and chips the Stables' way, and calves' liver and smoked bacon with bubble-and-squeak and apricot sauce.

The day's puddings, likewise listed on blackboards, encompass traditionals like strawberry fool and newer-wave desserts, along with cheeses and a glass of port. Remarkable for its value for money, Simon's brainchild has stellar aspirations.

 MEALS: L 12-2.30; D 7-10

44 Portmeirion

Hotel Portmeirion

Portmeirion
Penrhyndeudraeth
Gwynedd
LL48 6ET
Tel: 01766 - 770228
Fax: 01766 - 771331

Much time, effort and money has been lavished on Portmeirion in recent years and this magical place has never looked better. A stroll down to the hotel through Clough Williams-Ellis's fantasy village by the beautiful Traeth Bach estuary fills one with happy anticipation. And the hotel, with its log fire and floral welcome, does not disappoint as you pass through the elegant dayrooms and bar to the restaurant: your destination, all cream and white with its view across the water through bow-fronted windows, feels like the dining saloon of a grand ocean liner.

The food, like the setting, has a maritime Mediterranean feel for all that the menu is written in Welsh, and the best local ingredients are employed to good effect by Colin Pritchard and his team. You might be offered a thoroughly Welsh onion-and-potato soup to start, or a warm salade Nicoise with seared slices of fresh tuna, or a pungent terrine with sweet home-made chutney. Meirionnydd lamb and local beef or poultry appear with enterprising sauces; happily featured is a superb fillet of local salmon, topped perhaps with a rich baked crab crust.

Puddings too, like chocolate pie with first-rate chocolate and honey ice cream, are well up to the mark, as is the splendid Welsh cheese selection (full marks) and a comprehensive wine list – which for a hotel of this calibre marks up very generously in favour of the customer.

 MEALS: L 12.30-1.45 from £11.50; D 7-9.30 from £23.50
Set Sun L from £17.50
Special breaks: Dinner, Bed and Breakfast from £167

 WTB: 4 Crowns de luxe
34 En suite from £70 S; £88 D
Closed: L Mon; 3 weeks Jan

45 Pwllheli

Plas Bodegroes

Nefyn Road
Pwllheli
Gwynedd
LL53 5TH
Tel: 01758 - 612363
Fax: 01758 - 701247

A very special place, this beautiful small Georgian house with its stunning avenue of old beech trees is a true home of hospitality: Gunna Chown has returned to the helm after too long an absence in Bath and the place glows again with the sunshine of its chatelain. Since the recent addition of a partly covered courtyard with a Japanese-style garden and pond, both house and grounds have never looked more magically peaceful and enchanting. Shaun Mitchell, who cooked here for a year with Chris Chown, has returned as head chef after a spell at Fairyhill. He cooks wonderfully, with a daring touch of innovation in dishes where the components are married in excitingly seductive ways. His parcel of crab with coconut leeks, for example, is wickedly spiked with a sweet chilli salsa; baked local sea bream is perfection with Thai noodles and lime butter sauce; calves' liver is griddled with leek sausage, sage and onions and parsnip mash; while among the puddings you'd have to travel a long way to surpass Shaun's diaphanous banana cheesecake with caramelised banana and toffee sauce – a rare treat.

Preludes to a three-course dinner such as this include hot canapes served in the bar, before an amuse-gueule served at the table arrives with sensational onion marmalade bread. To follow there's a good selection of Welsh cheeses, cafetiere coffee with dainty petits fours, and a majestic wine list accompanies the meal.

 MEALS: D 7-9.30 from £28.50;
Set Sun L 12-2 from £14.50
Special breaks: Dinner, Bed and Breakfast from £140

 WTB: 4 Crowns de luxe
11 En suite from £50 S; £90 D
Closed: Dec-March

46 Rossett

Churton's

Chester Road
Rossett
Denbighshire
LL12 0HW
Tel: 01244 - 570163
Fax: 01244 - 570099

Just a few minutes into Wales, off the A483 from Chester, this longstanding, cheerful restaurant perennially offers good and generous fresh food to accompany the excellent wines, which may also be bought to take home by the bottle or case. It's a bustling place with an ever-changing blackboard menu at truly sensible prices, and the balconied restaurant gives off such a feeling of the Old West that one half expects Marlene Dietrich to descend the stairs at any moment.

Starters include hot, fresh garlicky prawns and chicken-liver terrine with, perhaps, a warm chicken salad or a skilfully-prepared tomato mousse decorated with prawns, and as well as steaks, stir-fries and pork meat balls, perhaps cooked Thai style, there's a strong fish section. Beautifully fresh cod, perhaps with a mustard and cheese sauce, is served with plentiful adventurously-prepared vegetables like carrot and onions in coriander-flavoured cream. Clearly enjoying the buzz as much today as when they set up here some eighteen years ago, James and

Nick Churton keep a watchful eye on both the quality and the service, neither of which ever appears to falter. The pleasure of eating lunch or dinner here – or at their sister restaurant in Tarporley – is enough to make one wish that more places in the Principality had a Churton's.

MEALS: L 12-2; 7-10.
Closed: L Sat; D Sun

47 St George

Kinmel Arms

St George
Abergele
Conwy
LL22 9BP
Tel/Fax: 01745 - 832207

The recently upgraded and enlarged Kinmel Arms is a charming, traditional pub, conveniently tucked away just off the A55 Expressway, which in addition to its good range of real ales and bar snacks has an elegant dining-room offering cooking of real distinction. The pub itself is a warm-hearted and unpretentious local but Gary Edwards's food is beautifully presented, his tendency towards "pictures on a plate" nonetheless setting off some serious cooking. At tables pleasantly laid with fresh flowers and candlelit by night, you'll be served hot canapes, such as a pork kebab with sweet chilli sauce, and warm home-made bread, before enjoying starters such as crab cakes with couscous or a winning tart of smoked haddock and leeks in a cheese and cream sauce.

Duck, chicken, steaks and lamb come in various guises as regularly changing main courses, while a constant feature is the fresh fish of the day with a choice, for example, of halibut with prawn butter sauce or generous portions of perfectly cooked tuna steak with a tomato and avocado salsa. Abundant helpings of vegetables are very good.

Desserts such as creme caramel and strawberry cheesecake are light and appealing, with many devotees of Gary's tangy lemon tart with strawberry sorbet and fresh stawberries. The beers are supplemented by some bargains on a comprehensive wine list, though regrettably this doesn't extend to any half bottles; so drivers will appreciate the coffee.

MEALS: Bar L 12-2; D 7-9.30
Restaurant 7-9

48 Talsarnau

Hotel Maes-y-Neuadd

Talsarnau
Nr Harlech
Gwynedd
LL47 6YA
Tel: 01766 - 780200
Fax: 01766 - 780211

With its prominent hillside position looking down on Tremadog Bay and out across to Snowdonia National Park, the imposing "Hall in the Meadows" is approached by a long, steep lane (from the B4573 just north of Harlech), so that few diners happen upon it by chance.

For those who come to stay relaxation is the key, and there is possible connection between Maes-y-Neuadd's splendid isolation and the unhurried approach in the dining-room, where dinner can technically run to a full seven courses and consume the entire evening.

Over canapes in the bar you choose between, say, soused mackerel with celery, walnut and apple salad or pan-fried chicken livers with rocket salad and mango to start, continuing with main courses of goose breast with caramelised apple, pea puree and thyme sauce; pork fillet with mushrooms, paprika and sour cream; or a vegetarian aubergine, tomato, garlic and courgette tower. Between these are optional (but rarely omitted) soup and fish courses, concluding with Diweddglo Mawreddog – The Grand Finale: a plate of Welsh cheeses such as Hen Sir and Pencarreg, home-made ice creams, and quite possibly two desserts offered as inclusives rather than alternatives! Local game in winter, and in summer vegetables, herbs and soft fruits fresh from the hotel gardens, complete the array of local produce.

 MEALS: L 12-1.45; D 7-9 from £24 (no children under 8); Set Sun L £14.94
Special breaks: Dinner, Bed and Breakfast from £152
 WTB: 4 Crowns de luxe
16 En suite from £55 S; £105 D

49 Tal-y-Bont

The Lodge

Tal-y-Bont
Nr Conwy
Conwy
LL32 8YX
Tel: 01492 - 660766
Fax: 01492 - 660534

At the Lodge, which stands beside the B5106 midway between Conwy and Llanrwst, Barbara Baldon's infectious enthusiasm for "taking care of people" keeps her at the centre of things, while her husband, Simon, has dedicated himself to the kitchen since they arrived in 1987.

Simon's table d'hôte dinners are planned and purchased on a daily basis with assiduous care to avoid duplication for those on extended stays, while the nightly menu reads like "Barbara Baldon's Diary" with regular references to the weather, local events and the current evening's dramatis personae. Choice starters are chicken livers sauteed with brandy, cream and herbs, thick lentil and ham soup, and a cocktail of dressed Conwy crab; Simon then gives rein to his ingenuity in the grilled salmon fillet with Thai spices, saddle of Welsh lamb with apricot and walnut stuffing, and pork fillet with apple and cider sauce. The home-made puds offer an equally appetising choice, and the friendly and persuasive waitresses make refusal out of the question.

Bedrooms are bedecked with cuddly toys, scatter cushions and rubber ducks for the bath. After Welsh cooked breakfast plus croissants and home-made jams, the performance concludes with hugs all round on departure – dogs not excepted.

 MEALS: L 12.15-1.45 from £6.25; D 7-8.45 from £15; Set Sun L £7.25
Special breaks: Dinner, Bed and Breakfast from £85
 WTB: 3 Crowns highly commended
10 En suite from £40 S; £70 D

50 Trearddur Bay

Trearddur Bay Hotel

Trearddur Bay
Nr Holyhead
Isle of Anglesey
LL65 2UN
Tel: 01407 - 860301
Fax: 01407 - 861181

Directly across the road from a broad stretch of sandy beach, the much-modernised Bay Hotel offers above-average family holiday accomodation overlooking the sea and is a convenient stopover for travellers to and from Ireland: the ferry terminal at Holyhead is little more than two miles away. The lounge and dining-room occupy the hotel's frontage without benefiting from the best seascapes and bearing with them an efficiently-run air without ever coming across as warmly hospitable.

At dinner, the lengthy a la carte menu, majoring in steaks and assorted fish dishes, is supplemented by a table d'hôte of commendable brevity but limited imagination. The latter offered lobster bisque, melon platter and a chicken mousseline of decent flavour and texture, followed by calves' liver, and an accurately grilled perfectly fresh salmon fillet with a rather tame saffron and prawn sauce. Alternative to the lemon meringue pie and chocolate parfait desserts was a cheeseboard bereft of any Welsh content and in a disappointing condition, with home-made biscuits ("like clay pigeons"!) served in place of walnut bread. We conclude that the food can be fine, but Trearddur's attention to detail requires more attention!

North Wales

MEALS: Bar L all day;
Restaurant D 7-9 from £18.50

WTB: 4 Crowns highly commended.
31 En suite from £68 S; £98 D.
Special breaks: Dinner, Bed and Breakfast from £120.

51 Trefriw

Chandlers

Trefriw
Nr Llanrwst
Conwy
LL27 0JH
Tel: 01492 - 640991

Trefriw is an outstandingly pretty village on the Conwy side of the valley across from Llanrwst, and this atmospheric little bistro sits unobtrusively on the High Street. Within, the white walls, interesting modern paintings and simple Van Gogh tables and chairs are warmed by blinds and candles at night. Penny Rattenbury welcomes and husband Adam cooks, both in a relaxed and informal manner, so that early expectations of a positive experience are readily met.

While the main menu highlighting local lamb, beef, duck, chicken and hare is a monthly one, Adam's fish selections are a daily affair which take precedence on the blackboard. All are treated simply to allow fresh flavours to speak out, though invariably there are well balanced sauces and confits to accompany – a classic beurre blanc with grilled sewin, for example. Rack of lamb comes with mustard crust and an onion sauce, and half a roast Barbary duck with a sauce of port and black cherries. Starters are treated with equal simplicity as in a winning warm salad of pigeon breast, walnut and Roquefort terrine, and monkfish deep-fried in apple batter: high praise is due, too, for the home-made granary bread with poppy seeds, generous portions of vegetables and soft, golden potatoes finished with nutmeg and cream.

Best desserts, also listed on the blackboard, range from Queen of Puddings with home-made damson jam to hot chocolate meringues with chocolate ice cream: it's all fresh, tasty and satisfyingly straightforward and there's a short wine list full of bargains.

MEALS: L 11.30-2 from £7.50; D 7-9.30;
Set Sun L 12 £12.50
Closed: L Mon, Tue & Sat; D Sun-Wed; Please call

52 Wrexham

Erddig Restaurant

The National Trust
Wrexham
Denbighshire
LL13 0YT

Tel: 01978 - 355314
Fax: 01978 - 313333

This remarkable family estate, whose previous owners never threw away anything they thought might come in useful, is now a wonderful monument to the early days of photography and farm mechanisation which merits a day's exploration. As well as the blacksmith's and carpenter's shops, cart sheds and displays of all manner of early horseless locomotion, the "Upstairs, Downstairs" tours of the main house are a revelation.

The original bakehouse and kitchen have been restored as museum pieces, but there's nothing old fashioned about the self-service restaurant which overlooks the old Stable Yard – a focal point for the entire complex.

From mid-morning until late afternoon the impressive range of home-baking, while not justifying alone the admission charge, is nonetheless well worth a detour. Bara brith liberally spread with Welsh butter is a perfect snack to accompany the diverse coffees, teas, mineral waters and cold fruit juices available all day, but it's well worth hanging on for more edible Welsh experiences at lunchtime.

Go for lamb casserole with prunes and raisins – adapted from "The Good Huswife's Jewell" published in 1596, then try the Welsh Border Tart for dessert, full of buttery sultanas and raisins topped with meringue. The Welsh dairy ice cream full of orchard and hedgerow fruits, commissioned by the National Trust in 1995, has proved a major hit with youngsters of all ages from nine to ninety.

MEALS: 11-5; L 12-2; T 2-5 from £2.95
Closed: Thur; Fri; Nov-Mar

MID WALES ENTRIES

53   Aberaeron

Hive on the Quay

Cadwgan Place
Aberaeron
Ceredigion
SA46 0BU
Tel: 01545 - 570445

The Holgate family's 21st anniversary here has been and gone with a summer-long celebration of everything that's good in Aberaeron. The restaurant itself, housed in a converted coal warehouse on the Wharf between the inner and outer, is integral to an operation which includes a fresh fish shop, famous honey-bee exhibition and the sea aquarium just along the quay.

Daughter Sarah's distinctive daily shopping list includes dispatching the family boat for Cardigan Bay crabs, sourcing organic flour and free-range eggs for home baking and collecting home-produced honey for their unique ice cream. Meringues, sesame biscuits, chopped nuts and Amerina cherries adorn the counters where fabulous sundaes are created and ice cream flavours change daily: passion-fruit, blackcurrant and mint, and fresh raspberry, for instance.

Lunches served from a buffet counter offer salads of crab and lobster, fresh prawns and curried chicken with home-made mayonnaise; chilled tomato and basil soup; frittata made with eggs and Parmesan and chock-full of vegetables, and crisp salads like cauliflower and red pepper. In July and August try supper of traditional cawl, Norwegian-style rabbit, salmon trout with wild sorrel and skate wings with caper butter.

Any time of day at this veritable hive of activity is good for plum and chocolate cake, espresso coffee or Welsh cream tea: then finish off with apple pie and Guernsey cream washed down with a glass of Welsh mead!

 MEALS: Meals all day 10.30-5; L 12-2.30
D 6-9.30 (in July & Aug)
Closed: Mid Sept - Spring Bank Hol

54   Aberdovey

Penhelig Arms Hotel

Aberdovey
Gwynedd
L35 0LT
Tel: 01654 - 767215
Fax: 01654 - 767690

Given its setting on the edge of the Dyfi estuary looking across to Ynyslas and beyond, it's small wonder that the Penhelig Arms is such a popular spot: however it's the efforts of its owners, Robert and Sally Hughes, that place it regularly amongst mid-Wales's award-winning hotels. Its team of women chefs produces food of genuine quality in both bar and restaurant – and out on the estuary wall in fine weather – with menus which are updated from one meal to the next.

Daily shopping spoils appear in starters like carrot and coriander roulade and fresh herb savoury cheesecake, with perhaps supreme of chicken with tarragon cream sauce, and roast rack of herb-crusted mountain lamb to follow. So close to source, naturally fish on the menu plays a prominent part: smoked haddock chowder and Cardigan Bay crab followed by halibut fillets with saffron cream sauce, and a medley of baked sewin, monkfish and haddock spiced, Thai-style, with coriander and ginger, black olives, tomato and fresh herbs. Rich, fruity

summer pudding, lightly-poached pears in fudge sauce and a commendable apricot frangipane flan are typical desserts, with farmhouse cheeses carefully chosen and in tip-top condition as an alternative or supplement.

Of equal merit is Robert Hughes's fine wine list. "Selections of the Month" are a regular education, while bottles and halves in bold type on the main list are his specially recommended personal favourites, according to what you can afford.

 MEALS: L 12-2; D 7-9 £19
Set Sun L 12-2.15 £12.50
Special breaks: Dinner, Bed and Breakfast from £100

 WTB: 4 Crowns highly commended
10 En suite B&B from £39 S; £68 D

55 Aberdovey

Plas Penhelig Country House

Aberdovey
Gwynedd
LL33 0NA
Tel: 01654 - 767676
Fax: 01654 - 767783

David Richardson's beautiful Edwardian mansion stands high above the village with stunning views through mature trees to the Dyfi estuary and the sea beyond. With its lovely panelled entrance hall and log fire the house is furnished as a private country house, with interesting oil paintings, family heirlooms and antiques. The sun-trap terrace lends a certain continental feel, with its ornamental pool and lush surrounding foliage overlooked by the main house's shuttered windows, and is an ideal spot for light lunches or afternoon tea. Dinner, in an elegant picture-windowed room looking out to sea, strengthens the continental impression with a strong French accent to the cooking: Nicole Ledet and her son have returned to the kitchens here every season for the last eight years.

Using the best local produce, daily-changing menus offer half-a-dozen starters of which a perennial favourite is a rich, French-provincial pork and chicken-liver terrine with onion marmalade. There are similar Gallic touches in main dishes like poached monkfish with wild mushroom sauce, and excellent Meirionnydd lamb herb-roasted with brandy, cream and pepper sauce and accompanied by unmissable boulangere potatoes. Puddings may include hazelnut meringues with toffee ice cream, creme caramel, and a thoroughly British pear and rhubarb crumble with creme anglaise. The cheeses, though, are distinctly Welsh – as is the warmth and efficiency of the service.

 MEALS: Bar L 12-2; T 3-5;
Restaurant D 7.30-8.45 £18.50
Special breaks: Dinner, Bed and Breakfast from £110

 WTB: 3 Crowns highly commended
11 En suite B&B from £50 S; £85 D
Closed: Mid Dec-mid Mar

56 Aberystwyth

Belle Vue Royal Hotel

Marine Terrace
Aberystwyth
Powys
SY23 2BA
Tel: 01970 - 617558
Fax: 01970 - 612190

This striking hotel of eminent Victorian origins enjoys a prominent position on Aberyswyth seafront with a magnificent view out across the broad expanse of Cardigan Bay. After some fifteen years at the helm, their own interpretation of a "family-run" hotel still sees the ebullient Alan and Marilyn Davies directing their crew with infectious enthusiasm, and the advantages of this are plain for all to see. Friendly staff here take rare pleasure in being of service and great loyalty is shown to the Belle Vue's restaurant by a local clientele whose tastes tend to be a little conservative.

Dining choices are divided between the Grill Room with its a la carte menu and a fixed-price table d'hôte which is properly employed here as a showcase for the kitchen's burgeoning talents. Alongside a daily soup, starters like local smoked salmon with avocado and cream cheese or ribbons of guinea fowl in sesame oil with braised spring onion jus precede an optional sorbet such as passion-fruit water ice on a poached pineapple base. Ystwyth lamb is used in a roast rack on a pillow of cressé potato with red wine and thyme sauce, paupiettes of marinated wild salmon with white wine vinegar and dill are paired with black olives and beef tomato, and medallions of pork fillet are baked in oatmeal over a creamed Stilton veloute. There follows a comprehensive selection of home-made desserts, hot and cold, and a selection of Welsh and Borders cheeses that is well above average.

*MEALS: L 12.30-2 from £8; D 6.30-9.15 from £19.50
Set Sun L £11.50
Special breaks: Dinner, Bed and Breakfast from £112*

*WTB: 4 Crowns highly commended
36 rooms 32 En suite B&B from £52 S; £80 D*

57 Berriew

The Lion Hotel

Berriew
Nr Welshpool
Powys
SY21 8PQ
Tel: 01686 - 640452
Fax: 01686 - 640604

Just off the A483 south of Welshpool the Lion stands at the centre of arguably the area's best-kept village, next to the churchyard which is overlooked by the quietest of the rear bedrooms. The Thomas family's distinguished stewardship over the last 14 years has passed most recently to son Lance, who copes manfully with a busy kitchen as well as keeping the house in order. With space on three sides for bar, bistro and restaurant this is a tall order, given the length of the blackboard menus which offer up to a dozen starters and main dishes daily, in addition to the popular market-fresh fish specials and a residents' table d'hôte at night.

Brecon venison makes regular appearances in steak or sausage form, with maybe roast haunch on a Sunday, and Welsh lamb loin – stuffed with lamb mince, onions, nutmeg and allspice – is a perennial favourite.

Lighter lunches include Thai spare ribs, lamb shoulder with mint gravy, and smoked bacon quiche with Y Fenni cheese, then gooseberry pie or bread-and-butter pudding for afters. From the table d'hôte, filo tart with leeks, cheese and tomato and basil dressing, venison steak with juniper and red-wine sauce, and cappuccino log with double-coffee-swirl ice cream are a fair display of Lance's skills.

MEALS: L 12-2; D 7-9 £18
Special breaks: Dinner, Bed and Breakfast from £110

WTB: Unclassified
7 En suite B&B from £50 S; £80 D

58   Brecon

Beacons Guest House

16 Bridge Street
Brecon
Powys
LD3 8AH
Tel: 01874 - 623339

Mid Wales

Peter and Barbara Jackson's first twelve months here have been marked by an ambitious refurbishment programme, including an extension of quality, en-suite bedroom facilities within this former farmhouse and its attendant stone outbuildings.

   Gastronomic innovations have included the arrival of a new chef and refreshing dinner menus in a modern idiom. Marinated octopus salad with tapenade dressing and chilled hummus with griddled artichoke were typical starters on an early menu, followed by honey-flavoured boiled ham on mashed potato and parsnips and grilled red-bream fillets with roasted Mediterranean vegetables; for vegetarians, mushroom fricassee with beetroot crust or home-made saffron pasta with chilli oil and char-grilled aubergine. To follow there might be a terrine of strawberries and Grand Marnier with roasted almond ice cream; a regular favourite is the accomplished chocolate and whisky bread-and-butter pudding served with a white chocolate sauce.

   Intriguing architectural features include the central spiral staircase and a vaulted bar, complete with ceiling meat-hooks, which once was the butchery store. The original pine doors have been stripped, in marked contrast to the varnished dining tables and chairs.

   Beacons is just a short walk from Brecon town centre across the Usk bridge and has private parking to the rear. Non-smoking bedrooms and restaurant.

MEALS: D 6.30-9 £15
Special breaks: Dinner, Bed and Breakfast from £66
Closed: D Sun & Mon

WTB: 3 Crowns highly commended
10 rooms 7 En suite from £25 S; £36 D

59 Brecon

Castle of Brecon Hotel

Brecon
Powys
LD3 9DB
Tel: 01874 - 624611
Fax: 01874 - 623737

Occupying the site and remains of Brecon Castle, this most civilised of family-run hotels exudes a comfortable lived-in air, its mood set by the strains of light classical music at meal times.

Similar and familiar themes permeate a nightly table d'hôte menu which is full of well-resourced local ingredients. Mussels cooked in a leek and saffron stew and fillet of sea bass with new potatoes and wholegrain mustard sauce, are typical of the fresh aquatic choices. Provencal mushrooms with feta cheese salad or creamy mushroom risotto for vegetarians, and chicken-liver pate with home-made chutney, followed by veal escalope with broccoli and asparagus sauce, more than satisfy tastes of other persuasions.

In addition, perhaps, to apple and plum tart, cherry mousse or steamed lemon pudding, a good selection of Welsh cheeses is always on offer to end with.

Single-course dishes of grilled fillets of plaice, venison cottage pie and a variety of steaks, with lighter alternatives like salmon and broccoli quiche, leek and mushroom tagliatelli and numerous open sandwiches are served in the lounge bar or out on the lawn which looks out over the lower town and beyond towards the Brecon Beacons.

Though handy for, but not easily found from the town centre, the hotel is best approached past the riverside promenade close to the Castle Street Bridge.

MEALS: L 12-2; D 6-9 £17
Set Sun L £8.90
Special breaks: Dinner, Bed and Breakfast from £84

WTB: 4 Crowns highly commended
43 En suite from £40 S; £60 D

60 Brecon

Waterfront Cafe and Bistro

Theatr Brycheiniog
Canal Wharf
Brecon
Powys
LD3 7EW
Tel: 01874 - 611866

The cafe and bistro at Brecon's new community theatre was a sure-fire hit from day one and has spent its first summer playing to packed houses. The bistro services the purpose-built, European-financed complex alongside the stunning new canal basin just a short walk from the town's centre. The complex incorporates a 430-seat theatre, conference rooms and art gallery.

Under the experienced and confident direction of Claire Graham, it has blossomed into a popular eating and meeting place for all age groups, with a growing clientele of local regulars, overseas tourists and visiting luminaries.

Food by day ranges from home-made cakes and scones and proprietary Welsh ice creams through filled freshly-baked baguettes and

jacket potatoes to hearty daily soups and lunch specials like lamb or vegetable lasagnes, cheese and potato pie and cold meats accompanied by imaginative self-served salads.

The evening operation, which has more recently got fully under way, takes in pre-theatre suppers and receptions, roast dinners, char-grilled organic beef steaks, lamb kebabs and hearty casseroles at truly applaudable prices.

Special events and theme nights staged in conjunction with the main theatre's programmes have already acquired a regular following, promising many an encore in years to come.

  MEALS: Meals all day 10-10
Please phone for winter opening hours

61 Builth Wells

Caer Beris Manor

Builth Wells
Powys
LD2 3NP
Tel: 01982 - 552601
Fax: 01982 - 552586

The illusions of antiquity suggested by the black-and-white magpie frontage and tall, brick Tudor stacks of this former home to the Earls of Swansea are quickly shattered as one crosses a stone threshold dated 1896 and enters Katherine and Peter Smith's cosy, lived-in mansion. There is, however, evidence of a Roman fort on this site overlooking the Irfon, and in an interior of great interest pride of place goes to the oak dining-room panelling which dates from 1570.

Similarly, the food is all genuine enough but exhibits a mixture of traditional and modern styles and techniques, of which some are more accomplished than others. The best local produce is used in a modern context, such as dressed mixed leaves under, and fillets of anchovy on top of, toasts of grilled goats' cheese, and a spiced, wild-rice timbale to accompany canon of Welsh lamb. Scallops are modishly pan-fried in olive oil but rather inappropriately paired with "Mediterranean garden vegetables" – mostly red peppers and onion – and sherry: vegetables are offered as a "panache".

Dessert choices mostly revert to traditional stuff like creme caramel with rum-soaked raisins and apple pie with creme anglaise. Had the curate eaten his egg here, he'd have loved it!

  MEALS: L 12.30-2; D 7.30-9.30 £19.95
Set Sun L 12.30-2.30 £9.95
Special breaks: Dinner, Bed and Breakfast from £105

  WTB: 4 Crowns highly commended
22 En suite B&B from £50 S; £80 D

62 Crickhowell

Bear Hotel

High Street
Crickhowell
Powys
NP8 1BW
Tel: 01873 - 810408
Fax: 01873 - 811696

Famous for the warm hospitality extended by Judith Hindmarsh and family for the past twenty years, the elegant, flower-decked Bear is a splendid all-round inn notable for its innovative cooking and high standard of accommodation. Charming courtyard rooms with thier own bathrooms are individually designed, as are the new, luxury suites housed in a rear extension where peaceful exclusivity is guaranteed.

Bustling bars with evocative oak panelling, antique furnishings, rug-strewn woodblock floors and warming log fires in winter make a splendid setting in which to enjoy eclectic pub food encompassing home-made lasagne, beef and Beamish pie and sausage jambalaya, and more-homespun dishes like Welsh rarebit with olive bread and bacon, Wye-salmon fishcakes and braised hock of Welsh lamb with rosemary and thyme.

In the three restaurant areas, the kitchen's creative talents come to the fore at night (and Sunday lunchtime) with an adventurous menu that highlights local fish, organic meats and game in season. Typical starters might be confit of duck with a caramelised pear-and-apple galette, or pan-fried scallops with carrot and sorrel mousse, followed by pigeon en croute over port and redcurrant sauce, or roast monkfish on black noodles with capsicum cream sauce. Home-made desserts feature apple and whinberry pie, summer-fruits and bread-and-butter puddings. Nine decent choices of wine are served by the glass, good cask-conditioned ales and single-malt whiskies by the score.

 MEALS: L 12-2; D 7-9.30
(Bistro till 10)
Special breaks: Dinner, Bed and Breakfast from £92

 WTB: 4 Crowns
29 En suite B&B from £42 S, £56 D

63 Crickhowell

Gliffaes Country House Hotel

Crickhowell
Powys
NP8 1RH
Tel: 01874 - 730371
Fax: 01874 - 730463

1997 marks the Brabner family's 50th year as hosts at their romantic Italianate mansion set in 32 acres of mature gardens overlooking the picturesque Usk Valley. With a third generation now joining the team all looks set fair for the next quarter-century. Guests return year after year to enjoy this seat of gracious country living, not least of their pleasures being dinner served in the relaxed atmosphere of a splendidly-proportioned dining room.

Menus display an easy balance between the firmly traditional and dishes with more modern influences, as displayed by starters such as oak-smoked salmon with basil-scented tomatoes, and chorizo sausage and mozzarella set on roasted pepper and olive dressing. Seared fillet of cod is served on a bed of traditional bubble-and-squeak, best end of Welsh lamb paired with Provencal vegetables and rosemary, pigeon breasts accompanied by Puy lentils, roasted red onions and pancetta. Afters are sticky puddings and fruit-based alternatives such as strawberry meringues with whisky cream, and there's a good selection of farmhouse cheeses.

Light lunches are popular and a real treat in summer, taken in the new conservatory or on a sunny, south-facing terrace overlooking the Usk way below: by any token a fine setting for eating well. Gliffaes also offers a superb afternoon tea.

MEALS: L 12-2.30; T 4-5.30 from £6.20;
D 7-9.15 from £21;
Set Sun L 12-2.15 £19.95

WTB: Unclassified
22 En suite B&B from £36.50 S; £73 D

64 Crickhowell

Nantyffin Cider Mill

Brecon Road
Crickhowell
Powys
NP8 1SG
Tel/Fax: 01873 - 810775

A long-standing foodie haunt, handily sited alongside the A40 at its junction with the A479, the Cider Mill dates partly from the 15th century, and the restored remains of a later mill-wheel form the centrepiece of its stylish dining-room. With little semblance to a traditional local pub, it offers nonetheless a range of draught beers and ciders and a sensibly-compiled wine list that finds room for an offering from Offa's Vineyard. Daily-updated blackboards indicate the kitchen's reliance on fresh supplies with organic vegetables, local game and butchers' meats and fish from Cornwall all in evidence.

The food is modern in style, with bags of flavour: deep-fried home-grown courgette flowers and a Swansea cockle and laverbread tart preceding char-grilled tuna with fine beans and black olives, pan-fried lamb's liver with olive oil mash and onion gravy, and supreme of local pigeon with risotto, chorizo and port sauce.

Service is chatty and informal in the bar areas at lunchtime and a little more restrained in the dining-room at night. The same partnership of Sean Gerrard and Glyn Bridgeman has this year acquired the Manor Hotel a mile down the road towards Crickhowell; their new-found capacity to offer quality accommodation as well as alternative dining of this quality augurs well.

MEALS: L 12-2.15; D 6.30-10
Set Sun L 12-2.15 £11.95
Closed: Mon

65 Cross Inn

New Quay Honey Farm

Cross Inn
Llandysul
Ceredigion
SA44 6NN
Tel: 01545 - 560822

Former dairy farmers Mariana and Gerald Cooper moved into beekeeping fifteen years ago and have since become notable authorities on the subject. They now have 35 hives in south-west Wales, on farms carefully selected to exclude from the bees' diet any traces of flavour-destroying oil-seed rape. At their farm and visitor centre the Coopers have created a fascinating exhibition and video display in the upper part of a disused chapel, above a shop offering all manner of bee-related produce and their adjacent tearoom.

Well worth a visit, this is an attractive, honey-coloured room with low ceiling and pine furnishings where a short menu offers pretty well everything home-made, with soup and a daily cooked dish at lunchtime as well as the more usual salads, cream teas, scones and cakes. Clever use of the farm's own honey is made in the baking of excellent bara brith and shortbread biscuits whose distinctively strong honey flavour comes clearly through. Organic cheeses and locally-made real dairy ice creams are used, while the jams are made locally by Wendy Brandon, who also supplies London's Ritz Hotel. The obvious choice for a teatime accompaniment, however, must be the sensational honey lemon curd that's so good you'll want to buy a pot from the shop to take home with you.

 MEALS: All day 10-6
Unlicensed
Closed: Nov-Easter

66 Cwm Taff

Nant Ddu Lodge Hotel

Cwm Taff
Nr Merthyr Tydfil
Powys
CF48 2HY
Tel: 01685 - 379111
Fax: 01685 - 377088

A former hunting lodge "by the black stream", Nant Ddu stands just above Llwyn-On reservoir in the Brecon Beacons National Park, little more than a half-hour's drive from the centre of Cardiff on the A470. Run by the Ronson family since 1992, the hotel is set almost to double in size by 1998: bedrooms, handsomely proportioned and individually designed, increase from 16 to 28 and new banqueting and reception areas and a lounge for residents are all being added.

With non-resident capacity already approaching 200, there's a noticeable buzz in both bars and bistro, where diners order from identical blackboard menus which are constantly revised and up-dated according to season. Char-grilled steaks, Welsh lamb cutlets and tuna loin retain their perennial popularity alongside more adventurous fare typified by smoked haddock fishcakes with shrimp and brandy bisque, guinea fowl breast with leg-meat sausage and Dijon mustard sauce, and venison sausages with onion gravy and spring onion mash. Fish supplies are especially good, contributing fresh crab for a gratinee and scampi tails for a coconut and Thai-spiced starter, and whole lemon sole with herb butter or perhaps brill fillets with prawns and capers as main dishes. Home-made desserts also help keep the kitchen on its toes: Scotch pancakes with summer fruits compote, chocolate praline terrine with orange anglaise, plum frangipane tart and sticky toffee pudding add to this commendably prodigious output, with which the Ronsons and their staff cope with unruffled geniality.

MEALS: L 12-2.30; D 6.30-9.30
Childrens menu available
Specail rates for 3 nights or more

WTB: 4 Crowns highly commended
28 En suite B&B from £45 S; £60 D
Bedrooms closed 10 days at Christmas

67 Cynghordy

Llanerchynddda Farm

Cynghordy
Llandovery
SA20 0NB
Tel: 01550 - 750274
Fax: 01550 - 750300

Staying on a working sheep farm is anything but dull at Nick and Irene Boynton's farmhouse set 200 metres above sea level in the southern foothills of the Cambrian Mountains. Standing on the edge of moor, mountain, woodland, wetland and flood plain, the farm attracts a multi-national cross-section of walkers and nature lovers, who after a long day out on the Cambrian Way often return to lashings of tea and crumpets by the roaring log fire and join in a convivial and polyglot evening.

Nick enthusiastically cooks anything he can procure locally: home-grown lamb (often served in a huge casserole of rosemary gravy), farm bacon, free-range eggs and pork and additive-free sausages – a particular dinner favourite. Everyone gathers round the farmhouse tables to tackle soup such as the richly inventive beetroot, apple and blackcurrant, followed by the tasty beef and Guinness casserole or freshly-caught sewin steamed with sorrel, and unexpected vegetable dishes such as carrots sauteed with fennel in honey and butter. Visitors sceptical of traditional British puddings are bowled over by the spotted dick, steamed ginger pudding or jam roly-poly often served up.

There are plenty of books and board games to amuse younger children (the Boyntons have four of their own). Housed in a former coach house and pig sty are some comfortable bedrooms of generous family size with bathrooms ensuite, two of which are on the ground floor, one with disabled facilities.

MEALS: D @ 7.30 £10
Special breaks: Dinner, Bed and Breakfast from £64

WTB: 2 Crowns commended
9 En suite from £22 S; £44 D
No credit cards

68 Eglwysfach

Ynyshir Hall

Eglwysfach
Machynlleth
Ceredigion
SY20 8TA
Tel: 01654 - 781209
Fax: 01654 - 781366

Queen Victoria's favourite hunting-lodge, now Joan and Bob Reen's beautifully ordered home, stands amid fine parkland in a peaceful valley next to an RSPB nature reserve. You could find no better place to relax than in this house hung with Rob's dramatic canvases, where the lounge bar, with its unique picture window, offers cocktails and canapes before an evening of gracious dining which has become integral to Ynyshir. Under Chris Colmer's confident direction meticulous shopping, inventiveness and spontaneious allowances for the vagaries of Welsh weather all contribute to menus whose handwritten descriptions hardly do justice to the experience that follows.

Chris's Thai spicing of classic moules mariniére is genuinely exciting, while his terrine of foie gras and Provencal vegetables with brushetta and tapenade is masterful, each an outstanding entree to main dishes equally assured in design and composition. Saddle of wild local rabbit with spring cabbage, herb cous-cous and sweet-and-sour sauce; fillets of roast John Dory with smoked haddock brandade; and breast of maize-fed chicken poached in vegetable *nage* with sage gnocchi and baby vegetables, are all full of exuberance and flair. Almond biscuits layered with chocolate mousse and praline custard are no less confidently flavoured, followed by delicate sweetmeats and coffee in the lounge - all leaving you with proof that there is genuinely exciting eating to be found in Wales's far west.

 MEALS: D 7-8.30 from £29.50
Set Sun L 12.30-1.30 £19.50
Special breaks: Dinner, Bed and Breakfast from £170

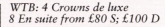 WTB: 4 Crowns de luxe
8 En suite from £80 S; £100 D

69 Elan Valley

Elan Valley Hotel

Elan Valley
Nr Rhayader
Powys
LD6 5HN
Tel/Fax 01597 - 810448

Just below Caban Coch, the last of four reservoirs which graduate spectacularly down the valley, this rejuvenated hotel stands among some of mid-Wales's finest scenery: for starters, just take the mountain road from here to Devil's Bridge.

In their first residential venture, the Boss/Johnson/Osborne/Ollman troupe indicate their theatrical background with interiors of striking originality and instant charm. This is evident in Anthony Ollman's Dish Dash Restaurant, whose name alone defies anyone to eat too solemnly and whose mid-Eastern decor and informal ambience set the tone for unusual eating. An evening's offerings might start with Spanish prawns with garlic, lemon and chilli; roasted red peppers with tomato and feta cheese; or "Anthony's famous fish soup" – and continue with fillets of locally-caught fresh trout on lime butter sauce; an ale and Guinness carbonnade of organic venison; chicken Jalfrezi or aubergine

Mid Wales

and red pepper moussaka. This thoughtful food is presented in an unfussy style: with five children between them, simplicity and family enjoyment go hand in hand. Bedrooms are being refurbished in the main house and additions among the outbuildings are on the agenda: as parents might reflect on their way upstairs past the series of animal cartoons – "all very commenda-bull".

*MEALS: Bar L 12-2.30; Tearoom 11-5.30 in summer
D 7-9.30 around £15
Special breaks: Dinner, Bed and Breakfast from £65*

*WTB: 3 Crowns commended
10 En suite B&B from £30 S; £45 D*

70 Kerry

Cilthriew

Kerry
Nr Newtown
Powys
SY16 4PF
Tel: 01686 - 670667

Mid Wales

Margaret and Gary Barbee's 16th century farmhouse lies in the pretty, unspoilt Vale of Kerry below Clun Forest. It's ideal as a touring or walking base and is only a mile or two from the Offa's Dyke path. The half-timbered magpie frontage and original interior, which includes a massive stone inglenook dominating the guests' lounge, create an impressive and enchanting setting. Diners are ushered together through a secret panelled doorway to encounter flickering candelabra, fresh flowers and silver cruets on the dining table.

One night's starter to what is literally the "table d'hôte" might be pink grapefruit grilled with brown sugar and cinnamon; the next, avocado and smoked bacon salad drizzled with vinaigrette. Main courses night by night might include poached salmon with fresh herb butter sauce, or a vegetarian feast of tortilla with re-fried beans, tomato, yoghurt and basil leaves; or pan-fried beef steak deglazed with mustard and cream, all served with a fine eye for detail. To finish, Margaret serves hearty fruit pies or simply conceived delicacies such as her elderflower and gooseberry honey hearts.

This is one of those comfortable, relaxed places with a little for everyone, from evocative Georgian bedrooms in the farmhouse (one is conveniently on the ground floor) to others in a listed barn across the courtyard. Here, the conversion has incorporated original ventilation panels (now craftily glazed) in the exposed brickwork, while the plain stripped doors and floors offset the new bedroom furniture.

*MEALS: D @ 7.30 £12
Special breaks: Dinner, Bed and Breakfast from £64*

*WTB: 3 Crowns highly commended
7 En suite from £23 S; £40 D
No credit cards*

71 Knighton

Milebrook House

Milebrook
Knighton
Powys
LD7 1LT
Tel: 01547 - 528632
Fax: 01547 - 520509

Formerly the home of the explorer Wilfred Thesiger who, incidentally, opened the smart new wing of de-luxe bedrooms in 1996, Beryl and Rodney Marsden's small country house hotel stands in three acres on the banks of the River Teme, on which it has fishing rights. In rolling, wooded Marches countryside two miles east of Knighton, it offers a relaxed, informal atmosphere, ten elegantly-furnished bedrooms and – more importantly – competently cooked food which makes a feature of home-grown herbs and vegetables from its own extensive kitchen garden. In addition, succulent lamb and tender beef from Teme Valley farms and fresh trout from nearby Presteigne are skilfully used by Beryl and her daughter Joanne in preparing their seasonally-changing fixed-price evening menus.

Choices might include smoked guinea fowl supreme with pickled damsons, Carmarthen ham with melon, and carrot and orange soup for starters, followed by lamb wrapped in bacon with rosemary and redcurrants, pork fillet with Dijon mustard and mushroom sauce, or poached lemon sole sauced with cream and vermouth.

Round off an enjoyable meal with iced almond mousse on a raspberry coulis, apple and blackcurrant sponge pudding with creme anglaise – or selected Borders and Welsh cheeses – then retire to the drawing-room, complete with deep sofas and open fire, for freshly-brewed coffee and petits fours. Good wines from Tanners are carefully selected by Rodney, whose enthusiastic tasting notes are informative and helpful.

MEALS: Restaurant L 12.30-1.30; D 7-8.30 from £17.50
Special breaks: Dinner, Bed and Breakfast from £98
Closed: L Mon

WTB: 4 Crowns highly commended
10 En suite B&B from £47 S; £68 D

Mid Wales

72 Libanus

Brecon Beacons Mountain Centre

Libanus
Brecon
Powys
LD3 5ER
Tel: 01873 - 623366
Fax: 01873 - 624515

This popular cafe and tearoom is part of the excellent Brecon Beacons National Park Information Centre, signposted from the A470 just south-west of Brecon. From its bench-filled terrace you can relax and savour the magnificent, panoramic views of the Beacons with Pen-y-Fan dominating the awe-inspiring scene. Be prepared to share your cake with the hordes of sparrows, chaffinches and blue tits which will eat off the plate in your lap if you let them. On inclement days, the picture windows in the spotlessly-kept cafe still allow parents to enjoy the view, while the youngsters can amuse themselves in a well-equipped playroom complete with wall mural, toy box and crayons.

A pleasing array of generously-filled baps includes home-baked ham and local cheeses alongside light, fresh scones, home-made carrot cake and Welsh specialities like bara brith and popular Welsh cakes. A monthly-changing Bwyd Cymreig menu lists a daily hot soup such as tomato and vegetable; carrot, walnut and broccoli flan, spinach pudding and perhaps Beacon Bake – a healthy potato, cheese, bacon and leek pie – all served along with freshly replenished salads by friendly, uniformed staff. Packed lunches are gladly prepared and boxed for walkers and to quench summer thirsts there's Frank's first-rate fruit-filled dairy ice cream.

MEALS: All day 10-6 (till 4.30 in winter);
L 11.30-3.30. Unlicensed
Closed: 25 Dec

73 Llandrindod Wells

Guidfa House

Crossgates
Llandrindod Wells
Powys
LD1 6RF
Tel: 01597 - 851241

A home-from-home run in exemplary fashion by Anne and Tony Millan, this white-painted former farmhouse stands by the junction of the A44 and A483 at Crossgates, some three miles north of Llandrindod Wells. Arrive in time for tea and bara brith in the chandeliered front lounge or for a stroll round the picturesque garden, either of which allow you to unwind before the evening's main event.

The three-course set dinner reflects Anne's careful shopping and menu planning, a baked goats' cheese with red pepper salsa preceding breast of chicken stuffed with spinach on a pungent saffron sauce, with generously boozy Tia Maria mousse to follow. Home-made gravadlax with beetroot salad, pork fillet stuffed with green peppercorns on a creme fraiche dressing and the much-requested apple pie might constitute a second evening's meal for those wise enough to take advantage of Guidfa's generous Special Break rates.

The seven spacious bedrooms are spotlessly kept (one is on the ground floor) and a self-catering apartment is available for rent by the week. Special dietary preferences are catered for and non-residents can book in for dinner by prior arrangement. As one observant guest noted: "The house plants looked so cared-for and healthy we were in no doubt that we'd have a memorable dinner – and so we did."

MEALS: D 7-8 £15.50
Set Sun D from £21
Special breaks: Dinner, Bed and Breakfast from £70

WTB: 3 Crowns highly commended
7 rooms 5 En suite B&B from £21 S; £48 D

74 Llanfihangel-nant-Melan

Red Lion

Llanfihangel-nant-
Melan
New Radnor
Powys
LD8 2TN
Tel: 01544 - 350220

The Johnses' frankly unpretentious roadhouse is a family affair which continues to attract a loyal following among food enthusiasts for the excellent quality and value of its food. Credit for this goes to chef Gareth Johns, who indefatigably hunts out Welsh produce equal to any in Mid-Wales. "*BWYD BLASUS IAWN*" proclaims a blackboard otherwise written in English – this being a largely non-Welsh-speaking area – which is updated daily.

For starters, or a light lunch, try grilled fresh herring with coriander and garlic butter, or pan-fried fillet of red snapper; other alternatives are Rhydlewis smoked trout, and inventive soups such as cream of fennel and onion. More substantially, Swansea cod is deep-fried in batter or grilled with saffron sauce, and there's wonderful farm lamb from Bwlch which appears as the sweetest spring cutlets simply grilled, rested and served with home-made rowan jelly. Later in the year the more mature rump is marinated and char-grilled with whinberries from nearby Radnor Forest. Gareth also combines wild whinberries with tiny, sharp cranberries in a peerless fruit tart, while this champion of Welsh cheeses offers half-a-dozen varieties as a ploughman's lunch or an after-dinner platter. His brother Paul (known as "The Badger") dispenses fine real ale and hospitality from the bar. Spotless, if modest, stopover chalet accommodation is available beside the beer garden.

 *MEALS: L 12-2;
D 6.30-9
(D Sun from 7, Sat till 9.30)*

 *WTB: 1 Crown
3 En suite B&B from £18 S; £35 D
Closed: Tue Nov-May; 1 week Nov*

75 Llanfyllin

Cyfie Farm

Llanfihangel-yng-
Ngwynfa
Nr Llanfyllin
Powys
SY22 5JE
Tel/Fax: 01691 - 648451

This remarkable 17th-century stone longhouse stands amid the 178 upland acres of a stock-rearing farm that also grows winter feedstuffs for the sheep and cattle. There are splendid walks in the surrounding countryside, which falls away steeply into the Meifod valley. Overnight accommodation in recent conversions of the former stables and barn offers an exceptional degree of comfort – a true home from home for guests who come back to stay by the week – and dinner (served at 7pm) is eagerly awaited with good reason.

Lynn Jenkins, for 30 years mistress of her own kitchen (George allegedly married her for her gravy!), is an accomplished and imaginative cook, producing a nightly four-course dinner full of textures and flavours to put many a more formal outfit to shame. Witness fresh salmon mousse, its rich and creamy saltiness balanced by

cool cucumber, Welsh mountain lamb on onion confit with mashed potato and leeks wallowing in richly-scented gravy, greengage fool accompanied by shortbread biscuits dressed with summer fruits, and a platter of Welsh and Border cheeses such as Llanboidy and Shropshire Blue: in a word, this is a feast! After a stroll round the garden or a visit to the nearby badger set, you're guaranteed a truly restful night at this peaceful spot – and next morning the leisurely farmhouse breakfast fortifies everyone for the day ahead.

 MEALS: D @ 7 £13
Special breaks: Dinner, Bed and Breakfast from £70

 WTB: 3 Crowns de luxe
Cottage suites from £44-£51 D
No credit cards

76 Llangattock

Ty Croeso Hotel

The Dardy
Llangattock
Powys
NP8 1PU

Tel/Fax: 01873 - 810573

Translated from the Welsh as House of Welcome, the Moore family's small and intimate hotel deserves its name. Set high into a hillside overlooking Crickhowell and the River Usk, this former workhouse infirmary of Victorian origins sports eight neat and comfortable en suite bedrooms – most commanding splendid mountain views. A peaceful, late-afternoon stroll beside the Brecon and Newport Canal just below the hotel should generate a healthy appetite for dinner. After drinks served by the fire in the cosy bar/lounge, or out on a pretty sun-terrace in fine weather, you'll find fresh local ingredients prepared with assiduous care on an unpretentious table d'hôte Tastes of Wales menu which gives excellent value for money.

Gower crab mousse, traditional Welsh cawl, and laverbread and bacon nuggets with rich tomato sauce are fitting precursors to carefully-worked main courses such as samphire-wrapped Teifi salmon baked in filo, saddle of wild rabbit with leek sauce and Brecon lamb steak with rowanberry and orange sauce.

For pudding try, perhaps, the Welsh whisky and chocolate cheesecake or indulge in a selection of well-kept cheeses which will generally include a St Illtyd or St Davids and possibly a Pencarreg. The wine list is extensive, well-chosen and equally good value.

 MEALS: L 12-1.30; D 7-9 from £16
Special breaks: Dinner, Bed and Breakfast from £80

 WTB: 3 Crowns highly commended
8 En suite B&B from £30 S; £55 D
Closed: 2 weeks Jan

77 Llanwrtyd Wells

Carlton House

Dolycoed Road
Llanwrtyd Wells
Powys
LD5 4RA
Tel: 01591 - 610248
Fax: 01591 - 610242

Wales's smallest town has Alan and Mary Ann Chilchrist to thank for its new-found prominence on the gastronomic map, where their former haberdasher's, grocer's and pub is arguably its best-known address. Mary Ann's consuming passion for food rules her day, which starts with finding the best ingredients for her two evening menus, a four-course table d'hôte with a choice of two main dishes, and an "Epicurean" set menu of three or four courses.

Uncomplicated baked goats' cheese and apple croustade, or an assorted leaf salad with crispy bacon, poached egg, balsamic vinaigrette and shaved parmesan, are preludes to main courses of singular inventiveness. Thai-spiced fish cake is backed by a formidable cast of rice noodles, stir-fried sugar-snap peas and a coconut cream with lime, lemongrass, ginger and coriander; roast cannon of Welsh lamb on a bed of mashed potato with Madeira and lamb jus, wild asparagus and steamed baby leeks is also a tour de force. Yet some of May Ann's best work is still to come, in a majestic chocolate parfait with forceful orange and Grand Marnier sauce, and an accomplished soft fruit mousse layered in shortbread biscuits on a raspberry coulis. This one-person show is a redoubtable performance, sometimes approaching grand Guignol - on top form, among Wales's best.

MEALS: *Light lunch 12-2 Tues-Sat;*
D 7-8.30 from £19.50
Special breaks: Dinner, Bed and Breakfast from £78

WTB: *Unclassified*
6 En suite B&B from £56 D
Closed: D Sun (residents only); 1 week Christmas

78 Llyswen

The Griffin Inn

Llyswen
Brecon
Powys
LD3 0UR
Tel: 01874 - 754241
Fax: 01874 - 754592

Among the oldest inns in the upper Wye Valley, and said to date from 1467, the Griffin exudes character throughout the bar and restaurant with their old beams and exposed stonework and open fires ablaze in winter. Comfortable bedrooms, the nicest opening on to an enclosed rear garden, make for a comfortable overnight stay. Richard and Di Stockton are the genial hosts of this family-run affair, presiding over a bar which is the focal point of village life, and supervising a kitchen notable for its reliance on the best local produce. The same seasonal menus in bar and restaurant feature Wye salmon and locally-caught wild trout in summer and a profusion of winter game delivered at the strangest hours to the kitchen door.

A Griffin ploughman's of Welsh cheeses and a warm salad borrowed from La Diége, their twin auberge in France, keep things light for a bar lunch supplemented daily by specials such as mussels in white wine, garlic and shallots, and braised oxtail in barley wine. At dinner, Penclawdd cockles with laverbread and bacon and the daily home-made

soups, pates and terrines are popular starters; then the salmon might be char-grilled with pesto and tomatoes, and Welsh lamb roasted with "the parson's Shrewsbury sauce". Leave room afterwards for sticky toffee pudding, apple crumble or lemon crunch among a heady list of home-made sweets. Or you can save up for a five-course blow-out Sunday lunch which includes cheese and coffee.

MEALS: L 12-2; D 7-9
Set Sun L 12.30-2 £13.75 (bookings only)
Special breaks: Dinner, Bed and Breakfast from £75

WTB: 3 Crowns highly commended
7 En suite B&B from £40 S; £55 D

79 Llyswen

Llangoed Hall

Llyswen
Brecon
Powys
LD3 0YP
Tel: 01874 - 754525
Fax: 01874 - 754545

It's widely believed that the legendary White Palace, original home to the 6th-century Welsh parliament, once stood on the site of the current house, dating from around 1600. It was redesigned by Sir Clough Williams-Ellis earlier this century and bought by Sir Bernard Ashley just ten years ago for conversion into a palatial country house hotel. Antiques, fine art and plush furnishings surround diners who encounter menus in the idiom of a modern diners' dictionary: fillet of rabbit marinated in thyme and served on a confit of potato and sweet pimento oil; a gateau of goats' cheese, aubergine and couscous with pistou sauce; assiette of Welsh lamb cutlet, leg and kidney with a "wanton of shoulder" and a lemongrass sauce; coconut parfait with caramelised bananas.

Cuisine moderne notwithstanding, the food is of fine quality and full of forthright flavours: lemon sole fillets on a saffron-infused couscous which brilliantly colours a salad of tomatoes and dill, and breast of guinea fowl on a rich, crisped rosti accompanied by diamonds of mange-tout in a succulent, buttery jus. Other offerings like the chilled garden-pea soup with mint and cucumber creme fraiche, strips of Welsh Black beef with a forestiere sauce, the delicious ice creams, Welsh border and Irish cheeses and a simple savoury Welsh rarebit can all be uncommonly good. Service is attentive and relaxed without erring towards intimidation and an excellent wine list contains good-value recommended selections with helpful tasting notes, alongside some classic Bordeaux vintages for the connoisseur.

MEALS: L 12.30-2 from £14; D 7.15-9.30 from £30
Set Sun L 12.15-2 £17.50
Special breaks: Dinner, Bed and Breakfast from £180

WTB: 4 Crowns de luxe
23 En suite B&B from £100 S; £165 D

80 Newtown

Yesterday's

Severn Square
Newtown
Powys
SY16 2AG
Tel: 01686 - 622644

The house that Jim rebuilt, Yesterday's almost became history during its restoration some six years ago, when the famous Shropshire earthquake struck. Today it houses comfortable B&B accommodation running through two upper floors beneath the original roof trusses, and a cosy open-plan restaurant at street level where the exterior walls have since been rebuilt from the footings up to the old pitched roof.

Jim Aston directs kitchen operations while Moyra deftly handles front-of-house with old-fashioned hospitality. Food is on the safe side of traditional with lots of roasts and grills. Also popular now, though, are Jim's marinated shank of lamb (cooked to order) and notable vegetarian options such as his Montgomery chestnut mushrooms with leek and cheese topping, and a Glamorgan pudding served with a choice of mushroom, pepper or cheese sauces. He is strong on nursery puddings such as steamed ginger or date and orange sponge served with rich, thick custard, though lighter fruit-based alternatives include Cointreau-soaked oranges. Pencarreg and Shropshire Blue are represented on the cheeseboard.

Yesterday's old fashioned theme is epitomised by framed advertisements for anthracite-burning stoves and carbolic soap and there's an old Mrs Beeton cookery book on the bookshelf for handy reference into the past. [No dogs (except guide dogs).]

MEALS: L 12-2; D 6.30-9.30
Set Sun L 12-2 from £7
Closed: L Mon; 2 weeks Jan

WTB: Welcome Host highly commended
3 En suite B&B from £25 S; £35 D

81 Pengenffordd

Upper Trewalkin Farm

Pengenffordd
Nr Brecon
Powys
LD3 0HA
Tel: 01874 - 711349

Expect a warm, traditional Welsh welcome and wholesome farmhouse fare at this 16th-century farmhouse at the heart of a working sheep farm far from the beaten track deep in the Black Mountains. Follow signposts from the A479 two miles south of Talgarth. An ambassadress for Wales and its indigenous cooking on her winter travels around the USA, Meudwen Stephens is a charming and entertaining host for whom nothing is too much trouble. Her three homely antique-furnished bedrooms, two with bathrooms en suite, are stacked with knick-knacks including teddy bears, and the sweeping views across Hay Bluff towards the upper Wye Valley fully justify the modest cost.

After producing pots of tea and Welsh cakes on your arrival, Meudwen re-emerges at around 7pm to serve an immaculate dinner that might start with creamy cauliflower soup, served with locally

baked sesame bread, followed by sweet tender lamb from the farm accompanied by vegetables picked that afternoon from her garden.

There'll be a choice of puddings, perhaps a delicious redcurrant pie or light bread-and-butter pudding bathed in farm-fresh cream, with mature farmhouse cheeses and cafetiere coffee to round off the meal. Next morning's hearty breakfasts of laverbread, farm bacon and locally-made sausages will set you up for a day's exploring.

 MEALS: D @ 7
Unlicensed; No credit cards
Special breaks: Dinner, Bed and Breakfast from £60

 WTB: 3 Crowns highly commended
3 En suite from £40 D
Closed: Nov-Easter

82 Pwllgloyw

Seland Newydd
Pwllgloyw
Brecon
Powys
LD3 9PV
Tel: 01874 - 690282

In May 1996, the talented Maynard Harvey and his wife Freya bought the rather run-down Camden Arms, beside the B4520 four miles north of Brecon, and set about transforming it into a stylish dining place offering some of the best pub food in Wales. Re-named Seland Newydd after Freya's country of origin, the 16th-century inn retains an unpretentious village-local atmosphere in the tile-floored bar where one can sample straightforward pub fare and wash it down with a good pint of Brain's.

Booking is required, however, for the new dining-room where Maynard's adventurous flair and imaginative presentation come into their own. A weekly-changing carte highlights fish fresh from Swansea and organic meats from local butchers.

Begin with a tasty seafood chowder or smooth chicken-liver parfait wrapped in smoked bacon with sweet-and-sour sauce; then follow with guinea fowl on braised red cabbage with redcurrant and lime sauce, supreme of salmon with avocado salsa and garlic-scented mussels, or white haddock with tomato compote, Welsh rarebit and sweetgrain mustard sauce.

For pudding try the black cherry and kirsch creme brulee or white chocolate fruit and nut torte, and finish with good, strong cafetiere coffee served with miniature Welsh cakes. Predictably new-wave, the single-supplier wine list also flies a Kiwi flag to complement this inventive contemporary cooking.

 MEALS: L 12-2.30; D 6.30-9
Closed: 25 & 31 Dec

83 Three Cocks

Three Cocks Hotel

Three Cocks
Hay on Wye
Powys
LD3 0SL
Tel/Fax: 01497 - 847215

There's a timeless warmth about this quiet, 15th-century hostelry and the old-fashioned hospitality dispensed by Marie-Jeanne Winstone and her husband, Michael, whose life is dedicated to his kitchen: any visit is an occasion to be savoured at leisure.

The four-course set-price dinner, served in the sedate, tapestry-hung dining-room, always begins with a soup: creamy vegetable, for instance, or lobster bisque (the latter at a noticeable supplement) are served from large tureens and "seconds" are proffered before the arrival of entrees such as Ardennes ham with honey-pickled onions, salmon hollandaise with mushroom duxelle or mixed-leaf salad with bacon lardons and warm blue-cheese dressing.

Main courses produce Wye salmon, wild boar and grouse or pheasant in their several seasons: tarragon sauce enhances a pinkly roast loin of lamb, while lobster is served on noodles with a mild curry sauce. Delicate individually portioned vegetables accompany - though preferably not when soy-based stir-fry chaperones a lobster!

Pretty traditional desserts include a formidable chocolate marquise, cold souffle of apple and cinnamon and glazed floating islands, all encircled by variously flavoured creams, to round off a dining experience which is comfortable, if short of passion.

MEALS: L by arrangement only,
D 7-9 £26
Special breaks: Dinner, Bed and Breakfast from £99

WTB: 2 Crowns highly commended
7 En suite B&B from £45 S; £65 D
Closed: Tue except July & Aug; Dec-mid Feb

84 Trecastle

Castle Coaching Inn

Trecastle
Nr Brecon
Powys
LD3 8UH
Tel: 01874 - 636354
Fax: 01874 - 636457

Since taking over last October at this substantial 17th-century coaching inn beside the A40 mid-way between Brecon and Llandovery, the enthusiastic Chamberlain family have worked hard to refurbish the place. Comfortable, well-equipped bedrooms are gradually being upgraded, and both the quarry-tiled Kitchen Bar and the homely dining-room next to it have undergone a warm and sympathetic revamp. The numerous pump-clips behind the bar indicate that it's found a loyal beer-drinking trade, but on the food side Bryn Chamberlain, the young chef, is still wisely assessing his market. At present a typically pubby menu in the bar, also written in Welsh, offers the likes of home-made steak and kidney pie, liver and bacon suet pudding and spicy chicken curry, alongside Brecon lamb shoulder with redcurrant and rosemary and Welsh Black sirloin steak with decent chips and peas or salad.

In the restaurant, a moderately-priced table d'hôte shows off Bryn's true skills to better effect, highlighting loin of lamb on rosti potato with haggis and port jus, and salmon with vegetable spaghetti on a saffron and dill sauce; local pheasant and wild duck are promised when in season.

Current indications are that careful attention is being paid to sources of supply, exemplified by the good selection of farmhouse cheeses and a straightforward, no-nonsense wine list: early reliance on bought-in puddings is understandable in the circumstances.

MEALS: L 12-2.30; D 6.30-9.45 £14
Special breaks: Dinner, Bed and Breakfast from £70

WTB: 3 Crowns highly commended
10 En suite B&B from £41 S; £44 D

85 Welshpool

Powis Castle Restaurant

The National Trust
Welshpool
Powys
SY21 8RF
Tel: 01938 - 554338

On the site of an original Welsh border fortress, Powis Castle is now famous for housing Lord Clive of India's unique collection of treasures. Perched high on a rocky outcrop above its celebrated gardens, it is approached by a long winding drive through extensive parklands; the final climb is by foot and not particularly suited to wheel- and push-chairs.

There is no admission charge to the courtyard leading to the restaurant, and the stone-floored refectory, with its large well-spaced tables and self-service counter, is popular from April to October and over the pre-Christmas period.

A perennial top-seller here is Clive's "Petits Pates", small sweet lamb pies from an original recipe he himself devised in 1768 in the French town of Pezenas, though there's a much wider range of locally-devised fare, including Cawl afal a chaws (apple and cheese soup), Welsh onion cake and Powis cheese pudding. The cheese platter consists of well-sourced Welsh farmhouse varieties, while the Isle of Anglesey double-cream ice cream is an ideal partner for a traditional blackberry and apple pudding. Nicely-baked fruit scones, bara brith and light sponge cakes accompany the Powis and Welsh Garden teas and the Welsh honey bread is made to Powis restaurant's own recipe.

MEALS: All day 11-5; L 12-2; T 2.30-5 from £2.95
Closed: Mon in Jun, Jul & Aug;
Mon & Tue in April-May & Sept-Oct;
Nov-end Mar except Dec (phone for opening hours)

SOUTH & WEST WALES ENTRIES

86   Abergavenny

The Walnut Tree Inn

Llandewi Skirrid
Abergavenny
Monmouthshire
NP7 8AW

Tel: 01873 - 852797
Fax: 01873 - 859764

Ann and Franco Taruschio's ancient inn almost defies definition. For 34 years it has never failed to fly in the face of convention and, for all its accolades, even today is still more of a people's pub than a haven for elitists. The Walnut Tree steadfastly remains its phenomenal self by constantly challenging trendy perceptions of good food: an innovator from day one, Franco has spent a lifetime at his stoves pursuing new ideas and trying out distinctive tastes that often have been a long time in gaining acceptance. True to his roots, he brought the 18th-century Vincisgrassi Maceratese to Wales yet, despite the irrepressible density of its flavours, it's a rib-sticking dish of pasta with porcini mushrooms, Parma ham and truffles which few "rising stars" today would deign to copy.

Franco is equally passionate about his adopted home, and his now-famous Llanover salt duck was adapted from Lady Llanover's 1837 recipe, while his recently-introduced laverbread soup accompanies roast monkfish with scallops and prawns in a classic reworking to much acclaim. Anything from the garden which can find a use *is* used – courgettes for griddling, their flowers stuffed as a starter or sweet-fried and served with cinnamon ice cream for dessert. Yet all of this happily co-exists in a pub that still has outside toilets and round three-legged bar tables which assault unwary shins; where you can't book a table at lunchtime or even pay by credit card. Food so original – old and new, Welsh-Italian, international and unique - owes nothing to fashion and everything to flavour and flair.

 MEALS: L 12-3.15; D 7-10.15
Closed: Sun & Mon; 5 days Christmas; 2 weeks Feb
No credit cards

87   Bassaleg

Junction 28

Station Approach
Bassaleg
Newport
NP1 9LD

Tel: 01633 - 891891

This is a restaurant where people can enjoy good food without having to dress up, so conveniently placed for its eponymous junction on the M4 that you can drop in on your way home from work. Hence the success of the early evening flyer menu, served between 5.30 and 7pm, which might offer spicy chorizo salad with a poached egg, followed by tender braised lamb shank with olive oil mash, or salmon with curry and coriander sauce, and finishing with banana bread-and-butter pudding. This is amazing value, having nobody feeling out of place or intimidated.

By contrast the huge carte menu of forty or more starters and main dishes is bound to stretch the kitchen. Fillet of red mullet dressed with ribbons of leek, perched on a mound of crab in gingery shellfish broth, followed by pork fillet with excellent savoy cabbage and bacon wrapped up into a bright green ball, come unadorned with the trappings of "haute cuisine", and there can be minor let-downs like an oversweet sabayon with an otherwise first-class strawberry tart. Service is relaxed, capable and down-to-earth, and the wine list offers a good range with quality and value: but reducing the menu options would allow more time for attention to detail and help to achieve the kitchen's obvious potential.

 MEALS: L 12-2; D 5.30-9.30 from £11.95
Set Sun L 12-4 from £8.95
Closed: D Sun

88 Bettws Newydd

Black Bear Inn

Bettws Newydd
Nr Usk
Monmouthshire
NP5 1JN
Tel: 01873 - 880701

Such is Stephen Molyneux's reputation that if you arrive without a booking you might be disappointed, and in any case you will need directions in order to find Bettws Newydd. Food is the priority here, the remoteness of the place demanding an inventive approach, with just enough produce on offer to see out the night – and when that runs out the kitchen closes. Molyneux responds handsomely with cooking that follows no particular theme, relying instead on his own skill and intuition – and just the hint of a sweet tooth. Thus he devises a lemon jelly to coat whole Dover sole before grilling, the result being an extraordinary caramelised crust to the moist, fresh flesh.

Powerful flavours abound in starters of pungent liver parfait or Stilton and chicken terrine, while for main course duck is roast as a half bird and served with crisp skin on a fresh plum sauce, and rack of local lamb is glazed with honey before roasting, then served with mint jus. Desserts are robust renditions of old favourites: both his sticky toffee pudding and glazed lemon tart are exemplary, while a butterscotch sauce (made unusually with dark sugar) offsets a Greek-yoghurt-and-honey ice cream with imperious intensity. Spontaneous, individual cooking such as this is definitely worth seeking out, for Molyneux remains a one-off with the power to amaze.

 MEALS: L 12-3; D 6.30-9.30
Closed: D Sun

89 Brechfa

Glasfryn Guest House

Brechfa
Carmarthenshire
SA32 7QY
Tel/Fax: 01267 - 202306

At the centre of pretty Brechfa village, Joyce Hart has been offering bed and breakfast at her family's old stone house for nearly ten years. The recent addition of a mahogany-floored conservatory extension, decorated in four shades of pink decor, has allowed her to expand her operation to offer food throughout the day in the summer months, and a simple "classic" menu of homely traditional dishes offers very reasonable value. With cawl as a starter and lamb hotpot as a main course there's extensive use of local ingredients, although as has been noted elsewhere in this area, a lack of good Welsh cheeses is attributed – rightly or wrongly – to supply difficulties.

Everything is kept sensibly simple, too, on the short a la carte menu offered year round at dinner: local pork chops with apple sauce, various trencherman's steaks and nicely cooked local sewin served with a simple butter sauce. To follow, apple pie and custard is as straightforward as it can get though a choice between packet custard and bought-in ice cream is perhaps keeping things too simple. Joyce is a charming and busy hostess who provides comfortable, homely accommodation and genuinely good value for money day in, day out, all week, all year. As the new restaurant operation finds its feet, more attention to detail – better breads, improved wine list - will make all the difference.

MEALS: All day 7-9.30
Closed: L Nov-Feb

WTB: 3 Crowns highly commended
3 Bedrooms £25 S; £45 D
No credit cards

  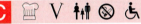

90 Bridgend

Martin's Bistro

Dunraven Place
Bridgend
CF31 1JF
Tel: 01656 - 767095

Martin's, which opened in March 1997, is a welcome and overdue addition to eating out in Bridgend. Although still developing its full potential, the restaurant's slant on seafood and informal dining have made a fine start. The blackboard list of specials from grilled sardines with garlic butter through grilled local lobster to baked red snapper with tarragon and orange butter, puts commendably uncompromising emphasis on quality ingredients shown in the "catch of the day" choices like sea bass from nearby Southerndown and wild Wye salmon when available.

Alternatively, look to the main menu for starters such as fresh calamari in garlic butter, white wine and cream with pistachios or Martin's spicy Szechuan prawns in a sauce of chilli, garlic, ginger, cider vinegar and brown sugar. Main dishes include classic bouillabaisse, Welsh hot oak-smoked salmon steak with vermouth and chive cream and an impressive sewin fillet in a ginger sauce that subtly complements the delicate fish flesh.

Desserts feature home-made crepes and a well-sculpted, crisp yet airy, fresh fruit Pavlova with heaps of cream. Plans are afoot to revamp the frontage with an awning and seats outside, adding al fresco eating to this bracing breath of fresh air in Bridgend.

MEALS: L 12-2.30; D 7-10
Closed: All Sun & Mon; 25 & 26 Dec

91 Brynmenin

Bryngarw House

Bryngarw Country Park
Brynmenin
Bridgend
CF32 8UU

Tel: 01656 - 729009
Fax: 01656 - 729007

Standing at the heart of Bryngarw's picturesque country park, the lovely old manor house was restored to its former glory as recently as 1995, and its immediate popularity for wedding parties comes as no surprise. A light, elegant conservatory houses the small bistro restaurant where you can relax facing the well-manicured lawns and lovely views of the park all around; evening candlelight adds a romantic touch. On days when the conference facilities are in use, the Bistro offers teas, coffees, treats and light lunches; it's advisable to check in advance that it is indeed open. When it is, a Bryngarw cream tea of large, fresh scones with heaps of whipped cream and preserves and light sponges or gateaux is a pure self-indulgence.

On Monday to Thursday evenings a table d'hôte menu operates, alternating with a la carte on Fridays and Saturdays. Medallions of pork fillet topped with a mushroom and St David's cheese sauce, or scallops in puff pastry, preceding by breast of magret duck served with honey and thyme, or canon of Welsh lamb with fondant potato and brunoise of vegetables, indicate the kitchen's well-balanced style.

Desserts can be as indulgent as you please - sticky toffee pudding with whisky and pecan nuts, or poached pear cheesecake.

Sunday lunch is a three-course fixed-price affair for which you should book.

 MEALS: All day 10-6; L 12-2; D 7-9 (Fri & Sat till 9.30)
Set Sun L 12-2.30 from £10.95
Closed: D Sun

92 Caerleon

The Priory Hotel

High Street
Caerleon
Newport
NP6 1XD

Tel: 01633 - 421241
Fax: 01633 - 421271

.A stylish new alternative to Cardiff's vast food emporia in the Benigno Martinez empire (see Cardiff entries) can now be found in the village of Caerleon. The listed 12th Century Priory has been transformed into a state-of-the-art 21-bedroomed hotel whose restaurant follows the formula whereby all manner of seafood, man-sized steaks and kebabs are displayed on shaved ice in a vast cabinet.

Your choice is cooked to order and accompanied with French or garlic bread, self-service salads and first-rate chips. Choose from informal seating close to, or away from, the long bar, in a panelled alcove that doubles as the breakfast-room, or in fine weather out on the tranquil patio.

Fish dishes lead the way, supplemented daily by specials such as halibut with sun-dried tomato and basil sauce, lemon sole with chive and coriander butter, and monkfish Provencal, where the kitchen's skills are shown at their best. Other assets include a substantial £5 lunch (grilled sewin with lemon and dill; minute steak "bonne femme"), a globe-trotting wine list with a dozen or more choices by the glass, and attentive service from smartly turned-out, friendly staff directed by another Cardiff emigre, Miguel Santiago.

MEALS: L 12-2.30 (Sun till 3);
T 2.30-5.30; D 6.30-10.30; D Sun 7-9

WTB: Unclassified
21 En suite B&B from £55 S; £75 D

 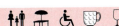

93 Cardiff

Angel Hotel
Castle Street
Cardiff
CF1 2QZ
Tel: 01222 - 252633
Fax: 01222 - 396212

Overlooking the Castle and only a drop-kick away from the Arms Park, this lovely old hotel is undergoing its own refurbishment programme to match the new stadium. The splendid baroque entrance hall with its soaring gold columns and painted angels floating across the ceiling symbolise the aspirations of a new kitchen team with fine ideas to set the Castell Restaurant up there with the best in Cardiff. Both menus and presentation are ambitious, at times recalling the days of Nouvelle Cuisine, and regardless of their origin the dishes work because the flavours are precise and clear.

Good home-made bread precedes interesting starters such as mashed sweet potato wrapped in spinach on a bed of roast peppers, and a tricky-sounding avocado mousse with watercress and wild strawbewrry vinaigrette in which the judicious spiking of the mousse with chopped shallot gives the balance.

Good puff pastry and a savoury tapenade make a simple tomato and basil tart a treat, and a perfectly-cooked best end of lamb is lifted by a fine mustard and herb crust.

Skilful and inventive desserts include a quite delightful assiette of strawberries, a mousse, a jelly, a tart and an ice cream all full of ripe flavour.

Along with some of the best bargain prices in the capital, the friendly and enthusiastic young staff contribute also to the general feeling that this Angel's star is in the ascendant.

MEALS: L 12-2; D 6.30-9.30 from £15.95
Special breaks: Dinner, Bed and Breakfast from £92

WTB: 5 Crowns highly commended
90 En suite B&B from £84 S; £95 D

South Wales

94 Cardiff

Armless Dragon

97 Wyeverne Road
Cathays
Cardiff
CF2 4BG
Tel/Fax: 01222 - 382357

The location on a road bend in Cathays might not be promising, but it's worth seeking out this long-standing yardstick of Cardiff's more informal dining scene. Like the heraldic Wyvern, the old armless dragon who got long in the tooth, the red, white and green decor here has rather lost its fire and any claim to be a definitively Welsh restaurant lies more in reputation than present fact. Though David Richards is Welsh his excellent front-of-house staff are French and the menus are a happy fusion of traditional Welsh ingredients with solid French provincial cooking. The basic menu contains such well-tried staples as mushrooms with laverballs and Provencal fish salad, but Dave's interest and creativity really lie in the two daily blackboards, carted round from table to table, which offer more adventurous alternatives such as octopus and grilled pepper salad or a chilli-hot escabeche of sardines and sand eels, the marinated fish sitting in a rich tomato sauce.

Lighter fish tastes can opt for simple fillet of sewin with sorrel sauce or fresh halibut with a good hollandaise, while the gamey may prefer wild rabbit, expertly cooked off the bone as a casserole with mustard sauce, and accompanied with punchnep, a delicious combination of swede and mashed potato. Finish with one of the chocolate classics – St Emilion or brandy ganache – and good espresso coffee, none of which will cost you an arm or leave you legless.

 MEALS: L 12.15-2.15 from £7.50;
D 7-10.15
Closed: L Sat; all Sun & Mon; 1 week Christmas

95 Cardiff

Benedicto's

4 Windsor Place
Cardiff
CF1 3BX
Tel: 01222 - 371130
Fax: 01222 - 255377

Conveniently situated near Queen Street and the New Theatre, this is a restaurant which is firmly attached to traditional values of cooking and service. Benedicto has been here 18 years, personally greeting every customer with charm and style and giving you confidence that you will be well looked after even as you are being seated. The dark-panelled room is suitably grand in the traditional Spanish style and the opulent dinner menu offers european cuisine with classic-sounding dishes such as crepe Alfredo, seabass Basquaise and entrecote Roquefort.

Twenty starters include baked eggs with smoked salmon and asparagus and warm salad of chicken livers, bacon and croutons with a good vinaigrette. Beside the extravagant veal, venison, turbot and lobster main dishes, a lowlier but nonetheless excellent hake baked in white wine is served with a good parsley veloute spiked with tasty clams and asparagus tips. Vegetables like spinach with nutmeg are served by attentive waiting staff who subsequently, and with a flourish, wheel out the chariot of desserts bearing chocolate and Grand Marnier truffle cake, mille-feuille of strawberries and a generous apple and almond strudel seasoned with cinnamon. Rather more modest menus, offering perhaps lamb kebabs with red wine, or a selection of deep-fried seafood, feature at lunch, including Sundays, for a fraction of the dinner price – which, like the setting, is pretty grand.

MEALS: L 12-2.30 £9.95; D 6-11.30
Sun L from £18.50
Closed: L Bank Hol Mon; 25 & 26 Dec

96 Cardiff

La Brasserie
61 St Mary Street
Cardiff
CF1 1FE
Tel: 01222 - 372164
Fax: 01222 - 668092

This is currently the largest restaurant in Wales since its recent expansion to 400 seats. It is a testament to founder/owner Benigno Martinez that his original concept – and the capital's seemingly insatiable appetite for it – keeps his raft of restaurants, including Champers and Le Monde, so consistently busy (total output more than 2000 covers per day). Despite superficial differences between individual outlets the formula throughout remains much the same – wine bar atmosphere, simple, fast cooking of fresh ingredients and friendly service. The apparently simple format disguises an organised regime based on good training, adroit purchasing and aggressive pricing – both La Brasserie and Champers offering a two-course lunch for just £5.

Although jugs hanging from ceiling beams speak more of Valencia than Versailles, La Brasserie's new extension is more Francophile, with cool marble floors, cast-iron lamps and tall doors folded open to the street in summer. The char-grill caters for a variety of fish, steaks and chicken, but meat is the major draw: suckling pig and leg of lamb are spit-roasted and game is casseroled. Main dishes come with first-rate chips or a jacket potato and help-yourself salad, and can be followed with cheesecake or Paris-Brest. The good-value set lunch typically offers marinated seafood salad or deep-fried chicken wings, followed by crispy plaice goujons or pork hock with lentils. As a wine-bar owner, Sr Martinez takes his wine very seriously indeed, listing more than two hundred wines of which a dozen or more are available by the glass.

MEALS: L 12-2.30; D 7-12
Closed: Sun; 25 & 26 Dec

97 Cardiff

Buffs Restaurant
8 Mount Stuart Square
Cardiff Bay
CF1 6EE
Tel: 01222 - 464628
Fax: 01222 - 480715

Conveniently situated for the burgeoning new developments in Cardiff Bay, Helen Young's two-tier wine bar and restaurant has in fact pre-dated them by some twelve years, and continues to attract a predominantly business crowd – as reflected by its daytime only, weekday opening hours. Stained glass and William Morris decor give an art nouveau feel, and pitch-pine church pews line the terracotta walls of the ground-floor wine bar, where the range of reasonably priced dishes runs from omelettes and baked potatoes to fishcakes with curry sauce, meatballs with tomato and pasta, and spicy vegetable parcels.

In the restaurant above, the pews are arranged railway-carriage style to create more formal booths and an atmosphere akin to a gentlemen's club. A similarly serious menu offers smoked salmon and scrambled egg and grilled Chevré with onion marmalade among a dozen starters, and some 20 hearty main dishes continue the theme: lemon sole with grapes, honeyed duck breast with ginger and orange, and nicely pink pan-fried calves' liver with creamed leeks and a pungent Madeira sauce. Speciality desserts are pancakes filled with cream and accompanied, perhaps, with apples in a Calvados sauce, and a brown-bread ice cream with toffee sauce. Forty reasonably-priced wines travel the world, while Helen controls operations from behind the bar.

MEALS: L 11-7
Closed: Sat & Sun; 1 week Christmas

98 Cardiff

Canadian Muffin Company

13 High Street
Cardiff
CF1 2AX
Tel: 01222 - 232202
Fax: 01222 - 373084

Only a quick stride down the busy street opposite Cardiff Castle, this smart little cafe instantly appeals to students, foreign visitors and jaded diners alike attracted by its light, inspirational menu and commendable coffee. The latter's range, rarely seen hereabouts, deserves superlatives with concoctions such as macchiato and senza schuma as well as cafe au lait, espresso and cappuccino, all in three sizes and decaffeinated if required. These and the muffins are not the only options here. A series of blackboards behind the counter advertise filled baguettes and ciabatta with plenty of fish and vegetarian choice, soups and filled potatoes, and for cool summer alternatives, frozen yoghurt, fruit smoothie and iced coffee.

Even so, the 140 or more varieties of oatbran muffins are still the main attraction: wheat bran, malted wheat flakes and flour, wholemeal oatbran and soda make up most of the fibre-rich organic mixture, along with raw cane sugar for the sweeter varieties. As franchisee Alun Richard emphasises to newcomers "These are not cakes!". But they are indeed special with their appealing coarse-grained texture, and taste is not sacrificed in savoury muffins such as pesto and olive or cheese and tomato. Double chocolate and banoffi are among the sweet favourites, blueberry, gingerbread and honey and raisin the most popular in the fat-free range. The warm yellow interior and circular racing-green tables proudly proclaiming "CMC's Muffins are Deliciously Healthy" add to the chic yet informal atmosphere.

MEALS: All day 8-6; Sat from 9; Sun 11-4
No credit cards
Unlicensed

99 Cardiff

Cardiff Bay Hotel

Schooner Way
Atlantic Wharf
Cardiff
CF1 5RT
Tel: 01222 - 465888
Fax: 01222 - 481491

The hotel, uniquely placed at the heart of Cardiff Bay's waterside development yet only minutes walk from the city centre, is currently in the throes of major extension work. In the Halyards Restaurant, where shipping motifs reflect the original building's Victorian past, diners attracted by excellent value table d'hôte lunches will be treated to fresh and well-balanced cooking prepared with a light touch. Daily soup such as cream of mushroom, and an accomplished chicken liver parfait, precede precisely grilled fresh mackerel fillets with tomato and basil sauce, and chicken supreme with lemon and thyme finished with glazed onions.

The three-course fixed-price dinner menu offers more complex, equally assured dishes: seared fillet of salmon with roquette and an oriental sauce, followed by rib-eye steak on Lyonnaise potato with béarnaise sauce and celeriac crisps, or red mullet and sautéed king prawns with light cucumber and ginger sauce, each confidently contemporary but not over-elaborate. Vegetarians are well served with starters such as potato and spring onion cakes with cherry tomato compote, and next perhaps baked yellow pepper filled with spinach, mushroom and feta cheese. Desserts - chocolate marquise with coffee sauce, steamed jam sponge with custard, or trifle - are comparatively traditional.

MEALS: L 12-2 from £5
D 7-9.45 from £15.50

WTB: 4 Crowns de luxe
158 En suite B&B from £93 S; £110 D

100 Cardiff

Le Cassoulet

5 Romilly Crescent
Cardiff
CF1 9NP
Tel/Fax: 01222 - 221905

Le Cassoulet claims to be Cardiff's leading French restaurant, and it remains reassuringly Gallic, with easy-to-follow French menus, a reliably good-value French wine list and, entirely justifiably in this context, French cheeses in preference to Welsh. The framed photographs of Toulouse rugby sides around the dining-room walls will scarcely go unnoticed by a Cardiff clientele who will applaud Gilbert Viader's mischievously paraded Gallic pride. After devoting his early years to his own culinary talents Gilbert has graduated smoothly to the front, keeping the same format while both content and style of the food are left – under his tutelage – to the Chef.

On a carte which offers half-a-dozen choices for each course, imaginative combinations of tastes and textures take a warm gazpacho dressed with pan-seared scallops, or a tartlet of mushrooms, quail egg

South Wales

and hollandaise to accompany smoked salmon, to start. Main dishes such as pork loin with lentils and black pudding in thyme and red wine sauce might be followed by an accomplished orange bavarois encasing pureed passion-fruit and served in an almond tuile with creme Anglaise. Daily fish dishes – briefly described on a blackboard as for instance "Ragout de poissons risotto beurre blanc" are assiduously explained by a genial host; the results meet expectations with style and flair. The responsibility for this is Andrew Reagen's: he won the Young Welsh Chef of the Year competition when working here in 1993 and has recently returned to Le Cassoulet as head chef – a fitting tribute indeed to both former pupil and his tutor.

MEALS: L 12-2 from £12.50
D 7-10 from £21 (Post theatre by arrangement)
Closed: Sun & Mon; 10 days at Christmas.

 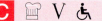

101 Cardiff

Celtic Cauldron

47-49 Castle Street
Cardiff
CF1 2BW

Tel: 01222 - 387185
Fax: 01222 - 708853

Situated opposite the Castle at the entrance to one of central Cardiff's charming arcades, this unpretentious little restaurant has as great a claim as any to be the standard-bearer for Welsh food. The charming menu highlights Welsh dishes with a daffodil – an excusable gimmick given the restaurant's culinary patriotism, a product of painstaking research into long-forgotten Welsh recipes. Glowing restaurant reviews from abroad cover the walls, together with Welsh memorabilia and heraldry, and the Cauldron's dragon logo is even on sale in T-shirt form.

As suggested by the name, soups and casseroles are a feature: cawl is the real thing, its lamb and vegetables simmered until tender and served with chunks of wholemeal bread with nary a garnish in sight. Laverbread, Glamorgan sausages, Penclawdd cockles and Anglesey eggs are among the authentically served traditional dishes; more conventional choices include omelettes, salads and an impressive range of vegetarian options. Befitting a dragon's lair, punch is the house beverage, the seven varieties including a Celtic Lovers' cup for two made with real Welsh mead. Cakes, pastries, puddings and scones are all baked on the premises, together with waffles, bagels and bhajis which add a perfectly acceptable eclectic flavour in the context of this cosmopolitan capital.

MEALS: All day 8.30-9 (Sat till 6)
Sun & Bank Hols 9.30-4
Closed: 25 & 26 Dec; 1 Jan

102 Cardiff

Champers

61 St Mary Street
Cardiff
CF1 1FE
Tel: 01222 - 373363
Fax: 01222 - 668092

The arched, shuttered windows, ornate wrought-iron grilles and friezes of hand-painted tiles showing peasant scenes add an authentic "bodega" touch to this most attractive of Benigno Martinez's chain of city-centre restaurants. The food sits happily with the decor, offering an edited version of the same splendid range of raw fish and meat as its sister establishments, plus a selection of good Spanish specialities and inexpensive wines along with a large range of tapas.

Arguably the best options, these include grilled chorizo with potato cubes cooked in the sausage fat, lambs' kidneys with onions, plain grilled sardines, and stews of tripe with chickpeas or beans with black pudding. Sliced Serrano ham is also offered, along with the rarer and superb Pata Negra wild boar ham, albeit at treble the price. These dishes make a reasonable meal accompanied by the help-yourself salad and plain bread to dip into the various juices. Better to finish with excellent Spanish Blue and Manchego cheeses than with the cosmetic gateau-type desserts, and wash it down with Rioja – of which twelve are available by the glass – or the eponymous Champers, the only French wine you'll find in the place.

MEALS: L 12-2.30 from £5
D 7-12
Closed: 25 & 26 Dec

103 Cardiff

Copthorne Hotel

Culverhouse Cross
Cardiff
CF5 6XJ
Tel: 01222 - 599100
Fax: 01222 - 599080

Extremely convenient for travellers on the M4 (from junction 33) and at the junction of the A4232 with the A48, the Copthorne is also a popular venue for the city, and locals take over from business delegates in the busy lounge bar at weekends. The two dining-rooms deliver contrasting levels of food, the day-long Beauchamps Brasserie specialising in snacks and international fast-food dishes such as nachos, baltis and a Caesar salad or two, while Raglan's Restaurant takes pride of place in the hotel with its lavish furnishings and large windows overlooking an ornamental lake.

As well as a straight forward table d'hôte, the a la carte menu is the focus of the kitchen's attention, and dishes with a Welsh flavour are annotated throughout. Start with Welsh cheeses in filo with cranberry coulis, or a timbale of leek and pistachio with butter sauce; either will come with mixed home-made breads. Main dishes range from shank of lamb, or beef fillet topped with Welsh rarebit, to crabcakes with guacamole and scallops with sorrel sauce. Desserts might be a decorative marbled chocolate teardrop or first-rate bara brith ice cream. Fifty or so wines, chosen like the food to suit most tastes and pockets, are served with professionalism by smartly turned-out staff who are both attentive and friendly.

MEALS: All day 12-10
D 7-10 from £18.95
Special breaks: Dinner, Bed & Breakfast from £150

WTB: 5 Crowns de luxe
135 En suite B&B from £110 S; £140 D

104 Cardiff

Gilby's Restaurant

Old Port Road
Culverhouse Cross
Cardiff
CF5 6DN

Tel: 01222 - 670800
Fax: 01222 - 594437

Purpose-built at Culverhouse Cross to the north-west of the city by restaurateur Anthony Armelin since his recent return to the area, Gilby's announces its intentions with a grand entrance, well-appointed bar and smart seating area. Service with a flourish produces an extensive menu including a comprehensive – for some superfluous – glossary to assist your choice of tempura of seafood or pasta of egg linguine to start, for instance, going on to savory pithiviers with red wine and mushroom sauce or Gilby's carpaccio of beef with truffle oil from among 20 or more main dishes.

High expectations raised by the fresh seafood displayed on crushed ice between dining-room and open kitchen are rewarded by starters like grilled oysters, seared tuna with salsa verdi, and excellent pan-fried scallops with ginger, mirin and coriander butter: no less so the lobster thermidor and roast salmon with samphire hollandaise which follow. For carnivores, peppered rib-eye steak comes with a cognac, cream and Dijon mustard sauce and a tender lamb shank is dramatically served with a seriously reduced sauce, accomplished by delicate creamed spinach. Fine home-cooked puddings include a light, tangy lemon tart with lavender ice cream, rice pudding de luxe and oeufs á la neige with honey and butter sauce.

MEALS: L 12-2.30 from £6.95
D 6.30-10.30
Set Sun L from £6.95

105 Cardiff

Gio's Restaurants

10 - 11 Mill Lane
Cardiff
CF1 1FL

Tel: 01222 - 645003
Fax: 01222 - 645005

Giovanni Malacrino's family of Italian restaurants has been at the cutting edge of popular catering in Cardiff since 1983. and he has been a leading light in the creation of the new cafe quarter that has brightened up the city's cosmopolitan image. Weather permitting, piazza dining is available all day, starting at 10am with breakfasts offering Pane al Ciocolata or a Cornetto (just one!) of jam and butter in a freshly-baked croissant. For main meals the "Al Fresco" menu lists a dozen pizzas and panine with generous toppings and fillings, and house specialities such as Pollo alla Cacciatora and Spezzatino Parmigiano – strips of beef in wine and tomato sauce.

The Continental Restaurant menu runs the whole gamut of popular favourites; house sauces such as Napolitana, Alfredo and Matribologna (bacon, mushrooms and cream) with four types of pasta; veal, poultry and fish in readily-recognised guises, steaks sauced or plain with potatoes and vegetables of the day, and large tossed salads or home-made bruschetta and ciabatta breads to accompany.

In addition, the two-course lunch for under £6 is a proven winner, with the inclusion of plaice goujons with fries and tartare sauce, and lambs' kidneys with onions, mushrooms and cream alongside the more predictable lasagne and canneloni. Gio's also operates "CiaoCaio" at 38, The Hayes (tel: 01222 220077), and the Continental function suites above Mill Lane (for details telephone 01222 - 645003).

MEALS: All day 11-11;
L 12-2.30 from £5.95; D 5.30-11
Closed: Sun; 25 & 26 Dec

106 Cardiff

Harry Ramsden's

Landsea House
Stuart Street
Cardiff
CF1 6BW

Tel: 01222 - 486300
Fax: 01222 - 460693

The Harry Ramsden story continues apace around the world, with branches now open in Australia and Singapore: Melbourne set a world record in 1996 by serving 12,105 portions of fish and chips in one day. You can expect a consistent product from "the world's most famous chippy" and the Cardiff branch is no exception. Be it cod, hake or halibut, the lard-fried fish will be moist and the batter crisp and light, with perfect chips to match, though the mushy peas are more of an acquired taste. Accept Harry's challenge to eat all the special giant cut of haddock, chips, bread and butter, peas and beans and you'll get a signed certificate and a free pudding thrown in.

Despite being part of a multi-national concern, "Harry's" makes a decent effort to reflect its locality in the restaurant quarter of the new Cardiff Bay development, supplementing the wood panelling, stained glass windows and chandeliers with posters of Welsh National Opera performances.

The menu includes Welsh faggots, a Welsh wine, and local fish on the supplementary "specials board"; salmon and haddock are perfectly poached and served with new potatoes.

Waiting staff are exemplary, and many a loftier establishment could do worse than follow their example; attentive and observant, they orchestrate the show to create an infectiously cheerful atmosphere.

MEALS: All day 11.30-11
(Sun & Bank Hols till 9.30)
Closed: 25 & 26 Dec

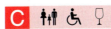

South Wales

107 Cardiff

Le Monde

60 St Mary Street
Cardiff
CF1 1FE
Tel: 01222 - 387376
Fax: 01222 - 668092

Despite being painted entirely in black, this upper section of the Martinez restaurant empire majors in art deco and fish. Its large windows and high ceiling make this the lightest of the three restaurants, brightened by mini-mirror tiles encasing the central kitchen like sequins while halogen down-lamps pick out the cactus flowers and 1920s motifs. The contrast between this Cardiff chic and the huge oak refectory tables and antique chairs emerges in a peculiarly Spanish way, accentuated by ubiquitous flamenco music and service from the red-and-black army of waiters.

A vast array of fish is displayed on ice: make your choice and watch it being cooked for you. Techniques accord to cut, so salmon and tuna steaks are char-grilled, squid and whitebait deep-fried and sole baked whole. Scallops pan-fried and served on a vegetable julienne with butter sauce is, perhaps, a trifle too ambitious in this context, but the whole sea bass baked in rock salt is a triumph – expertly broken open and taken from the bone at your table – and requiring nothing more than a lemon wedge as seasoning, it is a perfect dish for two.

The key to such simple cookery is freshness, which here is virtually guaranteed by the turnover. The hotchpotch of wines painted high up on boards are more likely to stretch the neck-muscles than to break the bank.

*MEALS: L 12-2.30; D 7-12
Closed: Sun; 25 & 26 Dec*

108 Cardiff

Museum of Welsh Life

St Fagans
Cardiff
CF5 6FB
Tel/Fax: 01222 - 566985

The fascinating Museum of Welsh Life is signposted both from the A48 and from the A4232 a mile or so from the M4 at junction 33, and its permanent displays and acres of parkland to explore merit a day out for the family. The old Toll House, thatched cockpit and circular pigsty has been rebuilt stone by stone within the grounds, and photographs showing them in their original locations hang in the museum's main restaurant. A visit to the old working bakery confirms that the bara caws, teisen lap and bara brith are all freshly produced, supplying daily both the restaurant and the outlying Castle and Gwalia tearooms.

The latter is housed above the recreated Gwalia Supply Company store where quality Welsh foods on sale include, traditionally, custard slices on a Friday. Counting the fruit and herbal varieties, there are 18 teas to sample in the cafe, plus sandwiches, Welsh cakes, Anglesey fruit cake and warm scones, butter and Welsh preserves to fill the gaps in a long day.

Main meals can be taken in the restaurant at lunchtime, where production runs from Welsh Cawl, faggots and peas and steak-and-ale pie to soup, salads and snacks, among which pride of place goes to the Dragon Sandwich - the colours of its smoked chicken filling with watercress and spicy home-made chutney recreating those of the national flag.

MEALS: Restaurant & Tearooms
All day 10-5; L 12-2
Closed: 25 Dec

109 Chepstow

Beaufort Hotel

Beaufort Square
Chepstow
Monmouthshire
NP6 5EP

Tel: 01291 - 622497
Fax: 01291 - 627389

In common with many modestly-priced community hotels the Beaufort is sometimes hard-pressed to provide comprehensive services to a wide-ranging clientele. The central bar of signal character is regarded with affection by its habitues, while a healthy mix of locals and travelling professionals enjoys the informality of a grill room and bar menu, and the comfort of the hotel's recently updated bedrooms.

Meanwhile the virtues of a pleasantly-appointed, panelled restaurant remain relatively unsung. Yet there is plenty of value in a table d'hôte menu whose choices might include a savoury Welsh rarebit or Stilton-filled breaded mushrooms, followed by fillet of pork in a filo basket glazed with hollandaise, chicken breast with chargrilled aubergine, or cod fillet baked in a herb crust with parsley and lemon butter.

There may be some overlap with the a la carte menu, further varieties of fishy starters such as smoked salmon roulade or scallop salad with mange tout and bacon. Substantial vegetarian and meaty main dishes include stuffed aubergine with ratatouille and mozzarella topping, duck breast with pear and cinnamon sauce, and rack of lamb with leek and celeriac rosti: plentiful fresh vegetables and two or more potato dishes of the day come at modest supplements.

A confident hand also applies stylish finishing touches to the cappuccino syllabub "dolci piedmontese" and strawberry creme brulee which follow, and the service is uniformly informal and friendly.

MEALS: L 12-2, D 7-9.30 from £12.95
Set Sun L from £7.95
Special breaks: Dinner, Bed and Breakfast from £70

WTB: 3 Crowns commended
19 En suite B&B from £43 S; £60 D

South Wales

110 Chepstow

Wye Knot Restaurant

18 The Back
Riverbank
Chepstow
Monmouthshire
NP6 5EZ
Tel: 01291 - 622929

The airy, palm-lined conservatory is separated from the Wye by little more than a pair of weeping willows, its relaxed atmosphere enlivened by cheerful strains of jazz. Chris Townend is the good-humoured front man while partner Kevin Brookes exercises his considerable talents in a small but highly productive kitchen. Dedication to their work is evident throughout, from the first-rate breads hot from the oven to fudges and soft fruits in white chocolate served with aromatic after-dinner coffee. Ten or more starters and main courses are described on a large blackboard, promising a challenging variety of combinations and flavours that is genuinely met in their execution.

Kevin's signature dish, his Thai crab-cake starter, has a classic sauce of chilli and coconut fragrant with coriander. To follow, a delicate filo parcel of Welsh goats' cheese and leeks lifts a soft fillet of pork with honey and rosemary jus to another plane, while crisped Parma ham, roast red peppers and quarters of lemon-infused new potato enhance baked monkfish and succulent shell-fresh scallops. This expertly-assembled yet unfussy and understated coooking supplants yesterday's cream-laden cuisine with an idiom just right for today. Largely unsung and not long past its first anniversary, the Wye Knot is among the most accomplished of South-East Wales's new restaurants and its future looks distinctly rosy.

MEALS: L 12.30-2; D 7-10
Closed: L Sat; all Sun & Mon;
1 week Oct; 26-30 Dec

111 Cowbridge

Off the Beeton Track

1 Town Hall
Cowbridge
Vale of Glamorgan
CF71 7DE
Tel: 01446 - 773599

The continuing success of this small family concern is founded on regular local trade, a well-worn track to Alison and David Richardson's door. Despite the unpretentious cobbled courtyard, quietly concealed off the High Street, and two small cottagey dining-rooms separated by a central stone chimney breast, a great deal of endeavour is packed into its long working day.

From 10am there are coffee and cakes, and through the afternoon from 2.30pm it's a popular haunt for deliciously naughty Welsh teas - with more cream cakes. Lunch and dinner are chosen from the same menu: choice can be as simple as bacon with laverbread on toast to start and hake cutlet with brown butter or gammon steak and pineapple to follow. However, tortellini carbonara or leek and Roquefort cannelloni may suffice for a single-course meal with a simple salad or crisp home-made chips, while a complete dinner treat could consist of home-made smoked trout pate and duck breast with a black cherry and kirsch sauce, finishing with lemon meringue pie or a tip-top selection of Welsh cheeses.

There's great value in the multi-choice Sunday lunch, which includes three roasts, and diners ordering before 7.45pm on Wednesday to Friday evenings are offered two limited-choice courses at truly unbeatable prices.

 MEALS: All day 10-5; L 12-2.30; D 6.45-9.30
Closed: D Sun & Mon; all day Mon in winter;
10 days Jan

112 Creigiau

Caesar's Arms

Cardiff Road
Creigiau
Cardiff
CF4 8NN
Tel: 01222 - 890486
Fax: 01222 - 892176

Incomers would be advised to follow the route from the A4119 at junction 34 of the M4. This densely populated part of Cardiff's hinterland is also an area of well-rusted signposts. Caesar's is by far the pubbiest of a brasserie-style empire which embraces three outlets in the city and offshoots in Caerleon and Swansea (see entries), and it's the only one with a beer garden, a heated al fresco eating terrace, and carpets in preference to wood-block floors and sawdust. Within the body of the pub the hard-pressed chefs perform wonders in full view of rows of diners. The consistency of their output allows you to choose with confidence from the array of fish and meats in the chilled cabinets and enjoy their uncomplicated flavours.

Crawfish tails, weighed before you buy, are split, grilled and soused in garlic butter; skate wings come with a classic caper butter sauce; half a roast duck crisped with honey, Welsh lamb steaks and pork kebabs are served with buttered Kenya beans and first-rate chips. From a third cabinet next to the self-help salads, desserts like strawberry mille-feuille and chocolate triolo with a certain conveyor-belt quality are dished up in gargantuan portions. In addition to Whitbread beers and lager on tap, a who's-who of the wine world displayed on boards behind the food counters handsomely rewards those who know their Chablis from their Rioja.

 MEALS: L 12-2.30; D 7-10.30
Closed: D Sun; 25 & 26 Dec

113 Crugybar

Glanrannell Park Hotel

Crugybar
Nr Lampeter
Carmarthenshire
SA19 8SA
Tel: 01558 - 685230
Fax: 01558 - 685784

Serene is scarcely an exaggerated description for the Davies family's lovely country house, whose dining-room overlooks well-tended lawns, a private lake stocked with carp and vistas of glorious countryside in the Cothi valley. There's scant enough passing trade here to justify vast or complicated menus: the evening's choices are displayed in the hall for guests to decide on in advance, and non-residents are offered the same nightly menu on arrival.

After starters, which always include fresh soup of the day, home-made pate and a fruit-based alternative, main courses are headlined in

Welsh, with the spring lamb and Welsh Black beef identified right back to their farm of origin. Look, too, for roasts of guinea fowl with game chips and pork loin with apple sauce served with their complementary rich roast gravies. Alternatives might be grilled fillet of cod topped with parsley butter or braised duck breast sliced over a red wine and orange sauce.

Hot apple tart, chocolate rum slice and black cherry trifle typify the range of homely puds on offer; the alternative cheeseboard guarantees at least one local variety. Late-evening conversation over coffee in the lounge is reminiscent more of a traditional house party than conventional hotel and is an excellent prelude to a tranquil night. Glanrannell is closed from 1st November to 31st March.

MEALS: L 12-2; T 3.30-5
D 7-8.30 from £17
Closed: Nov-Mar

WTB: 3 Crowns highly commended
8 En suite B&B from £41 S; £72 D

114 Cwm Gwaun

Tregynon Farmhouse Hotel

Gwaun Valley
Nr Fishguard
Pembrokeshire
SA65 9TU

Tel: 01239 - 820531
Fax: 01239 - 820808

Approached by fully half a mile of private driveway, the Heards' 16th-century stone farmhouse nestles in a world of its own among its neighbouring guest cottages high above Cwm Gwaun. Steep wooded paths lead down to the valley floor past the trout ponds and a 200-foot waterfall, the perfect way to work up an appetite for dinner.

No two nights' fixed-price menus are the same and you can stay two weeks without ever being served the same dish twice. That said, regular favourites like Tregynon's home-smoked gammon and rack of Pembrokeshire lamb are listed separately for a modest supplement; likewise such vegetarian options as Brazil nut and cranberry parcel with Madeira sauce.

Choose typically between cauliflower and broccoli soup, fried Pencarreg cheese with warm cranberry dressing, and chicory, orange and feta salad to start, followed by a main course ordered beforehand which might be beef olives stuffed with plums, walnuts and garlic cream cheese, mousseline of sole and prawns in prawn and cream sauce; or mushroom and aubergine lasagne with onion, garlic and tomato. Minted fine beans, Spanish crumb-baked sweetcorn and roast noisette potatoes with sesame seeds would be a representative selection of vegetables. To follow, exotic egg-free ice creams, summer fruit pancakes or lemon and ginger flan are typical alternatives to a discerning local Welsh cheeseboard.

For directions, signs to Cwm Gwaun are prominent a mile or so from the junction of the B4329 and B4313 at Tafarn Newydd ("New Inn"), and Tregynon is well signed thereafter: it is six winding miles along the B4313 for those driving from Fishguard.

MEALS: D 7.30-8.30 from £18
Special breaks: Dinner, Bed & Breakfast from £84

 WTB: 3 Crowns highly commended
8 En suite B&B from £28 S; £45 D

115 Dinas Powys

The Huntsman

Station Road
Dinas Powys
Vale of Glamorgan
CF64 4DE
Tel: 01222 - 514900

Look behind the recently refurbished Star Inn opposite the square to find this cosy neighbourhood restaurant in former outbuildings which share the pub car park. Hilary Rice cooks virtually unassisted, and her single-minded dedication to her kitchen produces a varied monthly a la carte menu which amply displays her skills.

Crispy duck and orange salad and light, crispy warm crab tartlets accompanied by a salad of white crabmeat, are enticing starters. Welsh lamb cutlets, maybe with a port and plum sauce, and breast of duck with Cumberland sauce, typify the style of the most popular main dishes, in which saucing is a strong point – chasseur, bearnaise and pepper sauces to accompany a 9oz Scottish fillet steak and an accomplished, silky hollandaise in perfect harmony with a lightly baked fresh salmon fillet. Sunday lunch of one, two or three courses is a family hit when Hilary applies her sure touch to sweets such as rich chocolate mousse, lemon souffle and apple and cinnamon crumble. Meanwhile, Peter Rice's assurance and attentive service keep his many regular customers at their ease.

 MEALS: L Thurs-Sat 12-2; D Tue-Sat 7-9.30;
Set Sun L 12.30-2 £10.50
Closed: D Sun; all Mon; L Tue & Wed

116 East Aberthaw

Blue Anchor Inn

East Aberthaw
Nr Barry
Cardiff
CF64 9DD
Tel: 01446 - 750329

One of the South's most ancient and celebrated pubs, the creeper-clad Blue Anchor looks every bit the smugglers' den it once reputedly was, its wealth of mysteries including a truncated spiral staircase to intrigue those of fertile imagination. There's no such mystery to the food here, a model of consistency under the tutelage of the Coleman family for forty years. The best onions and courgettes, we're told, still come from Pa Coleman's garden long after he's left his son, Jeremy, in charge of the more mundane aspects of running four bars and a restaurant.

Bar meals, available every session except Saturday and Sunday nights, are more of a challenge to appetite than inventiveness, freshly-cooked Wye salmon salads and chicken, ham and mushroom pie coming in huge portions with mounds of extra chips on request, while the traditional Welsh rarebit "starter" with bacon and black pudding is a meal in itself. Hidden away up flagstone steps from the pub proper, the

Anchor's restaurant food goes up a step, too; salmon cakes with saffron and dill sauce, guinea fowl galantine and baked mushrooms with garlic and chives are typical of the dozen reasonably-priced starters. Main courses include paupiettes of Cornish lemon sole and braised escalopes of Brecon venison alongside the more predictable steak selection, where the king-sized medallions of Welsh beef fillet finished with peppered shallot and madeira sauce are king, or rather a feast fit for one.

MEALS: Bar L 12-2, D 6-8; Restaurant D 7-9.30
Set Sun L 12.30-2.30 £9.45
Closed: D Sun; no bar food; D Sat & all Sun

117 Felingwm Uchaf

Allt-y-Golau Farmhouse

Felingwm Uchaf
Nr Carmarthen
Carmarthenshire
SA32 7BB
Tel: 01267 - 290455

Next door to the Felingwm pottery, Colin and Jacquie Rouse's sympathetic restoration of an old white farm cottage in a steep valley is comfortably furnished with antiques and a warm welcome awaits within. Meticulous preparation of the two small bedrooms, which share a bathroom, sees them stocked with masses of local information as well as seven different teas, home-made biscuits, bowls of fruit and fresh milk on arrival.

At breakfast, the old elm table is laid at one end of an open-plan living-room with home-made lemonade, dairy yoghurt, different cereals and dried fruits. Good home-made bread and muffins are complemented by Jacquie's jams and marmalade and Welsh butter. She cooks a fine breakfast with sausages and bacon from Carmarthen market and her own free range eggs – which she'll make into an omelette if you prefer; not to mention Manx kippers and Welsh rarebit. Finish with as much cafetiere coffee as you like while Colin chattily serves and clears around you. Breakfast is also offered to outsiders by arrangement, but the outstanding value of the rooms and breakfast together make it well worth staying here.

WTB: 2 Crowns highly commended. Breakfast only
2 bedrooms share a bathroom @ £17.50 per person.
No credit cards. Closed: 25 Dec

118 Fishguard

Three Main Street

3 Main Street
Fishguard
Pembrokeshire
SA65 9HG
Tel: 01348 - 874275

The elegant Georgian facade of No 3 in the heart of town stands high above the docks of Fishguard, formerly a herring port but better known these days for its ferry terminal. First-rate good food using the finest ingredients accurately summarises the approach of the formidable team of Marion Evans and Inez Ford, whose claims to home cooking at its best cleverly disguise abundant technical skill, especially in baking. The high spot of an outstanding breakfast was a crisp, buttery and ethereally light home-baked croissant.

Warmly welcoming surroundings with stripped pine furniture and comforting cranberry and evergreen walls produce a casual coffee-house atmosphere at lunchtime, with familiar yet thoughtfully prepared choices such as roasted pepper and tomato soup with delicious wholemeal rolls and Welsh butter, salade nicoise and broccoli and cheese tart served with a lightly dressed salad. The quality of Marion's baking is further exemplified by a wonderfully moist frangipane tart of apricots and fresh ground almonds decorated with physalis and hazelnut meringue topped with luscious unsieved raspberry sauce.

Mellower tones at night are accompanied by some more substantial but no less balanced main courses such as fillet of turbot, perfectly cooked and well matched by a sublime truffle and bacon sauce, and roast loin of lamb, carefully de-fatted and served with an understated rosemary gravy, adding up overall to some of the most accomplished cooking West Wales has to offer.

MEALS: L 12-2; D 7-9
Closed: all Sun & Mon; L Tue in Winter; Feb
No credit cards

WTB: 3 Crowns commended
3 En suite £30 S; £50 D

119 Glynarthen

Penbontbren Farm Hotel

Glynarthen
Cardigan
SA44 6PE
Tel: 01239 - 810248
Fax: 01239 - 811129

In unspoilt country above Carmarthen, former teachers Nan and Barrie Humphries have converted the outbuildings of her family's farmstead with sensitivity and style into a haven of Welsh hospitality. The peaceful courtyard has bedrooms in the former stables on one side, the bar and restaurant in an old barn on the other, and a museum of farm implements adjoining the farmhouse (still their home) at the end. This award-winning conversion successfully contrasts modern wood and glass with restored stonework and creature comforts with rustic simplicity. Pride of place goes to the splendid gold harp which is often used to augment piped background music in the dining-room.

Nan buys vegetables and cheese from the farm shop on the main road, and makes good use of local ingredients in her farmhouse rather than restaurant cooking. The bilingual fixed-price menu offers a substantial choice with plenty of vegetarian options. Starters range from traditional cawl and terrine of local smoked fish with fennel mayonnaise to laverbread pancakes with leeks and cheese sauce. Follow with parsnip and leek tartlets with honey, peppered fillet of Welsh Black beef, or herb-crusted lamb cutlets with port and redcurrant – all served with a comprehensive assortment of fresh vegetables. Home-made sweets served from the trolley include profiteroles, chocolate gateau and a champagne and strawberry syllabub; among the more popular wines is Ffynnon Lâs from nearby Aberaeron, and also on offer are first-rate local cheeses such as Penbryn.

MEALS: D 7-8.15 from £12
Special breaks: Dinner, Bed & Breakfast from £90

WTB: 4 Crowns highly commended
10 En suite B&B from £38 S; £68 D

120 Haverfordwest

The George's Cafe Bar & Restaurant

24 Market Street
Haverfordwest
Pembrokeshire
SA61 1NH
Tel: 01437 - 766683

Take a steep walk uphill from the High Street and past St Mary's Church to find this excellent cafe/bar and restaurant; motorists must make a short detour as Market Street is one-way coming down.

Converted from an 18th-century brewhouse pub by the present owners, The George's marks its change by housing beside the front door a Celtic Gift Shop (home of Pembrokeshire Primrose toiletries), while a delightful walled rear garden has recently been added to the two cavernous eating areas (upstairs for non-smokers) which positively buzz with activity.

Tasty light lunches take inspiration "from Cornwall to Canton", thereby embracing a deep-sea fish and prawn pie, Normandy crab pancakes, Thai-style chicken and Welsh lamb stew, and a legion of speciality vegetarian fare such as creamed garlic mushrooms in flaky pastry, pasta Milanese and George's vegetable hotpot topped with crisped potatoes. Night-time menu highlights consist mainly of exotic sauces to accompany grilled beef or lamb steaks and chicken breasts; further "pot dishes" include pasta bolognese, slow-cooked pork and apples in cider sauce and George's macaroni cheese with mushrooms, nuts and corn.

Generous desserts featuring Belgian ice creams fall into the naughty and nice category. A wide range of morning coffees and outstanding afternoon teas are served right through the off-peak hours and there's wine and good real ale aplenty. Booking is strongly recommended at night: closed on Sunday and Bank Holidays.

MEALS: L 11.30-2.30; T 2.30-6;
D 6.15-9.15
Closed: Sun & Bank Hols

121 Lampeter

Dremddu Fawr

Creuddyn Bridge
Ceredigion
Lampeter SA48 8BL
Tel: 01570 - 470394

The only way to find this secluded little haven is if you ring first for directions from Anne and Dilwyn Williams Jones. Their working farm sits above the Lampeter valley – as lush and unspoilt a part of Wales as you could find – Anne cooks and serves everything herself, from the treacly bara brith offered on arrival to the marmalade at breakfast.

At dinner you'll sit with the other guests around a single table in the farmhouse dining-room; remember to bring your own wine. Anne delights in surprising guests with her "amateur" prowess, starting with a roulade of smoked salmon and prawns set in cream cheese with dill or a meltingly delicious souffle of Welsh cheeses dressed with tangy blackcurrant vinaigrette. Follow with chicken Veronique with grapes in a rich wine sauce, or in winter pheasant breasts wrapped in bacon from her mother's nearby pig-farm.

Desserts could be ginger meringues with a perfect foil of sharp rhubarb sauce, and in the heart of Welsh cheese country, Anne comes up with seven choices, including a local goat varietal and the marvellous Acorn ewes' milk cheese, served with oat cakes. At the moment it's dinner, bed and breakfast only: the rooms are delightful, with fresh milk left outside your door for morning tea, and breakfast includes oven-fresh home-made bread and rich yellow scrambled egg.

MEALS: D 7-8
Special breaks: Dinner, Bed & Breakfast from £32.50

WTB: 3 Crowns highly commended

122 Laugharne

The Cors

Newbridge Lane
Laugharne
Carmarthenshire
SA33 4SA
Tel: 01994 - 427219

Don't be deterred by the mysterious drive leading over a little humpbacked bridge and through plantations of huge gunnera and weeping willow which apparently signal the approach to some rarefied country house hotel where best behaviour is de rigeur. In fact this perfect little Regency villa houses one of the most stylish and relaxed restaurants you'll find anywhere. "Water- meadow" in Welsh, Cors's stunning gardens are the creation of multi-talented owner Nick Priestland, who trained as an artist in London before returning to Laugharne some ten years ago. His abstract paintings, matching the bare white floorboards, cast-iron furniture and strong wall colours – cherry red in the dining-room, turquoise in the bar – characterise the stylish, eclectic surroundings just as confidently as the beautiful embroidered linen tablecloths and candlelight show off his highly accomplished modern cooking.

There is more to admire in starters encompassing fresh local crab with tangy sorrel mayonnaise, char-grilled peppers with basil and olive oil crostini and a brilliant potato and dill pancake with creme fraiche, Brechfa smoked salmon and lumpfish caviar. Follow these with broccoli, dolcelatte and walnut crepes, rack of Welsh lamb with rosemary and Parmesan crust, or sea bass fillets on red pepper sauce dressed with the simplest steamed samphire, harvested to order by Nick himself. Finish with a full-flavoured lemon tart with rich, buttery pastry or good cheeses from Wales or France. The smiling, friendly service is from Nick's sister, whose own B&B near the castle is in easy walking distance should the two delightful bedrooms here already be taken.

MEALS: D 7.30-9.30
Closed: D Mon & Tue; D Wed in Winter
5 days Christmas

 WTB: 2 Crowns highly commended
2 En suite B&B from £20 S; £40 D

123   Little Haven

Whitegates

Little Haven,
Haverfordwest
Pembrokeshire
SA62 3LA
Tel: 01437 - 781552
Fax: 01437 - 781386

This is almost certainly the only bed-and-breakfast establishment in the land which boasts its own ostrich farm and hatchery, and no visit would be complete without a conducted tour to meet the birds. The restored 16th-century farmhouse has a superb position high on the clifftops and each of the comfortable, modestly-sized bedrooms has a view over the Pembrokeshire coastal path and across Little Haven Bay.

Guests on arrival are appraised of other eating establishments with easy walking distance, while dinner "at home" is strictly by prior arrangement, cooked jointly by Richard and Marian Llewellin and exploiting locally-obtainable produce: Welsh lamb, cheeses from Llangloffan Farm, and wine from Pembrokeshire's premier vineyard at Cwm Deri. Out of season, you are invited to organise your own house party for a gastronomic weekend which includes a suggested day trip followed by dinner tailored to your choice. Breakfast the following morning, complete with a glass of Buck's Fizz, offers a gastronomic start to the day with local smoked kippers, haddock and poached egg, Scotch woodcock and devilled kidneys. Special ostrich meat and egg dishes are there for the tasting, and recipes are provided for those wishing to sample the products at home. A complete farm shop and gift centre is planned as a possible addition to this remarkable enterprise.

 MEALS: D £15 (by prior arrangement)

 WTB: Unclassified
Farm/Guest House
5 En suite £25 S; £45 D

124   Llandeilo

Fanny's

3 King Street
Llandeilo
Carmarthenshire
SA19 6AA
Tel: 01558 - 822908

The strength of this appealing little town-centre restaurant and tea room over the years has been its consistency and the care taken over food which appeals to a clientele of all age groups.

The daily blackboards reveal a vegetarian emphasis; lunchtime specials may well include asparagus crepes, and sweet potato and chick-pea curry, alongside long-standing favourites like Red Dragon and Green Dragon pie, based in turn on red kidney beans with lentil bolognese and white beans, spinach, eggs and cream. While meat-eaters

are by no means ignored, prime beef in their version of Desperate Dan's cow pie is balanced with the assorted vegetables and flaky crust. Fish lovers are catered for with prawn and tuna pie topped with savoury crumble and fresh Towi salmon or local trout in season. There are lots of good ingredients in the spinach and nutmeg, leek and cream cheese, and chicken and sweetcorn quiches (to name but three), as well as in first-rate puddings and teatime treats like egg custard tart, raspberry brulee, caramel meringue and warmed toffee pudding.

Recently taken on by Sue Toller and her son Rick, who is clearly an accomplished young chef, Fanny's has progressed further, and now provides evening meals and Sunday lunches of a more ambitious nature, offering on one early menu parfait of chicken livers with toasted brioche, loin of fallow deer with red onion marmalade and warm chocolate tart with rich chocolate and brandy sauce; or alternatively queen scallops with chive and tomato butter sauce, fillet of Welsh Black beef with roast shallots and garlic, and exotic mango mousse as a finale.

MEALS: Tue-Sun all day 10-5; Thu-Sat D 7-10
Set Sun L 12-3 £10.50
Closed: D Sun & all Mon; 2 weeks Jan

125 Llandeloy

Lochmeyler Farm

Llandeloy
Nr Solva
Haverfordwest
Pembrokeshire
SA62 6LL

Tel: 01348 - 837724
Fax: 01348 - 837622

Lochmeyler is tucked away among the maze of high-hedged lanes threading the hinterland of the St David's peninsula, but once you're there you'll be impressed by the quality of accommodation offered. The farmhouse bedrooms are large and well-equipped, with videos in every room and a video library between the two lounges, and the newer suites next door are even more spacious. To cap this, the value is outstanding: Morfydd Jones does accept non-resident diners, but the dinner, bed and breakfast rate makes it sensible to stay.

"I don't cook fancy stuff!" laughs Morfydd. Instead she concentrates on offering simple dishes appropriate to a good farmhouse holiday. She insists on good ingredients: local salmon and sea trout are cut as steaks and poached with dill, and only Welsh beef is used, obtained from the butcher in Welsh Hook. This might be fillet, baked individually in puff pastry, or slices from a whole silverside, braised for five hours in the Aga until it melts in the mouth, and served with horseradish gravy and simple vegetables. Accompany this with wine from the Cwm Deri vineyard or home-made elderflower fizz. Home-made apple pies, fruit crumbles and steamed puddings complete a true farmhouse meal.

MEALS: D @ 7 £10
Special breaks: Dinner Bed & Breakfast from £50

WTB: 4 Crowns de luxe
12 En suite £15 S; £30 D

South Wales

126 Llanrhidian

Welcome to Town Bistro and Tavern

Llanrhidian
Gower
Swansea
SA3 1EH
Tel/Fax: 01792 - 390015

After gaining wide recognition at their former restaurant, Fanny's at Llandeilo (see entry), Robert and Sheila Allen "came home" to Llanrhidian when offered the chance to buy a moribund free-house in the village where they lived some ten years ago, and a faithful clientele has followed them to the Gower.

Their admirable philosophy of "trading locally but thinking globally" sees this new enterprise putting it into practice in terms of food sourcing and staff. Gower potatoes, cockles, laverbread, organic greens, free-range eggs and wonderful home-baked breads are all obtained within a few minutes' drive, meat is collected from Colin Davis, the local butcher and the choicest fish is delivered from Swansea market by Coakley Green. These ingredients cannot fail in dishes like smoked haddock cakes with tomato and basil and Llanrhidian Bun, a brioche-based version of Swansea Tart with leeks, bacon, cockles and laverbread. Wild boar (delivered from Surrey) and venison with port and redcurrant sauce vie for attention alongside hot smoked salmon with mango mayonnaise, and spinach risotto tart topped with Welsh rarebit: to follow, an accomplished raspberry creme patisserie tart, dark and white chocolate cup or berry fruit crumble.

As we went to press, informal light menus only were operating on Tuesdays and Wednesdays, while reservations were becoming essential for the rest of the week, including Sunday lunch; a heavily subscribed Welcome Regulars Club further indicating the Welcome's instant popularity.

 MEALS: L 12-2.30; D 6.30-8.45 (no children under 14 after 7pm); Set Sun L 12-2 £12.50 Closed: D Sun; all Mon in Restaurant; Oct

127 Llantrisant

La Trattoria

11 Talbot Road
Talbot Green
Llantrisant
CF72 8AF
Tel/Fax: 01443 - 223399

A short distance from junction 34 of the M4 is a recently-opened ambitious restaurant whose owners, Massimo and Daniela Berzolla, aspire to reproduce an authentic and rustic taste of Italy. The repertoire is based on the produce of the northern Italian region of Parma, Massimo's home province, whence slow-cured meats, including the superior culatello, and regional cheeses are imported directly. His menus are still evolving and it will be interesting to see whether more risotto or some polenta dishes appear in time.

Time-consuming old-fashioned cooking methods are used to prepare his native dishes, hence the menu is fairly concise. Among the eight or so starters carpaccio di salmone – fine slices of salmon and turbot with a spinach and basil pesto – is particularly commendable, while both the pan-fried sardine fillets in herbed breadcrumbs and, of course, the cured meat platters are well worth trying. Pasta choices include a rich maltagliata allo speck e spinaci – smoked ham, spinach and cream combined with home-made egg noodles – while ever-popular veal in the scallopine di vitello ai funghi porcini comes in a creamy wild mushroom sauce. Massimo's own semifreddo all' Amaretto is an aromatic and decadently creamy end to an enjoyable meal, accompanied by choice from two pages of Italian wines, followed by fine, strong espresso.

MEALS: L 12-2.30; D 7-9.45
Closed: D Sun; all Mon; 24-26 Dec; 2 weeks Jan

128 Llantrisant

Woods Bistro

79-81 Talbot Road
Talbot Green
Llantrisant
CF72 8AF
Tel/Fax: 01443 - 222458

Proprietors Martyn and Deborah Peters have steadily built up a loyal following since opening Woods in 1993, and their two-course mid-week lunch remains exceptional value. The earthy mustard-and-brick decor of the dining areas in this oasis of good food create a bistro ambience reinforced by the professional service and by Martyn's first-rate cooking.

Though self-taught, his style is light and creative, leaning towards bright, modern flavours with a hint of the exotic: Woods' house salad, a rich alternative similar to Caesar's is an updated combination of avocado and spicy chorizo sausage which works very well as a starter, as do shellfish risotto with ginger and coriander, and pan-fried chicken livers with fresh marjoram, Serrano ham and Parmesan biscuits.

Main courses range from a vegetarian cep risotto with truffle oil and Parmesan flakes to breast of duck with crushed peppercorns, honey and spicy oriental sauce. A typical special of supremely moist sea bass fillet with sweet, seared queen scallops and a perfectly congruent pesto is spot-on, the lightness of the fish supported by a satisfying bed of mash and a side dish of deep-fried cauliflower with sprightly gremolata.

Home-made desserts feature cherry and almond tart and unusually flavoured ice creams such as basil, and a memorable toffee and praline.

MEALS: L 12-2 from £5.95; D 7-9.30
Closed: L Mon; all Sun; all public hols;
25 & 26 Dec

129 Llanvair Discoed

The Woodland Tavern

Llanvair Discoed
Nr Penhow
Newport
Monmouthshire
NP6 6LX
Tel: 01633 - 400313

The James and Gibbs families joined forces in early 1997 to take over Llanvair Discoed's local, which stands in a well-heeled hamlet just below Wentwood Forest – handily signed nonetheless from the A48 between Penhow and Caerwent. Robert and Keith's combined culinary skills have brought new life and an appreciative regular clientele to the business: it took just six months for booking to become necessary for Friday and Saturday nights, Sunday lunch and the regular theme evenings.

Popular starters are the mussels in wine, herbs and cream, grilled sardines with herb butter, and home-made soups such as tomato and basil served with a hot freshly baked roll. Roast rack of lamb with leeks, applejack and red wine, and wild boar with mustard and herb glaze are a big hit, and there's also roast duck Chinese style with kumquats, seared monkfish on pasta Provencale and sirloin of Welsh beef sauced or plain.

Simpler variations appear on the bar meals board, alongside good gammon steaks and cod fillets in beer batter. As further work upgrades the tattier parts of this rambling old building, early portents are highly encouraging.

 MEALS: L 12-2; D 7-9.30; Set Sun L 12-2 £7.95
Closed: D Sun
No credit cards

130 Mumbles

High Tide Cafe

61 Newton Road
Mumbles
Swansea
SA3 4BL
Tel: 01792 - 363462

Live Wire award winner Emily Cosgrove celebrated the first anniversary of her opening the High Tide by collecting Wales's Young Entrepreneur title for 1997. A long stay in Italy converted her to cafe culture, and after more trips she returned with a mission to "realise my vision".

You enter a friendly decor of Spanish terracotta tiling, simple pine-topped tables and chapel chairs, pots and paintings by Annabel Dann and animal-character cut-outs by Justin Harris, all enriched by the aroma of Fair Trade coffee wafting from the Gaggia.

Any time of the day, you can order pain au chocolat, open BLT sandwiches, Welsh smoked salmon bagels and Emily's home-made "yummy scrummies, pastries and treats".

Mealtimes have the added appeal of a "Low Tide" pricing policy for lunch chosen from the blackboard, offering two or three courses at prices London cafe society would not believe. Choose here from tomato and olive salad with pasta, or mozzarella and fresh garlic bread; then stuffed red pepper with sun-dried tomato and basil rice, or pizza with toppings such as onion, bacon and prawn, or chargrilled gammon with crushed pineapple and ginger: to finish, say, Bakewell tart or pineapple and passionfruit cheesecake.

Carefully selected organic produce and house wines, and complete commitment to her cause, mark Emily's new enterprise as a real winner.

 MEALS: All day 10-6 (Sat from 10; Fri & Sat till 10)
L 12-2 £6;
Closed: Sun; 25 Dec. No credit cards

131 Mumbles

Hillcrest House Hotel

1 Higher Lane
Mumbles
Swansea
SA3 4NS
Tel: 01792 - 363700
Fax: 01792 - 363768

Follow the Langland signs from the top of Newton Road to Yvonne Scott's compact, meticulously-kept hotel perched high on a hill behind Mumbles. It's a fair climb from the parking place to the paved terrace leading to the reception hall and lounge, beyond which the dining-room, discreetly draped and garlanded with fruit motifs, looks over a sylvan setting. A dozen varnished pine tables are set in the two-tier room, divided from the kitchen by a free-standing wine-rack.

Comfortable with what she does best, Yvonne offers cooking to match the friendly, informal, entirely unpretentious setting. Her nightly two and three-course table d'hôte menus confidently rely on Welsh ingredients in, for instance, laverbread and cockle filo parcels, or herbed Welsh goat's cheese grilled with honey and pink grapefruit for a refreshing and original starter. Traditional main dishes such as skate wing with black butter and capers, or duck breast with sour cherry sauce, illustrate her straightforward approach to flavours. Simple desserts specialise in the fine home-made sorbets such as melon or mint and blackberry, or a delicate cardamom ice cream served on a chocolate brownie, with local cheeses and fresh fruit as an alternative.

 MEALS: D 7-9 from £15

 WTB: 4 Crowns de luxe
7 En suite B&B from £50 S; £60 D
Closed: Sun

132 Mumbles

Norton House Hotel

Norton House
Mumbles
Swansea
SA3 5TQ
Tel: 01792 - 404891
Fax: 01792 - 403210

Elegant and homely, this Georgian master mariner's house has long steered a serene course with Jan and John Power at the helm, promising guests a smooth passage. Comfortable bedrooms and a certain understated opulence in the bar and dining-room are much in keeping with their philosophy of an informally-run family cruise.

Welsh hospitality is typified by a dinner menu translated from the mother tongue for those who might find Corgimwch Eidacaidd indecipherable; this being none other than linguini pasta in basil and saffron sauce topped with sauteed king prawns! Other starters patriotically include laverbread, cockles and bacon in filo pastry and smoked haddock topped with glazed Welsh rarebit, while prime Welsh lamb and beef feature among half-a-dozen main dishes – a best end with herb crust on rosemary and garlic jus and a Black fillet, perhaps, on toasted brioche with brandy, cream and peppercorn sauce. Fish dishes vary daily, with local sewin a favourite in season.

Lemon ricotta cheesecake and whisky bread-and-butter pudding are typical of some well-honed sweets; in another linguistic somersault the Crempog gyda Oren would appear on most menus as crepes Suzette! Keeping the service comfortably at ease are son Gareth, and his partner

South Wales

Emma, whose attention to customer care provide a strong argument to board again soon.

 MEALS: D 7-9.30 (Sun till 9) from £15.95

 WTB: 4 Crowns highly commended
15 En suite B&B from £55 S; £65 D
Closed: 25 & 26 Dec

133 Mumbles

P.A.'s Wine Bar

95 Newton Road
Mumbles
Swansea
SA3 4BN

Tel: 01792 - 367723

Wine bar more in name than by nature, Steve and Kate Maloney's sophisticated little watering hole has many good things on offer in an informal setting with its intimate small-town atmosphere. Good teamwork among their experienced chefs ensures that standards are maintained throughout a long working week (no food only on Sunday nights), and results in a consistently high standard of cooking.

First-rate supplies of local fish ensure variety and quality starters like sauteed scallops with ginger-and-lime-infused noodles and a cocktail of smoked salmon, fresh crab and hot, garlicky shrimps. Alongside main course choices such as char-grilled sea bass flamed with Pernod, and salmon served with a hollandaise cream, the daily special might be baked lemon sole, with which portions of buttered new potatoes and fresh vegetables (the latter charged extra) are nothing if not generous. Carnivorous choices on the regularly-changing blackboard menu include beef fillet with wild mushrooms and bearnaise sauce and the ever-popular rack of Welsh lamb laid on garlic potatoes.

The eye-catching home-made desserts displayed in a chiller cabinet include such temptations as Queen of Puddings, creme brulee and a superb chocolate caramel cake. Careful thought, too, has gone into a wine list that offers an agreeably distinctive selection of house varieties by the glass.

 MEALS: L 12-2.30; D 5.45-9.30
Set Sun L 12-2.30 from £9.95
Closed: D Sun

134 Nantgaredig

Four Seasons Restaurant

Nantgaredig
Nr Carmarthen
Carmarthenshire
SA32 7NY

Tel: 01267 - 290238
Fax: 01267 - 290808

Jenny and Bill Willmott have created a lovely retreat at their attractively converted complex of farm buildings, the Cwmtwrch Hotel, whose popular swimming pool is an added attraction. The farm itself houses the breakfast room and half the bedrooms; the rest are in the old barn next door beside a landscaped meadow which entices you out for a leisurely stroll before dinner to take in some spectacular views across the valley. The Four Seasons Restaurant run by daughters Maryann and Charlotte is a whitewashed former cowshed with a slate flagstone floor, exposed beams and natural stone walls hung with old farm implements;

adjoining are a cosy bar and a wine merchants' shop, also run by the Wilmotts, in the old pigsty.

A fixed-price dinner runs to four courses with plenty of choice at each stage and encompassing several inventive dishes which suit the style of the place. Good use is made of fresh local ingredients, as in a starter of field mushrooms stuffed with hot crabmeat, a nicely-cooked chicken breast filled with leeks and rolled in Carmarthen ham, and Llanboidy cheese in a tart of spinach and leeks. Alternatively, Brechfa smoked salmon is served with blinis and creme fraiche and a plain rack of Welsh lamb dressed with redcurrant jelly. Home-made desserts include a light and tasty pear and almond tart; there's an optional course of Welsh cheeses and a pot of good Italian coffee included in the price. Service is informal yet informed and friendly, and the peace and quiet of the bedrooms contributes to a most relaxing break.

MEALS: D 7.30-9.30 from £20

WTB: 3 Crowns highly commended
6 En suite B&B from £33 S; £52 D
Closed: D Sun & Mon

135 Newcastle Emlyn

Emlyn Arms

Bridge Street
Newcastle Emlyn
Carmarthenshire
SA38 9DU

Tel: 01239 - 710317
Fax: 01239 - 710792

This dowdy-looking, sprawling old town pub, unkindly treated by the years, is being given an ambitious facelift by new owner John Retallick. The restyled bar is a bit plain and is dominated by a brooding bust of Wagner, but the dining-room has a pleasant enough feel to it, with whitewashed stone walls and burgundy carpets and tablecloths. An experienced and well-respected caterer, John has drafted in a head chef from Cardiff who has brought an unexpectedly cosmopolitan feel to the menu. On a good-value, five-course "fine dining" menu descriptions tend towards the prosaic flavour as in "pan-fried fillet of seabass presented on olive oil and dill mashed potato with pine nuts, cordoned by a passion-fruit butter sauce" which begs no questions as to its content, but may intimidate the uninitiated.

Equally good value, however, can be found on the simpler table d'hôte, which might be smoked salmon, tuna, lime and anchovy salad followed by pork tenderloin with an apricot and rosemary mousse and mustard sauce, finishing with peppered pear baked in filo. Good use is made also of cheaper ingredients in bar snacks such as braised lamb shank with tomato sauce and bubble-and-squeak. Technique in abundance is further displayed in a well-made mango bavarois and decent home-made breads like saffron and raisin-and-walnut, but there may yet follow a long, hard road to popular acceptance.

South Wales

MEALS: L 12-2 from £8.50;
D 7-10 from £13.50
Set Sun L 12-2.30 £10.50

WTB: pending
27 En suite B&B from £38 S; £50 D

136 New Inn

Tate's at Tafarn Newydd

New Inn
Nr Rosebush
Pembrokeshire
SA66 7RA
Tel: 01437 - 532542

Hard by the junction of the B4313 and B4329, the plain buff exterior of this old coaching inn leaves you unprepared for the treasures within. The slate flag floors, random mix of antique tables and gate-leg chairs, stained-glass panels and candles-in-bottles represent four variations on an "ideal pub" theme, with Crown Buckley's (still!) and a brace of guest ales to try. The adjacent dining-room is scarcely less informal but rather more spacious, with rag-washed walls and more subdued lighting at night: at weekends the bars come alive to the strains of some very good folk music.

As well as interesting bar snacks, the daily set menus posted around offer an eclectic mix of three or more dishes like bruschetta of duck livers with pine nuts and sherry followed by Greek-style marinated lamb leg steak, or far-eastern-inspired Korean pork patties and monkfish satay with coconut milk. Other fish dishes, including sewin gravad lax and a spot-on grilled plaice are consistently good, and Tate's scores further with its terrific vegetables – carrots with lovage; braised lettuce with juniper – and home-baked breads. Pride of place, though, goes to a simple but superbly finished pudding of marinated dried peach on hazelnut shortbread and light caramel sauce: for sheer perfection, add a scoop of the inventive Diana Richards's own-recipe brown-bread ice cream, and round off with a pot of strong espresso and home-made fudge.

MEALS: L 12-2.30; D 6-9.30
Set L from £7.50

137 Newport

Cnapan

East Street
Newport
Pembrokeshire
SA42 0SY
Tel: 01239 - 820575
Fax: 01239 - 820878

A striking plum-and-pink exterior sets this small hotel apart from the many other hostelries on Newport's main street; many equally bold colours inside confirm the abundant individuality of the delightfully eccentric Eluned Lloyd and her family – three generations take a hand. They insist they're amateurs, and that's the attraction: Eluned's daughter Judy handles most of the cooking, her husband Mike Cooper organises the front and Eluned serves drinks accompanied by charming chat. A vegetarian herself, she's devised dishes like Leopard Pie, a feast of spinach, mango, pinenuts, feta and cinnamon that ensures those of like mind aren't treated as second-class citizens. Elsewhere the menu focuses on imaginative use of local ingredients, as in duck breast cooked

in elderflower with a bitter cherry sauce, or breast of chicken glazed with marmalade, filled with pesto and served with tomato and orange sauce. The cooking is neither fussy nor pretentious, however; everything is done with unforced easy charm and everyone is made to feel at home.

Lunch is a good option too: daily specials such as fresh lobster appear on a blackboard with two or three different soups and flans such as sardine and tuna or broccoli and orange from Eluned's repertoire. On Sundays a more traditional line-up might start with a tasty bacon and chicken terrine with spicy apricot relish, followed by a roast or a perfectly cooked fillet of salmon with light herb hollandaise.

 MEALS: L 12-2; D 7-9
Set Sun L 12-2 £12.95
Closed: Tue; L Mon & Sat; D Mon & Thur in winter; Feb

 WTB: 3 Crowns highly commended
5 En suite from £28 S; £48 D

138 Pembroke

Henry's Coffee Shop

5 Main Street
Pembroke
Pembrokeshire
SA71 4JS
Tel: 01646 - 622293
Fax: 01646 - 622728

Opened just two years ago on licensed premises that had seen better days, Henry's today looks well set for a brighter future in years to come. Through the street-facing Gift Shop selling linen and lace, cards and candles, pots and pot pourri, the Coffee Shop is at the back and open all day.

Its daily dishes won't set the world alight, but a suitably warming effect is guaranteed by the hot soups served daily, and a genuine flow of guilty conscience by the exceedingly sticky cakes.

Home-made fruit scones, Welsh cakes and bara brith are popular snacks, while a light lunch might consist of baked potato with tuna filling, cheese and broccoli quiche with a salad and crunchy coleslaw or a generous portion of plain Welsh Rarebit. Salmon and cucumber, smoked salmon and cream cheese, egg and cress and coronation chicken are typical fillings for baguettes, hoagy rolls and granary cobs while the sweet-toothed can indulge in fruit Pavlova, chocolate and hazelnut log or toffee crunch cheesecake loaded with whipped cream.

Plans are afoot to add to the menu, and to extend the cafe further into a courtyard and dining conservatory.

 MEALS: All day 9-5
Closed: Sun; Bank Hols in winter; 25 & 26 Dec
No credit cards

139 Pembroke

The Left Bank

63 Main Street
Pembroke
Pembrokeshire
SA71 4DA
Tel: 01646 - 622333

The imposing granite building – formerly a bank – strikes a serious note, implying that this restaurant means business, and indeed it does: Andrew Griffith is an ambitious and capable chef with a good team around him. The influences of others are currently strong, and cappuccino of white mushrooms, guineafowl poche grille, potage of shellfish with fresh herbs and truffle oil are dishes out to impress. At our first-ever visit a splendid array of home-made breads, including olive, thyme and red pepper, showed the kitchen's potential. Spring vegetable broth with penne and coriander pesto was tasty with well-cooked root vegetables, but the penne were actually commercial spaghetti and the pesto had used parsley, while a tasty pork belly, perfectly cooked and seared, was served in a pool of intense soy-based liquor which proved too strong for it. A fine rhubarb flan, though, was nicely offset with home-made vanilla ice cream. There's excellent espresso coffee, and a short range of interesting wines. Relaxed service is both confident and friendly.

A cool modern feel, with a terracotta-floored bar area, clean walls absorbing the light through trendy stained glass windows and bright green and turquoise seat-covers shows that no expense has been spared to put this restaurant on the gastronomic map, and despite an early inclination to over-gild the lily, Left Bank is set fair to be the table talk of West Wales.

 MEALS: L 12-2.30; D 7-10.30
L from £11.95
Closed: Sun & Mon

140 Pembroke

Woodhouse Restaurant

40 Main Street
Pembroke
Pembrokeshire
SA71 4NP
Tel: 01646 - 687140

Cheeseplants, knick-knacks and oriental artefacts at the front jostle for position with the tables and chairs, adding a Portobello Road effect which is reinforced by the background of 1960s pop-rock with your breakfast and coffee at 10am. The main restaurant is more conventional, with pine dresser, screen prints and a pleasant view over Pembroke's millpond; but the Baylisses don't take themselves too seriously, and provide toys to entertain the kids and board games for the less gastronomically inclined.

The menu is essentially good bistro fare with plenty of lighter lunch dishes like pasta bolognese (made with minced turkey) and creamy spinach and mushroom curry. Lynn Bayliss takes care to use fresh local ingredients for dishes like scrambled eggs with cockles and oregano, and venison steak with blackcurrant and red wine sauce. Vegetarians are imaginatively catered for, as in stir-fried vegetables with laverbread and noodles, and daily fish from Milford Haven might include grilled fillet of turbot or a huge whole crab, freshly boiled and spiked with black bean sauce: served with a generous rocket salad for only £4.50

this is an absolute bargain. Pancakes and home-made sponge pudding are popular desserts, a simple fruit salad is served with tasty honey ice cream, and well-kept Welsh cheeses include Acorn and Y Fenni.

MEALS: B 10-12; L 12-2; D 7-9
Closed: Sun (except Mothers Day); 25 & 26 Dec

141 Penally

Penally Abbey

Penally
Nr Tenby
Pembrokeshire
SA70 7PY
Tel: 01834 - 843033
Fax: 01834 - 844714

Just a dozen years ago the listed mansion at Penally – on the site of the original sixth-century abbey – was rescued from decay by Steve and Elleen Warren and gradually converted into the serene hotel it is now. With a clear sense of direction that has stood them in good stead since, their earliest purchases from a miniscule budget included the four-poster beds which continue to grace the Abbey's most stylish bedrooms. The tranquil setting in five acres of garden and woodland overlooking Camarthen Bay, and elegant day-rooms and dining-room, are matched by menus which Elleen devises on a daily basis with spontaneity and flair. This is a tall order, given the choice of 20 starters and main courses she offers, yet the food she produces is constantly improving.

Broccoli and cream-cheese roulade with ratatouille, leek and prawn crumble and a terrine of smoked trout, salmon and mackerel typify one evening's choice of starters; next there might be goujons of sweet and sour duck, Chinese-style, cod mornay with crispy bacon, and Brecon venison with red wine and juniper. Equal care goes into luscious and generous-sized desserts highly suited to Pembrokeshire appetites, and there are good Welsh cheeses either as an alternative or to follow. The Warrens' hard-working and versatile crew which turns a hand to anything – including the painting in winter – engender a friendly, relaxed family atmosphere. No pets.

MEALS: D 7.30-9.30 from £24
(no children under 7)
Special breaks: Dinner, Bed & Breakfast from £144

WTB: 4 Crown de luxe
12 En suite B&B from £68 S; £96 D

142 Penarth

Caprice

The Esplanade
Penarth
Nr Cardiff
CF64 3AU
Tel: 01222 - 702424
Fax: 01222 - 711518

So well-known is the Caprice that it apparently sees no need to publicise its telephone number to the average passer-by who wanders past a dozen feet below on Penarth's esplanade; yet booking is advisable to ensure a window table at this mecca of good taste founded by the Rabaiotti family back in 1963. Having negotiated the stairs by Chandler's Pub and Wine Bar, you can then sit back and take in serene seascapes towards the Holms, Sully Island and the sweep of Cardiff Bay through picture windows opened up to the elements in rare perfect summer weather. While other foodie fads and fashions have come and gone, Caprice remains remarkably unchanged, its style epitomised by good old-fashioned courtesy and smooth ocean-liner service.

The range of daily menus, a la carte and set-price "Patron's Choices", is little short of encyclopaedic and full of instantly recognisable classics, from native pasta and veal dishes to duckling with orange sauce, Wiener Schnitzel and a flambe of Tournedos au poivre. Perennial favourites major in all manner of seafood from baked calamari to lobster and avocado salad starters, and from enormous helpings of hake in crispy batter – or with sauce meuniere – to whole sea bass, fresh sewin hollandaise and fillets of sole bonne femme. It's only to be expected that a calorie-laden trolley of profiteroles, Pavlova and tiramisu will follow, unless you're bold enough to plump for more sugar, butter, fruit and fire with a classic crepes Suzette. With its echoes of a Blue Riband era, Caprice is unsurpassed.

MEALS: L 12-2.15 from £9.25; D 7-10.30 from £25.95
Set Sun L 12-2.30 £13.55
Closed: L Sat; D Sun; Bank Hols; 25 & 26 Dec

143 Pentyrch

De Courcey's

Tyla Morris Avenue
Pentyrch
Nr Cardiff
CF4 8QN
Tel: 01222 - 892232
Fax: 01222 - 891949

The original De Courcey's, a sort of Scandinavian log-cabin affair, a short step from junctions 34 and 32 of the M4, was razed by fire in 1994 and totally rebuilt, amazingly, in under six months. Its air-conditioned re-incarnation is a neo-Georgian building in yellow brick with double glazing and double-festooned drapes which, while providing insulation from the world outside, also succeed in obliterating some fine views of the surrounding woods. In this rarefied setting, a little drama is scarcely out of place and the performance of Thilo Thielmann and his team readily rises to the occasion. A cooking style little altered from before offers a fine tian of crab with rich black olive dressing, herb-coated cutlets of lamb with an accompaniment of ratatouille, basil jus and other vegetables stylishly served.

The house menu offers chicken liver and bacon salad, steak, mushroom and Guiness pie followed by strawberry creme brulee at a fixed price; the Gourmet menu expands into boudin of lemon sole and tiger prawns, fillet of beef on celeriac rosti with lardons, oyster mushrooms and a red wine jus, with hot passion-fruit souffle to finish. Diners are promised a leisurely pace of eating, dark meats cooked pink, generous selections of market-fresh vegetables and freshly brewed coffee prepared at the table with a fair degree of finesse and showmanship: if one small spark were called for now, it would be one of genius.

MEALS: D 7-10 £22.50
Set Sun L 12-2 £14.95
Closed: D Sun & Mon; 1 week Christmas

144　Penycwm

Whitehouse

Penycwm
Nr Solva
Haverfordwest
Pembrokeshire
SA62 6LA
Tel/Fax: 01437 - 720959

After the loving restoration of this collection of farm buildings over the last ten years, Ken and Patricia Cross now entertain guests in the comfort of their own home and also provide half - or full-board or self-catering accommodation in arguably the best-appointed Youth Hostel anywhere in Wales. Standing at the fringe of the Pembrokeshire National Park, it's best found by following the brown-painted YHA direction signs from the A487 at Penycwm.

Guests readily confess to returning for Patricia's set three-course dinners, served nightly at 7.30pm, which represent outstanding value. Begin perhaps with a fan of fresh pear with blue cheese dressing before enjoying a fine chicken and mushroom pie, encased in the lightest crunchy pastry, with extra jugsful of mushroom sauce.

On Sundays Pat might serve a traditional Welsh Black beef roast with Yorkshire pudding and assorted roast roots, preceded by Ken's famous sprout-and-chestnut soup. Her desserts are generally fruit-inspired, based on the best shopping available: rhubarb and ginger brown Betty or maybe "crunchie pears with Welsh honey, white wine and cinnamon" bringing a balanced meal to a highly satisfactory conclusion.

Next year they are planning several "Good Food and Wine Weekends" based at the hostel and including organised tours to Llangloffan Farm to see cheese being made and to the Cwm Deri Vineyard, enabling guests to hone their knowledge as well as their appetites for another dinner at the Whitehouse.

 MEALS: D @ 7.30 £8.50
Special breaks: Dinner, Bed & Breakfast from £49
No credit cards

 WTB: 3 Crowns highly commended
£17 S; £34 D

145　Porthcawl

Atlantic Hotel

West Drive
Porthcawl
Bridgend
CF36 3LT
Tel: 01656 - 785011
Fax: 01656 - 771877

On the western fringe of town, by an expansive sweep of the bay, the Atlantic makes full use in summer of its south-facing frontage looking out across the Bristol Channel to the North Devon coast and slopes of Exmoor. In a short season it copes gamely with being most things to all people, serving bar food on the patio in tandem with local bar trade and various catering functions.

The pick of restaurant fare can be found on the chef's seasonal carte, which offers well-sourced marine products in the salmon and crab pancakes and seafood thermidor, which appear alongside more mundane dishes such as whitebait and fresh grilled plaice. Citrus fruit and pine nuts adorn a brandied liver pate and classically-based saucing such as bigarade with Barbary duck breast provides a sound alternative to Atlantic specialities like venison tournedos with Madeira wine, star anis, woodland mushrooms and chestnut puree.

Residents on inclusive terms are offered a weekly table d'hôte, including Sundays, where you need to choose carefully to get the best results: chicken satay with garlic mayonnaise, chicken supreme with asparagus and tomatoes, and mushroom stroganoff supplement the fish and roast of the day. Further roasts and a long list of hot and cold sweets make the Atlantic a popular family choice for Sunday lunch.

MEALS: L 12-2.30; D 6.30-10.30 £12.95
Set Sun L 12-2.30 £8.95
Special breaks: Dinner, Bed & Breakfast from £80

WTB: 4 Crowns highly commended
19 En suite B&B from £54 S; £72 D

146 Porthgain

Harbour Lights

Porthgain
Nr St Davids
Pembrokeshire
SA62 5BW
Tel: 01348 - 831549

Dominated by the ruined brickworks and huge harbour building, Porthgain lacks the immediate appeal of other coastal havens, but its industrial past is reflected by the boats that land their catch at the door of Annie Davies's delightful restaurant, housed in two small adjoining quayside cottages. The long dining-room is decorated with paintings for sale by Pembrokeshire artists and a local theme runs through the menus on which laverbread collected and cooked by Huw and Annie is a permanent feature.

Annie's laverbread and bacon gratin is a firm favourite as a starter, as is fresh Porthgain crab with fennel mayonnaise. Pancakes are strong vegetarian options, filled with roasted peppers, spinach and pine nuts and topped with Parmesan. Main courses naturally major on fish: perfect, simple grilled sewin comes with lemon butter sauce, and wild salmon is wrapped in puff pastry with prawns and served with a shellfish sauce. Imaginative vegetables include braised cabbage with caraway and a potato and celeriac gratin. A pancake may appear again for dessert, filled this time with black cherries, while a deliciously fresh, crunchy elderflower water ice is a highly agreeable lighter option. Huw, who runs front-of-house with calm authority, takes delight in the gem of a wine list – ruled by the Davieses' decision to offer wines that they themselves enjoy – and there's not a duff bottle among them.

MEALS: D 7-9.30 from £19.50
Closed: Sun; Mon; Tue; Nov-Feb
Please call

147 Porthkerry

Egerton Grey

Porthkerry
Nr Barry
Vale of Glamorgan
CF62 9BS
Tel: 01446 - 711666
Fax: 01446 - 711690

Standing in a secluded vale not far from Cardiff International Airport, Anthony and Magda Pitkin's comfortable hotel was once a Victorian rectory and their laid-back, unhurried service suits its tranquil atmosphere. The hallway's parquet floors are muted with Persian rugs and the dining-room's oak-panelled walls softened by candlelight at night. Equally muted strains of Mozart and Vivaldi accompany an ambitiously composed, sometimes elaborately embellished country-house dinner.

A terrine of salmon and scallops, laid on asparagus and mussel salad with lemon and red pepper oils and anchovy toast, beckons pictorially but fails to capture the essential seafood flavours. A soup course - smoked chicken and leek, or perhaps celeriac and apple cream with smoked cheese and paprika glaze - precedes rack of Welsh lamb wrapped in basil mousse with boulangére potatoes and rosemary jus, or a more complex fillet of marinated black bream on truffle risotto with shellfish oil, sweet chilli and soya dressing and a tempura of asparagus. Equally carefully contrived are steamed toffee and banana pudding with rum sauce, and a first-rate mango and pineapple brulee with homemade hazelnut biscuits.

MEALS: L 12-1.45; D 7-10 from £22
Set Sun L 12-2 from £18
Special breaks: Dinner, Bed and Breakfast from £125

10 En suite B&B from £60 S; £90 D

148 Port Talbot

Aberavon Beach Hotel

Swansea Bay
Port Talbot
SA12 6QP
Tel: 01639 - 884949
Fax: 01639 - 897885

The hotel is a solid 1960s block overdue for a bit of a facelift, but makes the best of its location across the road from the vast beach with views stretching from Mumbles Head to the Devon coast.

Reception is hung with modern prints of Welsh landscapes and two red dragons adorn the glazed partitions in the conservatory dining-room, but sadly such Welsh touches are lacking in an unambitious table d'hôte featuring the likes of prawn harlequin salad and pan-fried chicken breast with tarragon and white wine. Better attempts at regionality appear on the a la carte menu – baked monkfish tails with honey and mustard sauce (disguised as pescado Alta Maria!); fillet steak with Caerphilly cheese and walnut sauce – and on a locally-sourced cheeseboard.

Our inspection meal produced simple but tasty devilled mushrooms, excellent rack of Welsh lamb (nicely trimmed, cooked and rested) with a decent rosemary sauce, and flavourful home-made delice of forest fruits followed by good cafetiere coffee. The professional and friendly service, particularly attentive to the many children present, indicated the Aberavon Beach's deserved popularity with family groups as well as with solo businessmen. Wouldn't it be nice, though, to see such a potentially fine ambassador fly the Welsh flag with a little more self-confidence?

MEALS: D 7-10.15 (Sun D till 9.30) from £14.50
Set Sun L 12.30-2 £9.95

WTB: 4 Crowns commended
52 En suite B&B from £59 S; £62 D
Special breaks: Dinner, Bed and Breakfast from £90

149 Reynoldston

Fairyhill

Reynoldston
Gower
Swansea
SA3 1BS
Tel: 01792 - 390139
Fax: 01792 - 391358

The understated sumptuousness of Fairyhill is so tastefully done that you hardly notice the sheer comfort of the place, from the simple, elegant entrance hall to the well-appointed bathrooms stocked with Penhaligon bath accessories. The beds are superb, and every room has a CD player, with discs supplied by a library in reception. The menu and wine list mean business, too, offering an unrivalled range of Welsh produce: where else can boast two pages of Welsh wines?

Dishes that show off Welsh ingredients in a modern style include laverbread tart with tomato chutney and bacon, and fillet of Welsh Black beef with beer-batter onions and beer and onion sauce, while the crisp deep-fried cockles are such fresh and tasty appetisers that the rest are almost superfluous.

Elaborately presented starters of marinated salmon with blinis, sour cream and caviar, and warm salad of skate and bacon are followed by for instance, "sea bass with greens" – two fresh moist fillets with a mound of spring greens, spinach and parsley flavoured with ginger. A fine meal might conclude with caramelised banana creme brulee or red berry soup with port and claret jelly. Delicious home-made petits fours include chocolates with freshly chopped mint. Service throughout is perhaps a little formal, but then again this is a grander place than you might think.

MEALS: L 12.30-1.45 from £11.50;
D 7.30-9.15 from £24.50; Sun L £19.50;
Special breaks: Dinner, Bed and Breakfast from £190

WTB: 4 Crowns de luxe
8 En suite B&B from £75 S; £85 D
No children under 8

150 Reynoldston

King Arthur Hotel

Reynoldston
Gower
Swansea
SA3 1AD
Tel: 01792 - 391099
Tel/Fax: 01792 - 390775

It's well worth the slow approach along the winding South Gower roads to the legendary King Arthur's Stone and, nearby, this informal inn, to unwind in this area of outstanding beauty just below its high point, Cefn Bryn. Landlord Len O'Driscoll travelled a little less far when he moved into his old "local" on the same day that the bailiffs moved out. Six years on, following a total refurbishment and completion of seven en suite guest rooms, he's installed a new state-of-the-art kitchen so that food which was initially constrained by size and equipment is now moving swiftly into another dimension.

Much of the everyday fare extends little beyond predictable curries, casseroles and ploughman's, but a growing choice of fresh fish and butchers' meats from the main specials board is now the better bet. Start with home-made soup, grilled sardines or a pint of prawns before choosing between salmon fillet with tarragon sauce, fresh local sewin, Texan rib-eye steak, chicken breast with white wine and mushrooms, and a home-made cheese, tomato and basil quiche with salad; then finish off in season with fresh Gower strawberries or Pencarreg and St David's Cheddar.

The clientele is as varied as the menu: a steady stream of walkers and outdoor types sharing space with local farmers and professional folk in the bar by a roaring fire, or braving the elements in the garden.

MEALS: L 12-2.30; D 6-9.30

WTB: 3 Crowns commended
7 En suite B&B from £30 S; £40 D

151 Roch

Hilton Court Garden Tearoom

Roch
Nr Haverfordwest
Pembrokeshire
SA62 6AE
Tel: 01437 - 710262

Just off the A487 close to Simpson's Cross you need to persevere down the narrow lane, along a farm track and through the farmyard car park to enter a different world. First you find an attractively laid out garden centre with creeper-clad trellises; then beyond is a treasure in the great tradition of British gardens, with banks of Azaleas and herbaceous borders taking one out to tranquil lakes surrounded by irises and bullrushes. Overlooking this is Cheryl Lynch's tiny tearoom, most of whose tables are set on the open-air terrace.

In the words of its creator, this is "just a little garden shed that went out of control", and only lack of space limits home-production of her first-class cakes. The delicious pecan pie and "very best carrot cake" are based on American recipes, while lemon and walnut and the apple and sultana are very much her own, and the Welshcakes and bara brith fiercely traditional. Several varieties of teas are served, and excellent cafetiere coffee over which to relax with the Sunday papers. This delightful refuge has become so popular that there are plans to convert the nearby stable block into an altogether larger affair. Watch this space!

MEALS: All day 10-5
Unlicensed. No credit cards
Closed: Oct-Mar

152 St Brides Wentloog

The Elm Tree

St Brides Wentloog
Newport
NP1 9SQ
Tel: 01633 - 680225
Fax: 01633 - 681170

The Elm Tree's "two old barns and a cowshed", thus described by proprietor Mike Thomas, have become established over ten years as a popular dining place where it is truly fun to eat.

Arrivals who have zig-zagged across the Gwent levels (on the B4239) from Castleton or Tredegar House will be impressed by Pat Thomas's massive hanging baskets and flower tubs, and inside by colourful bistro-type blackboards displaying divers aquatic fare, from the mixed seafood broth – a worthy single-course lunch in itself – to whole Cornish crabs and lobster.

A menu choice which runs to some sixty items taxes the kitchen's ability to cope in the space available, but there's consistent quality in the cooking of griddled goats' cheese en croute, a vast chicken-liver muffin topped with scrambled eggs, Finnan haddock with Welsh rarebit, and rump of Welsh lamb roasted with fresh garlic and rosemary and served over buttered leeks with Madeira sauce. Mountainous helpings of vegetables defeat many a trencherman's appetite and the frenetic pace of the chatty service makes the experience seem somehow larger than life. Next year's addition of twelve bedrooms with bathrooms in the vast roof-space above is likely to see a doubling of activity (and a bigger kitchen), but none of this will alter the ebullient Mike's greatest claim to fame: he sells his home-made faggots to the local butcher!

MEALS: L 11.30-2.30; D 6.30-10
Set Sun L 12-2.30 £11.95
Closed: D Sun; 1 week Christmas

153 St Davids

Morgan's Brasserie

20 Nun Street
St Davids
Pembrokeshire
SA62 6NT
Tel/Fax: 01437 - 720508

With its bentwood chairs and maroon tablecloths, the ambience is more bistro than brasserie; the small bar leads through to a dining-room decorated with paintings and fine woodturnings by local artists. A typical menu offers five starters and eight main courses of which a good half will be fish, allowing Ceri Morgan to exploit the latest catch landed at nearby Milford Haven. Go, then, for a starter of steamed queen scallops in a white port, lime and ginger sauce served with perfectly cooked jasmine rice, followed by monkfish wrapped in smoked salmon with a laverbread sauce, the salmon successfully standing up to so

strong a partner and the fish within agreeably fresh and moist. Alternatives might be fillet of salmon in filo with Thai spices, sea bass with a simple garlic butter, or the Morgan version of Red Dragon Pie – mixed beans and vegetables under a cheese crust.

Ceri is duly proud of his presentation of desserts which might be framed in sugar baskets; Celtic Crunch – a sort of crunchie-bar ice cream – is served in a tuile basket. A small selection of good Welsh cheeses includes Llangloffan and Caerphilly; Welsh butter is served with the fresh granary bread and the cafetiere coffee is excellent. Service throughout is relaxed, informative and smiling, and it is perhaps a tribute to Elaine Morgan's stewardship that the evening waitress, who also does breakfasts at a nearby hotel, was not a patch on her evening self when serving our breakfast the next morning!

 MEALS: D 6.30-9
Closed: Sun & Mon (except Bank Hols); Jan & Feb

154 St Davids

Ramsey House

Lower Moor
St Davids
Pembrokeshire
SA62 6RP

Tel: 01437 - 720321
Fax: 01437 - 720025

At the last house on the Ramsey road out of St Davids, Mac Thompson will probably greet you outside with his German Shepherd, to guide your parking. Their 1960s house has been extended to provide seven high class double bedrooms (singles are discouraged) and day rooms furnished with velvet sofas and modern pine in the dining area. The three-course set menu is posted in the morning to allow for special requests. The quiet patio garden beyond the bar is a pleasant spot for a drink before Mac ushers guests to their seats at 7pm sharp.

Start with smoked trout pate and oatcakes or cawl with grated cheese and a home-made roll, graduating to stuffed leg of lamb, simply grilled fish or chicken breast with a mustard and parsley farce and mustardy lemon sauce, all accompanied by potatoes from the farm next door and local leeks or greens; finish off with puddings such as The Dean's Cream, a tipsy trifle topped with syllabub, or apple pie with Welsh whisky custard. Sandra and Mac are enthusiastic about Welsh ingredients and wines, and there's a nightly recommendation from the shortlist, which includes Cariad dry or rose, to accompany dinner. Mac entertains the while with local anecdotes and walking or excursion tips, encouraging an early start in the morning to explore the spectacular coastline for yourself.

 MEALS: Set D @ 7 pm
Special breaks: on application

 WTB: 3 Crowns highly commended
7 En suite £82 D

South Wales

155 St Florence

Bramley's Tea Room

Plough Penny Nursery
St Florence
Nr Tenby
Pembrokeshire
SA70 8LP
Tel: 01834 - 871778

Here is a tearoom with a difference, housed in a wood cabin in Plough Penny Field Nursery – but "tearoom" hardly begins to suggest the goodies within. Liz Hainsworth is a skilled and experienced caterer, and her enthusiasm for her craft helps raise her spotless little emporium well above the norm. Certainly, this tearoom offers tea, but it also serves an amazing range of 23 different cakes and gateaux from flapjacks and scones to passion cake and chocolate brandy slice – all home-made. It does not stop there: rolls, jacket potatoes and toasties come with a variety of fillings and hot lunchtime dishes include home-made pies, Glamorgan sausages and home-cooked ham with parsley sauce.

Though it wasn't even on the menu, we fell upon a divine raspberry frangipane tart – melting pastry, sharp fruity raspberries and the lightest sponge: "I just made that for fun," quoth Liz. On Sundays a traditional three-course roast lunch includes alternative vegetarian options, and there are speciality evenings with national themes: ring Liz for further details. A recent Welsh evening menu included mushrooms stuffed with laverbread followed by roast lamb with cider, honey and rosemary or Glamorgan sausages with mushroom and sherry sauce and rounded off with rhubarb and apple crumble. It's unlicensed, but bring your own wine – and plenty of it: this is some tearoom!

 MEALS: All day 10-5; L 12-3;
Set Sun L 12-2 £6.95 (children £3.50).
Unlicensed. No credit cards.
Closed: Mon-Thurs; Nov-Mar; 25 & 26 Dec

156 Shirenewton

Tredegar Arms

Shirenewton
Nr Chepstow
Monmouthshire
NP6 6RQ
Tel: 01291 - 641274

The secret of this very successful little village pub lies not simply in the expectation of a good meal. Attention to detail in so many other aspects of innkeeping sets the Tredegar Arms apart: witness the care lavished on the flower-filled tubs and hanging baskets that make the pub such a picture in summer; and within, the spotless home of a house-proud landlady, cheerful well-turned-out helpers and a genuinely warm welcome from Rob and Val Edwards.

There's an easy sense of humour to the best dishes described on the Specials boards: Long Meadow Beef, Pant-y-Cossin Pork and even Venta Silurum Lamb derive their names from local places of note and carry short if somewhat fanciful descriptions of their content. Lamb Rumpus, a new addition to this repertoire, turns out to be a near-pound-sized leg steak of succulent locally-reared lamb accompanied by a rustic gravy formidably infused with fresh garden mint.

For starters and lighter midday snacks commendable alternatives include tiger prawns and mussels in garlic, wine and cream; hot-smoked peppered mackerel; and crispy bacon and tomato salad on dressed leaves. Sunday lunch weighs in with hearty roasts accompanied by crisp, fresh vegetables aplenty, followed – first come first served – by Veronica's unique lemon meringue pie. I'd book if I were you!

MEALS: L 12-2; D 7-9.30.
Set Sun L £7.95
No credit cards.

WTB: 3 Crowns commended
2 En suite B&B (shower only) £25 S; £40 D

157 Simpson's Cross

The Victorian Conservatory
Simpson's Cross
Nr Haverfordwest
Pembrokeshire
SA62 6EP
Tel: 01437 - 710465

Conveniently situated by the A487 between Haverfordwest and St Davids, Monica Hemming's conservatory is almost larger than the traditional stone and brick house it's attached to. Huge bunches of grapes hang from the ridge-piece, and a mass of flowering baskets and fuchsias adorn an interior where even the white wicker tables are shaded by parasols.

Savoury snacks, light lunches, home-made soups and beverages are served from mid-morning but, unsurprisingly, cream teas are the major draw. Home-made scones and jam with local clotted cream and a choice of quality teas compete for attention with a superior Victoria sponge, and a wide range of gateaux and pastries is available at any time. Leading from the car park are a pleasant rear garden with an ornamental pond, the tables around it well sheltered from the main road, and an eighteen-hole putting green to occupy the more energetic. On Sundays be sure to book for lunch, and bring your own wine to drink with the weekly roast, sandwiched between the likes of country vegetable soup and apple crumble.

Two quite modest, simple rooms are available for bed and breakfast but beyond the 6pm closing time (7pm in high season) no evening meal is provided.

MEALS: All day 10.30-6 (till 7 in Jun, July & Aug)
Unlicensed. No credit cards
Closed: Nov-Easter

158 Southerndown

Frolics
Beacon Road
Southerndown
Bridgend
CF32 0RP
Tel: 01656 - 880127

Formerly an unassuming corner-shop, Frolics combines its idyllic setting just a pebble's throw from the dramatic Southerndown cliffs with a small, intimate interior which hits the spot when dining a deux. Martin Dobson carefully sources local produce for his seasonal menus from sea bass caught just down the road to muddy, uneven courgettes grown in a neighbour's garden. However, not all is local, as the menu's listing of "Scotch beef" and "Norfolk duck" will testify.

The ambitious menu, which relies on careful preparation, imaginative saucing and accomplished presentation for its impact, describes its mouth-watering creations at length: "shortcrust pastry tartlet filled with braised leeks in cream, layered with fresh scallops and glazed with a hollandaise and sherry sabayon" is followed by "pan-fried tenderloin of pork served with a piquant raspberry, fresh ginger and shallot butter sauced garnished with a glazed banana". While leaving precious little room for surprises on the plate, Martin delivers what he promises, and the sewin from West Wales served on a cream-rich lobster bisque is as good as anybody's, though at a fair mark-up for these parts. You'll follow with a carefully constructed strawberry sable and accompany with reasonably-priced wines with a French bias. The fixed-price three-course table d'hôte is a less expensive option, where tasty amuse-gueules and chocolates with coffee help to soften the blow.

 MEALS: D 7-9 £6.50
Set Sun L 12-2 £11.95
Closed: D Sun & Mon; 5 days Christmas

159 Southerndown

The Old Stable Tea Shop

West Farm
Southerndown
Bridgend
CF32 0PY

Tel/Fax: 01656 - 880068

Built as a single-storey oxen barn some three centuries ago, the Stables sits atop 150ft cliffs overlooking the Bristol Channel with views of the Somerset coastline from Watchet to Ilfracombe. Over the past ten years it has been lovingly restored to its present state with exposed timbers, mangers, stalls which make cosy dining areas, wooden farm implements on the walls and a cobbled floor. What better place to take Granny out for a hearty lunch or cream tea, confident she'll be pampered by the friendly young staff?

Veronica Craig's home cooking is evident throughout the small regular menu of ploughman's lunches, jacket potatoes and sandwiches, as well as on the short specials board listing freshly-cooked cold meats and main meals like chicken, mushroom and ham pie, all served with fresh salads. For those who can find room, there are fresh fruit pies served with cream, custard and ice cream, while well into the afternoon the celebrated Special Cream Tea has customers queuing for Veronica's scones the minute they come out of the oven. Although the 70 or so seats inside are augmented by plenty of picnic tables in the small paddock, if your party wants to sit in comfort, especially on summer weekends, you'd be well advised to book ahead of time.

 MEALS: All day 11.30-6
Closed: Mon; Tue; Wed; Oct-Feb
No credit cards

160 Spittal

Lower Haythog

Spittal
Haverfordwest
Pembrokeshire
SA62 6LL

Tel/Fax: 01437 - 731279

A working dairy farm five miles from Haverfordwest between the A40 and B4329, Lower Haythog makes an ideal base for a Pembrokeshire holiday. The handsome centuries-old farmhouse has been discreetly converted to offer accommodation, and more is available in converted outhouses. An attractive conservatory leads through to the drawing-room with its exposed beams and open hearth, where Nesta Thomas's warm welcome invites discussion of the day's activities before the evening meal.

There's no menu: Nesta is a keen amateur cook and the evening has the air of a lively dinner party (Bring your own wine as it's not licensed, and do let Nesta know if you're vegetarian). In winter, starters are often soups such as lentil and parsnip, followed by a hearty chicken and leek pie or lamb and apricot stew with cumin, finishing perhaps with baked apples. Salmon features in summer, in a pate with smoked salmon or the whole fish poached with a rustic tomato sauce and served with fresh-picked mange-tout and flavoursome celeriac and sprout bake. Generous spicing in the best tradition of Welsh baking features in desserts such as caramelised apples with marzipan, baked in a puff-pastry heart with rich cinnamon custard. By this time the farm's working day will be over too, adding convivial conversation to the coffee in a homely place designed to make you feel among friends.

 MEALS: D @ 7.15 £12.50
Unlicensed. No credit cards.
Special breaks: Dinner, Bed and Breakfast from £60

 WTB: 3 Crowns highly commended
4 En suite from £25 S; £40 D
Closed: 5 days Christmas

161 Swansea

La Braseria

28 Wind Street
Swansea
SA1 1DZ

Tel: 01792 - 469683
Fax: 01792 - 470816

This archetypal Spanish bodega can be a bit bewildering to newcomers who are shown to their tables with a degree of Mediterranean macho but handed no menu or wine list. So, back at the bar to look at the various blackboards, you then choose your fish or meat in its raw state from the vast array displayed on ice, and return to your table to await its arrival, grilled, baked or fried to order. Two long air-conditioned rooms – fish upstairs, meat down – are furnished with huge upturned barrels, beams and pillars are all festooned with Rioja labels, wicker baskets hang on the whitewashed walls as lampshades and red-and-black-clad waiters stalk the sawdust floors with giant peppermills. The atmosphere may be theatrical, but the food is real enough. The popularity of this 200-seat emporium guarantees the freshness of meat and fish bought daily from Swansea Market, and the simplicity of its preparation ensures that ingredients speak for themselves.

Steaks – be they beef or marinated swordfish – are char-grilled; squid and hake are battered, deep-fried and served with tartare sauce; whole sea bass are baked in rocksalt, sole and turbot skinned, sauteed, briefly baked and served with lemon wedges and crisp chips, and you help yourself to accompanying salads at the counter. Be sure, though, to check the weight of the fish you choose, as per-pound pricing can lead to a shock when the bill arrives. A vast array of Riojas is on offer and Armagnacs are a house speciality; no draught beers.

MEALS: L 12-2.30; D 7-11.30
Closed: Sun; 25 Dec

162 Swansea

Ty Llen Restaurant

The Dylan Thomas Centre
Somerset Place
Swansea
SA1 1RR
Tel: 01792 - 465392
Fax: 01792 - 463993

The Dylan Thomas Centre, opened as a joint project by the City and County of Swansea in the European Year of Literature, 1995, is housed in Ty Llen (literally "the home of literature") on the east bank of the River Tawe.

Developments in progress include a permanent exhibition recalling the poet's roistering days which will house a typical old Swansea drinking den of Dylan Thomas's day.

For today's more respectable visits, the first-floor restaurant and lecture theatre are much in demand for weddings, corporate functions and literary events. Mid-week, however, it provides a temptingly serene location (overlooking Swansea Marina) for a light lunch or bar snacks of exceptional value.

Starters on the fixed-price menu may well include duck and orange pate or seafood salad alongside the daily soup, followed by pan-fried lamb cutlets, braised liver with bacon and thyme or smoked haddock with roasted peppers and soft green peppercorns. Handily placed for the town centre and market, these young chefs pay meticulous attention to their shopping.

In the bar area there's usually a dish of the day, a braised lamb and mint casserole perhaps, for under £4, open sandwiches such as chicken Indiennne or smoked salmon, and Welsh rarebit is always available. Sticky cakes and doughnuts, chocolate mousse cups and scones with jam and cream add calories – and a pot of tea or coffee, a beer or glass of wine assuage one's thirst.

MEALS: All day 10-5; L 12-2.30
Set Sun L 12-2.30 from £7.95
Closed: Mon; 10 days Christmas

163 Swansea

Number One

1 Wind Street
Swansea
SA1 1DE
Tel: 01792 - 456996

Near Swansea's old dockland – and pronounced as in the winding cables pulling cargo ashore – Wind Street now delivers the goods to its restaurant-goers. Recently enlarged, this unpretentious restaurant has a light and airy feel, its neutral walls displaying prints and paintings by local artists, with fresh flowers and Haydn completing the scene. Maggi Munday and Peter Gillen provide a cheerful welcome front-of-house while behind the scenes Kate Taylor is loyal to the best local ingredients, combining these in traditional recipes, some modern flourishes, illustrated by polpette of lamb with rocket salad and baked fillet of hake with a herb crust and Provencale sauce.

Excellent for lighter lunchtime appetites, the half-dozen starters such as smoked duck with red cabbage, and warm terrine of local lobster with sauce Maltaise, can be taken with a full salad as main courses. More substantially, a beef, shallot and mushroom pie or fish dishes such as monkfish fillets with prawn risotto and lemon butter sauce are also excellent value.

The evening menu offers a greater range of dishes at set prices, including canapes such as leek, laverbread and Stilton tartlets and main dishes like venison with juniper, ceps and home-made tagliatelli, and roast breast of duck with glazed shallots and petits pois. Desserts include a creamy white chocolate mousse with strawberries and amaretto biscuit; coffee is excellent. Peter's personally selected wine list offers great value.

 MEALS: L 12-2.30 from £7; D 7-9.30 from £17; Closed: Sun & Mon; 1 week Christmas

164 Swansea

Windsor Lodge Hotel

Mount Pleasant
Swansea
SA1 6EG
Tel: 01792 - 642158
Fax: 01792 - 648996

Just minutes' walk from the bustling city centre, Windsor Lodge is as peaceful a haven as you'd wish to find and its well-heeled business clientele is made to feel very much at home by the resident owners, Pam and Ron Rumble. The interlinked lounge and bar, where light classical music plays in the background, and a spotless, intimate dining-room are given an extra feeling of space by strategic wall mirrors, the latter coming to life at night by flickering candlelight.

The fixed-price dinner menus are kept sensibly short to allow the day's shopping to come to the fore. Among the starters, Tina's Thai chicken soup with shallots and coriander, and crab cakes with tartare sauce are a tribute to one who has graduated over the years from kitchen assistant to senior chef on all but the busiest nights.

Main courses of sauteed duck breast with plum and ginger sauce, cod fillet grilled with a herb crust, or fillet of Welsh beef with wild mushroom sauce are competently handled and served with individual dishes of potatoes and fresh market vegetables. Orange and passion-fruit mousse with blackcurrant sauce, and Merlyn's Magic – a cleverly-blended soft cheesecake with Welsh whisky – are equally accomplished desserts.

Having recently marked their first quarter-century at the helm, the Rumbles continue to evolve and expand, and four new executive bedroooms will come on line in 1998.

*MEALS: L (by arrangement) 12.30-2.30
D 7-10 from £17.50*

*WTB: Unclassified
19 En suite B&B from £47 S; £62 D*

165 Tenby

Plantagenet House

Quay Hill
Tenby
Pembrokeshire
Tel: 01834 - 842350
Fax: 01834 - 834915

Barney Stone's establishment is hard to pigeon-hole, but whatever time of day or night you visit it feels like a place where things are happening. You can start the day in the downstairs bar with laverbread, bacon and cockles, traditional Welsh cawl or a "Rat in a Loaf" – which the cheerful crew will readily explain to you. Or, bathed in candlelight, you can dine romantically on pan-fried tiger prawns and Welsh lamb fillet at a table under the stars, shining far above the huge 12th-century Flemish chimney that rises straight through the roof and dominates the upper restaurant.

Among a variety of menus you'll find much to admire in the choice and the freshness of what's on offer. While there's no obligation to choose more than a fresh crab salad or sandwich through the day, there will also be fresh local asparagus, lobster and king scallops in season, and careful shopping extends to Pembrokeshire new potatoes and organically-farmed Welsh beef.

The kitchen offers six varieties of home-made sausage – served with creamy mash and onion gravy or roasted red pepper sauce; makes its own burgers and felafels; and offers five types of bread in a genuinely eclectic sandwich selection. The cooking, in which Barney personally has had a hand for 18 years, is admirably consistent given the breadth of its skills and endeavour – a remarkable achievement.

*MEALS: All day 9.30-11
L 12-3 (Sun till 4); D 6-11
Closed: D Sun; all Mon-Thurs in Nov; Jan & Feb*

166 Trellech

The Village Green

Trellech
Nr Monmouth
Monmouthshire
NP5 4PA
Tel: 01600 - 860119

Part-pub, part-bistro and self-professed restaurant, The Village Green cheerfully defies fashion with its mid-1980's decor of exposed stonework, stuffed beasties, enamelled pre-war advertisements and rugby memorabilia.

Proprietor and chef Bob Evans's food is comfortable and substantial, characterised by starters of spicy local lamb sausage with mango sauce, or baked potato skins with sun-dried tomatoes and mozzarella, each more than enough for a mid-day snack. Main dishes could challenge any appetite - whole hock of Welsh lamb, roast and served with honeyed mint sauce, rib of beef with pizzaiola sauce, and loin chop of wild boar served with creamy wild mushrooms. This traditional cooking, plentiful and full of flavour, is not without subtlety in the oven-baked monkfish with Thermidor sauce, and classic duck breast Montmorency. Jane Evans produces an accomplished citron tart and toothsome iced chocolate and Drambuie terrine; hardy trenchermen shouldn't miss her formidable pineapple upside-down cake. There are two self-catering bedroom suites next to the pub, with cooked breakfasts provided on request.

MEALS: L 11.45-2; D 7-10
Set Sun L 12-2 £11.75
Closed: D Sun; all Mon; 1 Week Jan

WTB: Unclassified
2 En suite B&B from £45 D
Closed: 1 Week Jan

167 Usk

Bush House of Usk

12 Bridge Street
Usk
Monmouthshire
NP5 1BQ
Tel: 01291 - 672929

Unassuming, yet steadily growing in confidence, Steven Rogers has run his informal, low-key bistro for ten years now, its eclectic background music, wall posters, decorative ceramics and bric-a-brac reflecting the character of its owner. Wholefoods and pulses, herbs and spices, oils and vinegars, available in Bush House's speciality shop, add a similarly broad church to the food he produces; while his varied menus result from careful research into customers' demands and sympathy with vegetarian tastes.

Each day's freshly made soup (perhaps a punchy puree of fresh tomatoes finished with yoghurt and purple basil leaves) is a meal in itself with generous helpings of fresh bread; or there'll be pasta with queen scallops and vermouth, Glamorgan sausages with fruit coulis, grilled Chevré salad with crispy bacon and croutons and corn-fed chicken Dijonnaise with lightly-sauteed vegetables. To these add char-grilled dab with sea salt and lime, or warm game salad with crispy

leeks, followed by gigot of Welsh lamb with asparagus spears and mint vinaigrette, roast Wye salmon with salsa verdi and aioli, or spinach and pistachio strudel, as examples of equally well-sourced evening dishes. There are plenty of home-made desserts to go for, such as bread-and-butter and sticky toffee puddings or creamy lemon tart; alternatively choose a cheese or two of excellent quality from the cabinet display. Speciality teas, coffees, seltzers, wines and bottled beers are available along with cakes, scones and cream teas sold during normal shop hours throughout the week.

 MEALS: L 11.30-3; D 7-9.30 (Fri & Sat till 10)
Set Sun L 12.30-3.30 £11.95
Closed: D Sun in summer; 3 days Christmas

168 Welsh Hook

Stone Hall

Welsh Hook
Nr Haverfordwest
Pembrokeshire
SA62 5NS
Tel: 01348 - 840212
Fax: 01348 - 840815

Stone Hall is an atmospheric U-shaped mixture of 15th and 19th century simple country architecture standing in a leafy, rambling garden. The fine blue-and-white entrance hall with its stunning art nouveau clock reminds you of proprietor Martine Watson's French origins, confirmed by the maison's food. The menu reads well and is full of French classics like cassoulet and confit served with traditional onion marmalade, but Martine no longer cooks every evening – a pity, since results are most successful when the food sticks to her repertoire.

Everything is home-made: good fresh bread and cheese straws lead in to salade gourmande of home-smoked duck breast and goats' cheese, or lambs' sweetbreads and local wild mushrooms (including Jew's ears and Trompettes) in a rich, deep sauce with buttery puff pastry, both representing Stone Hall at its best. Brave, but less successful on our visit, were an over-sweet monkfish with vanilla and a tarte Tatin that had failed to crisp up. However, the Celtic Crunch ice cream and chocolate truffles with the coffee redeemed the performance.

Alan Watson's predominantly French wine list offers good value, and for overnight guests a communal breakfast with home-made bread and marmalade constitutes an agreeable start to the next day.

 MEALS: L by arrangement,
D 7-9.30 from £16; T from 5.30
(No children under 10 after 7pm)

 WTB: unclassified
5 En suite B&B from £ 45 S; £68 D
Special breaks: Dinner, Bed and Breakfast from £98.

169 Whitebrook

The Crown at Whitebrook

Whitebrook
Nr Monmouth
Monmouthshire
NP5 4TX

Tel: 01600 - 860254
Fax: 01600 - 860607

Arguably the only restaurant in Wales to claim the epithet auberge, the Crown is hidden away in the narrow, wooded Whitebrook Valley a mile or so up from the River Wye (turn off the A466 at Bigsweir Bridge).

Sandra Bates's nightly menus may have a French slant, but the local produce – from goats' cheeses to luscious summer fruits – is diligently sourced and handled with care and affection, while Roger Bates's supervision of the restaurant possesses that cheery informality which helps to transform one's evening into a memorable dining experience.

Among six or more starters, the soup may be cream of fresh asparagus; lamb's offal is crafted into a trio of kidney, liver and sausage with onion marmalade and mustard sauce; and a pristine red mullet fillet, marinated in lemon juice and olive oil, is served with crisp, piquant pickled vegetables. Welsh lamb, Wye salmon and locally-reared venison seasonally head some classy main courses, the last perhaps a roast loin served with roast shallots and creamed hazelnuts in a puff pastry case. Alternatives might include a delicate boned quail roast with chicken, tarragon and pistachio farce on a bed of baby leaf spinach, and a herb and hazelnut croustade filled with wild mushrooms on a herb beurre blanc. Equal care goes into exquisite presentations of souffle au citron vert, tarte au chocolat and the extensive predominantly Welsh cheeseboard.

The fixed-price three-course lunch offers if anything even better value for money, while lighter lunches served in the lounge or on the terrace in fine weather offer toothsome individual dishes such as Welsh lamb sausages in puff pastry with rosemary gravy, and smoked haddock fishcakes on a herb and cream sauce.

 MEALS: L 12-2 from £16; D 7-9 from £27
Closed: D Sun (residents only); L Mon
Special breaks: Dinner, Bed and Breakfast from £130

 WTB: 3 Crowns highly commended.
12 En suite B&B from £50 S; £80 D
Closed: 25 & 26 Dec; 2 weeks Jan.

170 Whitemill

Pantgwyn Farm

Whitemill
Carmarthen
Carmarthenshire
SA32 7ES

Tel: 01267 - 290247
Fax: 01267 - 290880

Call ahead and Tim Giles will give you accurate directions to his lovely farm where whitewashed barns and immaculate homestead beside a hillside stream provide an idyllic retreat. Tim masterminds the operation with self-assurance, offering knowledgeable advice and opinion when requested and producing menus which speak of the same quiet confidence.

This is excellent farmhouse cookery, the flavoursome soups and simple stews all the better for being made with local ingredients. Pretty well everything comes from nearby, from the good, doughy bread made with flour from an ancient mill down the road through the excellent ice cream and breakfast marmalade to Tim's home-produced honey.

His three-course, set-price dinner might start with smooth cream of sweetcorn soup or field mushrooms with Welsh rarebit and follow with Welsh Black beef braised in Double Dragon beer, roast salmon with a mustard crust or a vegetarian option such as tagliatelli with Stilton and walnuts. At the heart of this cheesemaking country, the cheese selection is always a good option, though equally tempting desserts will include, perhaps, an apricot and almond tart, elderflower syllabub with gooseberries and a choice of ice creams – the lemon is a star. Hand-churned butter and lamb sausages continue this concept of excellence through an award-winning breakfast, and with plenty to explore on the farm this makes an excellent base for family holiday-making.

MEALS: D 7.15-8
Special breaks: Dinner, Bed and Breakfast from £86

WTB: 3 Crowns de luxe
5 En suite £36 S; £50 D
Closed: 1 week Christmas

171 Wolfscastle

Wolfscastle Hotel

Wolfscastle
Nr Haverfordwest
Pembrokeshire
SA62 5LZ

Tel: 01437 - 741225
Fax: 01437 - 741383

Conveniently situated by the main A40 seven miles south of Fishguard, this reasonably appointed hotel is popular with seasoned travellers' and its many facilities include squash courts for the energetic and Sky TV for couch potatoes.

Though not presented as Welsh, the menu makes use of local and fresh ingredients. Superb white rolls and Welsh butter make a good start to accompany warm local smoked salmon with lime and dill vinaigrette, from among a dozen first courses which might also include seafood pancakes and a highly successful confit of duck leg with ginger and soy rather like Peking duck. A similar number of main courses ranges perhaps through broccoli and mushroom cobbler and fillet of local sewin with a smooth watercress sauce, new potatoes and decent greens, disconcertingly served with a rather inappropriate ratatouille.

Typical sweets might be a rich if somewhat heavy chocolate and Grand Marnier terrine with a light vanilla sauce; good home-made fudge accompanies the coffee. Sage Derby, Red Leicester and Stilton among the "selection of Welsh cheeses" indicate, however, a somewhat uneven overall approach.

MEALS: Bar L 12-2.30; D 6.30-9
Restaurant D 7-9
Special breaks: Dinner, Bed and Breakfast from £98

WTB: 4 Crowns highly commended
20 En suite B&B from £40 S; £70 D

The Youth Hostels of Wales

By Chris Chown

If you were thinking that Youth Hostels are hard tack and hobnails, and only the province of student back-packers, then think again. They may not be the last word in luxury but, for those willing to embrace the communal atmosphere, the rewards can be great. Locations are often spectacular, value is outstanding and simple cooking can hold its own with far grander operations.

Youthful tastebuds and staffing constraints do necessitate some bought-in foodstuffs, but all those we have selected below cook a range of their own dishes. The dinner format is usually a simple fruit juice or soup starter, a hot or cold dessert and a larger choice of main dish: vegetarian choices are always plentiful, and often the most imaginative options.

The hostel at Llangollen is also a Study and Activity Centre – one of only two in the UK – and so is well geared to the needs of the private individual or family. An added bonus for 1998 is the family "Great Escape", a multi-activity break of two to seven nights with membership of the YHA thrown in. A varied menu features speciality dishes of mushroom and lentil canneloni and carrot cake.

Three hostels encircle Mount Snowdon. At Llanberis, a simple building above the village looks over to the vast slate quarries beyond the lake, and is ideally positioned for the Snowdon Railway. Here, try the chicken and vegetable tikka masala. In the lovely Nantgwynant valley, Bryn Gwynant is a solid Victorian villa surrounded by rhododendrons, with additional accommodation in the grounds. The smell of home-baked apple pies with a wholemeal crust will greet you as you return from a mountain day. At the Snowdon Ranger near Rhyd Ddu, charming Kath Woods makes almost everything herself. "I couldn't afford to buy it in!", she laughs as she takes an old-fashioned spiced bread pudding out of the oven. The modesty of a natural cook points out this basic economic truth – let's have more like her!

In Ceredigion, the seafront location at Borth could scarcely be more different, with its rooms looking out to sea over a vast expanse of beach. Salads and vegetables, perhaps for the creamy vegetable pie, come from Ynyslas market garden, and you may even be offered fresh mackerel for breakfast!

Way above Libanus, in Brecon, stands the perfectly peaceful old longhouse of Llwyn-y-Celin, where Suzanne Hall chirpily controls the operation, offering her own lasagne or a courgette and leek bake in the lovely flag-floored dining-room with its splendid views across to the Beacons.

Of the three hostels on the Pembrokeshire coast, Whitehouse at Pen-y-Cwm provides arguably the best-appointed accommodation in its converted farm buildings, and Pat Cross's catering is almost legendary. She rounds off her working day, after serving three generous courses in the hostel, by cooking dinner for residents at her guest-house next door. It's worth the trip just for her pastry and homemade mushroom gravy. The Broad Haven hostel faces the broad expanse of surfing beach and is less picturesque than some, but they offer very good home-cooked lamb cobbler and Glamorgan sausages. Manorbier is at the southern tip - in a spectacular location only a minute away from the coastal path – where an old army building has been cleverly converted into a high-tech venue. Here, Deb and Matthew Roberts offer an all-in price, with packed lunch as well as home-made dishes like toad-in-the-hole and puff pastry parcels of Mediterranean vegetables.

Individual hostel addresses and telephone numbers are as follows:

BORTH	Youth Hostel, Morlais, Ceredigion SY24 5JS	Tel: 01970 - 871827
BROAD HAVEN	Youth Hostel, Broad Haven, Haverfordfordwest, Pembrokeshire SA62 3JH	Tel: 01437 - 781688
BRYN GWYNANT	Youth Hostel, Bryn Gwynant, Nantgwynant, Caernarfon, Gwynedd LL55 4NP	Tel: 01766 - 890251
LLANBERIS	Youth Hostel, Llwyn Celyn, Llanberis, Caernarfon, Gwynedd LL55 4SR	Tel: 01286 - 870280
LLANGOLLEN	YHA Study and Activity Centre, Tyndwr Hall, Tyndwr Road, Llangollen, Denbighshire LL20 8AR	Tel: 01978 - 860330
LLWYN-Y-CELYN	Youth Hostel, Libanus, Brecon, Powys LD3 8NH	Tel: 01874 - 624261
MANORBIER	Youth Hostel, Manorbier, Nr Tenby, Pembrokeshire SA70 7TT	Tel: 01834 - 871101
PEN-Y-CWM	Youth Hostel, Pen-y-Cwm, Nr Solva, Haverfordwest, Pembrokeshire SA62 6LA	Tel: 01437 - 720959
SNOWDON RANGER	Youth Hostel, Rhyd Ddu, Caernarfon, Gwynedd LL54 7YS	Tel: 01286 - 650391

A Welsh Wine List

The wine industry in Wales is in remarkably good health. With more than a dozen vineyards in production, there are now enough Welsh wines to make a wine list. Despite the fact that it only takes one late frost, dull summer, hailstorm or wet autumn to write off most of the crop, and that after Customs and Excise taxes are added the retail price seems high compared to the many imported wines, Welsh wines are holding their own.

Almost all the vineyards are found in the south, where the Romans planted one of the largest vineyards in Britain in the Vale of Glamorgan. The Normans encouraged viniculture in monasteries and it was only the success of the Plantagenets in France that demoralised wine production in Wales. The Marquis of Bute challenged the French with his vineyard at Castell Coch just north of Cardiff: in 1876 he sent his head gardener, Andrew Pettigrew, for a year to Bordeaux to study viticulture in order to produce red wine from a grape variety called Gamay Noir. By 1905 the total number of vines planted exceeded 63,000 and the wines were sold commercially in London with prices higher than imported Burgundy wines (60 shillings per case for the Castell Coch 1893 vintage).

A new burst of wine-making enthusiasts emerged in the 1970s and today the Welsh wine industry thrives. There are more than a dozen vineyards, some of whose wines achieve a standard of quality equal to any made in the British Isles. These are mainly white wines, with a few light reds and some promising rosés, as well as some sparkling wines now available. The grapes used are generally hybrid Alsace varieties, such as Madeleine Angevine, Seyval Blanc, Reichensteiner, Leon Millot and Triomphe d'Alsace, which can withstand the Welsh climate. The Welsh wines are light, dry and fruity in character. Many of the vineyards welcome visitors and offer wine tastings.

Croffta

One of the first vineyards to be planted in the present revival in Wales. In the mid 1970s, John Bevan planted 1,500 vines over 3 acres of farmland when he retired from the steel industry. Grapes used for Croffta are Muller-Thurgau, Seyve Villard and Madeleine Angevine.

Glyndwr

Brothers Robbie and Richard Norris produce 3,000 to 6,000 bottles of white, red, rosé and now a Glyndwr sparkling wine on their five-acre vineyard. It was established in 1983 and is set among rolling hills with a small wood to the west, enjoying a very mild maritime climate four miles from the sea. The vineyard soil is limestone with a topping of loamy clay, and the vines are trained on the double Guyot system in rows 6ft apart. Glyndwr has sold its wine to France and Switzerland.

Pant Teg

Cardiff city's own vineyard at Lisvane on the north east. The vineyard of 1¼ acres has produced white wines since 1991 under the capable hands of Kynric Lewis and John Albert Evans. New from Pant Teg is a sparkling wine from Kerner and Kernling grapes.

Andrac

The first wine was produced in 1990, and today still and sparkling wines are made from Chardonnay vines under this label.

Wyecliff

The vineyard overlooks Hay Castle and was first planted more than a decade ago. The wine is made from Madeleine Angevine grapes.

Monnow Valley

The vineyards, now extending to four acres, were first planted in 1979 on the sheltered slopes of the Monnow Valley just outside Monmouth. Production exceeds 3,500 bottles, including 500 sparkling from Seyval Blanc; the other grape variety is Huxelrebe/Seyval. The Baker family have taken over this vineyard recently.

Sugar Loaf

Three white wines are produced from a five-acre vineyard situated above Abergavenny on the southern slope of the Sugar Loaf mountain. This vineyard was planted in 1992 with Reichensteiner, Seigerrebe, Madeleine Angevine, Seyval and Triomphe Alsace grape varieties.

Mewslade

A vineyard of just over an acre above Mewslade Bay in Rhossili on the Gower Peninsula. The warm micro-climate helps growing conditions for white and an experimental light red wine ably produced by Pam and Mark Keegan. Grape varieties are Madeleine Angevine, Seyval Blanc and Triomphe D'Alsace.

Cariad

Planted on the slopes of the Ely valley at Pendoylan, Vale of Glamorgan, Llanerch vineyard has become perhaps Wales's premier vineyard. Diana and Peter Andrews have perfected the skills of viticulture and viniculture since retiring as pharmacists, and produce a range of award winning wines – whites, rosés, sparkling and even a fumé. Visitors welcome for wine tasting and a cup of tea in the cafe.

Cwm Deri

This family-run vineyard is in Martletwy, Pembrokeshire where the Cowburns make four white wines and a light red on the farm. Fourteen grape varieties include Madeleine Angevine and Seyval Blanc. Country wines also available. Visitors welcome to look around and taste.

Ffynnon Las

A small well-established vineyard of about an acre in size overlooking Cardigan Bay, that now produces two still table wines from Madeleine Angevine, Schonburger, Reichensteiner and Seyval Blanc grapes. The wines are dry and medium dry with two new wines, one a red, in the pipeline.

Brecon Court

Barbara and Desmond McElney run their large vineyard in conjunction with a deer farm and visitors are welcome to see the wine-making process. The grapes grown are Seyval Blanc, Reichensteiner and Schonburger and the McElneys produce several white table wines as well as a sparkling white and a light ruby red.

Offa's

Produced from grape varieties Faber and Schonburger, wine under the Offa's label is available in South Wales.

A Welsh Cheeseboard

Produced on a number of farms in Wales – mainly in Dyfed – Welsh cheeses are available throughout the year, and today they offer enough variety of taste and texture to constitute a competent Welsh cheeseboard.

These cheeses are not cheap because making small quantities by hand takes time; and the maturing process takes more time, which again costs money. But the best Welsh farmhouse cheeses are among the finest made anywhere and deserve to be treated as such. Some are sold in Harrods, some abroad, and many are available through good delicatessens throughout Britain or at the cheese counter in supermarkets. Although distribution in Wales is variable, almost all hotels and restaurants now serve local cheeses.

Here are some of the best Welsh farmhouse cheeses available....

Acorn
Unpasteurised ewes' milk cheese made with vegetarian rennet. Natural rind, semi-hard with mild flavour and pleasant texture.

Brecon Blue
Mixed goat' and cows' milk blue, newly in production, very promising.

Caerfai
Organically produced hard cows' milk cheese matured from 4 months. Also smoked, with garlic and leeks, apricot and brandy.

Caws Ffermdy Cenarth
Traditional unpasteurised Caerphilly, semi-hard with a crumbly texture. Mild, mature and smoked, plus various added flavours.

Celtic Promise
Hard cheese with washed rind, made from unpasteurised cows' milk. Strong individual character with powerful smell and flavour.

Cwm Tawe Pecorino
Traditional Sardinian semi-hard cheese, made from unpasteurised sheep's milk, with good salty flavour. Ricotta is also made by Cwm Tawe.

Franjoy Cheese
Unpasteurised hard Cheddar-style cheese, made from organically produced milk from Jersey cows. Aged between 3 and 12 months.

Gorwydd Caerffili
Recently available traditional Caerphilly, semi-hard with exceptionally good flavour.

Hen Sir
Mature Cheddar with nutty flavour, popular and reasonably priced.

Lady Llanover
Saffron washed rind ewes' milk cheese. Fine flavour.

Llangloffan
A hard, pressed cheese made to an original Cheshire cheese recipe from the unpasteurised milk of Jersey cows. Good flavour. Also available with added garlic and chives.

Llanboidy
A hard, pressed farmhouse cheese with a rich nutty flavour made with unpasteurised milk from Red Poll cows. (Laverbread Llanboidy also available.)

Merlin
Unpasteurised hard goats' milk cheese, with a texture between Cheddar and Gouda and creamy flavour. Natural, smoked, with olives or walnuts and other flavours.

Monks of Strata Florida
A range of flavoured cows' milk cheeses.

Nantybwla
Unpasteurised Caerphilly made and matured to traditional recipe. Smoked variety also available.

Pant ys Gawn
Soft fresh goats' milk cheese available plain or flavoured with herbs, black pepper, garlic with chives, and lemon rind. Clean fresh texture and taste.

Penbryn
Another fine hard Gouda cheese made with organically produced cows' milk and matured for 3 to 6 months by a Dutch cheesemaker.

Pencarreg
Welsh Brie, a soft rind cheese made from organically produced cows' milk.

Pencarreg Blue
Blue version of the above. Creamy with good flavour.

Pen-y-bont
Natural rind, with organically produced goats' milk, semi-hard with pleasant texture and flavour.

Skirrid
Semi-hard ewes' milk cheese, marinated in mead.

St. David's
Washed rind Chaume-type cheese with lots of character when ripe.

St. Florence
Firm cheese, based on traditional Cheshire cheese recipe. Made with unpasteurised milk and vegetarian rennet, wrapped in muslin and aged. Also flavoured with chives and leeks.

St. Illtyd
Mature Welsh Cheddar milled with Welsh wine, garlic and herbs.

Teifi
Traditional unpasteurised Gouda made with vegetarian rennet. Available in garlic, garlic and onion, celery, nettle, sweet pepper, chives, laverbread, mustard and cumin seed flavours. Look out for the mature Teifi.

Y Fenni
Milled Cheddar with Welsh ale and mustardseed. Very popular.

Recipes

Anthony's Famous Fish Soup

by Anthony Ollman
at the Elan Valley Hotel
near Rhayader

The secret of a really good fish soup is a good fishmonger and a degree of flexibility. Warwick, a sympathetic and helpful fishman, supplies me with all sorts of off-cuts and then I let my taste buds do the rest. My aim - the fishier the better!

4 fish heads and tails and assorted trimmings (salmon and tuna are excellent, avoid anything too oily)

2 Spanish onions, roughly chopped

1 head of garlic, roughly chopped

6 celery sticks, chopped

4 peppers, red and green, roughly chopped

4 carrots, chopped

a bunch of parsley, well washed

1 tablespoon concentrated fish stock (bouillon)

1 heaped tablespoon tomato puree

1 tablespoon chopped dill

2 teaspoons turmeric

2 teaspoons paprika

1 teaspoon piri-piri, or a finely-chopped chilli

½ bottle dry white wine

seasoning

450g (1lb) pieces of fish or assorted fish (salmon, tuna, swordfish)

1. Put the fish trimmings into a large pan with all the other ingredients except the whole fish pieces. Cover with water, add a lid and bring to the boil, and simmer for half an hour.

2. Remove the lid and boil for a further 1½ hours to reduce the liquid, stirring occasionally.

3. Leave to cool before sieving all the liquid into a smaller pan. Pick out any meaty bits from the fish trimmings and add these to the liquid. Press all the cooked vegetables through a sieve and add the puree to the fish liquor in the small pan.

4. Bring this remaining stock back to the boil, add the whole fish pieces and simmer for ten minutes.

5. Using a hand held blender, liquidise the soup to achieve a thicker, rich consistency.

6. Serve steaming hot with garlic croutons.

Llanrhidian Bun

by Sheila and Robert Allen, at The Welcome to Town, Llanrhidian

This is the speciality dish of our new restaurant. A savoury mixture of cockles, laverbread, leeks and bacon, it is a version of the traditional Swansea Tart – but ours is served in the hollow of a toasted brioche-style bread roll and not a pastry case.

Ingredients to fill 4 rolls to overflowing

2 large rashers streaky bacon, finely diced

4 brioche-style buns

50g (2oz) leeks, washed and finely sliced

225g (8oz) cockles, boiled and well rinsed

50g (2oz) laverbread, fresh, frozen or tinned

fresh ground pepper to season

25g (1oz) butter

1. Dry fry the bacon for one minute then add the leeks and cook for a further 3 minutes. Add the cockles and laverbread and heat through.

2. Cut the top of the brioche. Hollow out the bun leaving a reasonable thickness for the walls. Brush with a little butter and put the brioche and lid in a hot oven to bake until golden.

3. Fill with the cockle mixture and place the lid back on top. Serve with a selection of salad leaves.

Pressed Tongue Terrine

by Jason Hornbuckle, Tyddyn Llan Country Hotel, Llandrillo.

This terrine is very good served with a warm madeira sauce

1 ox tongue (soaked in brine)

3 carrots

2 onions

3 sticks celery

2 bay leaves

1 sprig of fresh thyme

2 cloves garlic

6 peppercorns

small bunch of parsley

2 tablespoons capers

6 shallots, chopped finely

1 tablespoon white wine vinegar

salt and pepper

2 leaves gelatine

1. Put the tongue into a large pan with the carrots, whole onions, celery, bay leaves, thyme, garlic and peppercorns. Cover with cold water, bring to the boil and simmer for 3 hours, or until cooked.

2. Remove the tongue from the pan and immerse in ice for a few seconds, which will help remove the skin. Remove all the vegetables from the liquid and keep to one side. Reduce the stock over a high heat by ³/₄ then pass through a fine sieve and leave to cool.

3. Skin the tongue and dice into cubes, and dice the carrots, which will now have absorbed the flavour of the tongue. Put in a bowl with the chopped parsley, shallots, capers and vinegar.

4. Add the gelatine to the stock and then pour over the ingredients in the bowl, mix well and check for seasoning. Spoon the mixture into a terrine mould and leave overnight to set.

Breast of Corn-fed Chicken on Tagliatelle with Tarragon Sauce and Deep-fried Leeks

by Steven Rogers
at The Bush House,
Usk.

This is one of those recipes that has stood the test of time at the restaurant and is still one of the most popular dishes on the menu.

4 corn-fed chicken breasts, boned but with skin on

4 nests of good quality tagliatelle

2 large leeks, green part only

1 tablespoon olive oil or garlic butter

salt

1 dessertspoon cornflour

For the Sauce

3 wine glasses (18 fl oz) good dry white wine

1 wine glass (6 fl oz) good meat or chicken stock

2 wine glasses (12 fl oz) whipping cream

1 heaped tablespoon chopped fresh tarragon

1. Heat the oil or butter in a pan and sear the chicken breasts on all sides for a minute. Transfer the chicken, skin side up, to a baking sheet, cover with garlic butter or olive oil and sprinkle each with a pinch of salt. Roast in a very hot oven for 8 - 10 minutes.

2. Boil the tagliatelle in well-salted water until al dente. Drain and keep warm.

3. Cut the leeks into 3" lengths then into thin strips, lengthways. Toss the strips in the cornflour and deep fry until golden brown, sprinkle with salt and keep warm.

4. Make the sauce by boiling the wine and stock until reduced by half. Add the cream and reduce until the sauce thickens. Add the tarragon and take off the heat.

5. Remove the chicken from the oven when the skin is crisp and brown, slice each breast into 3 pieces and return to the oven to finish cooking.

6. To serve: Arrange a nest of tagliatelle on each of 4 hot plates, place a sliced chicken breast on each and pour the sauce over, topping with a liberal mound of fried leeks.

Roast Cannon of Welsh Lamb in an Oatmeal and Laverbread Crust with a Creamy Leek Sauce

by Mary Ann Gilchrist,
Carlton House,
Llanwrtyd Wells

I have always viewed laverbread with a certain degree of revulsion. I find it resembles slimy, overcooked spinach, and on its own it is quite horrid. However, I decided that I must overcome my prejudice and invented this dish which is eaten to great acclaim in my restaurant.

Recipe for 2

1 boned best end of lamb

50g (2oz) pinhead oatmeal

1 heaped teaspoon prepared laverbread

1 teaspoon Dijon mustard

1 tablespoon olive oil

100g (4oz) thinly-sliced leeks

25g (1oz) butter

125ml (4fl oz) double cream

50ml (2fl oz) lamb stock

salt and pepper to taste

1. Pre-heat the oven to 200c, Gas 6, 400f. Trim the lamb of all visible fat and gristle and seal in a hot pan brushed with a little oil. Remove and leave to cool.

2. Spread the mustard all over the lamb. In a bowl mix the oatmeal, laverbread and the olive oil. Roll the lamb in the mixture and place in a roasting tin and cook for 7 - 10 minutes. Remove from the oven and rest for 5 minutes before carving.

3. While the lamb is roasting sweat the leeks in the butter till soft, add the lamb stock and reduce by half. Add the cream and boil down till the sauce will lightly coat the back of the spoon, then season to taste with salt and pepper.

4. To serve, carve the lamb and divide between two warm plates, pour a little of the sauce on each plate and accompany this dish with some lovely Pembroke new potatoes tossed in a little butter and chives.

Moroccan Lamb

by Alison Whowell,
Goetre Isaf Farmhouse,
Bangor

We were first given this dish on a riding holiday in the Atlas Mountains in Morocco. Our meal was cooked in the traditional tagine over a charcoal cooker on the floor by our young Moroccan-Berber guide. At home I cook this recipe in a casserole and it goes down particularly well with guests.

1k (2.2lb) cubed lean lamb (from shoulder)

50g (2oz) butter or oil

1 large onion, diced

2 cloves of garlic, crushed

Braised Brisket of Welsh Black Beef

from Andrew Addis-Fuller
at The Griffin Inn,
Llyswen, Brecon

We now have a good supply of well-matured, superb-quality Welsh Black beef and we use the brisket because when cooked slowly with wine and herbs it acquires a rich deep flavour and is remarkably tender. We feel this is a real Griffin special – although it is quite rich, it is so popular and makes a fine supper.

1 whole brisket 2.5 - 3kg (5½ - 6lb)
1½ lt of red wine
6 carrots, roughly chopped
2 large onions, chopped
1 tin chopped tomatoes
1-2 red peppers, sliced
1 heaped teaspoon paprika
1 heaped teaspoon ground ginger
1 heaped teaspoon cinnamon
2 tablespoons honey
50g (2oz) whole unblanched almonds
1 tablespoon herbs or fresh chopped oregano and basil
1 teaspoon salt
black pepper to taste
600ml (1 pt) stock
2 tablespoons lemon juice
1 tablespoon tomato puree for colour (optional)

1. Heat the oil in a large casserole and fry the onions and garlic. Add the lamb and brown well.

2. Add the tinned tomatoes then all the other ingredients. Bring the contents of the casserole to the boil and simmer gently in the oven at 170c, Gas 3, 325f for 1½ to 2 hours.

3. Taste for seasoning and thicken the sauce if desired.

4. Garnish the dish with toasted pine nuts and serve with saffron rice, couscous or potatoes.

To accompany: okra, fresh beans, broccoli, courgettes, broad beans.
Unleavened or garlic bread.

1 head of celery, roughly chopped

1 bay leaf

6 peppercorns

1.2 lt (2 pt) beef stock

Garnish

100g (4oz) button mushrooms

100g (4oz) shallots or pickling onions

100g (4oz) smoked bacon, chopped

1. Put the vegetables in the bottom of a roasting tin and sit the meat on top. Pour over the red wine and season. Cover with foil and braise very slowly for 4-5 hours at 150-170c, Gas 2-3, 300-325f until very tender.

2. Carefully lift out the meat in one piece and keep warm. Add the stock to the pan and cook down for 20 minutes to reduce by half, squashing the vegetables to release all the juices. Strain the juice and keep.

3. Saute the button mushrooms, onions and lardons of smoked bacon to garnish the dish.

4. Carve the meat and serve with the juice and garnish

Elderflower Ice Cream

by Sue and Tim Giles,
Pantgwyn Farm,
Whitemill.

A delightful, refreshing and tangy ice cream full of the flavours of the country springtime and very healthy!

Elderflower Syrup

Although elderflower syrup is now available in delicatessens and health food shops we make our own in early summer when the glorious elderflowers are at their peak of creamy perfection.

Pick about 30 full heads of the best elderflowers you can find – best gathered just after the morning dew has evaporated but before the flowers have become really hot. They must be picked dry, and do remember that the best flowers are the

169

female ones – unfortunately the male flowers can spoil the flavour!

Combine 50 g (2oz) citric acid, 1.75k (4 lbs) sugar and 250ml (9 fl oz) water. Heat gently to dissolve.

Boil 1 litre (1¾ pints) of water and pour over 2 sliced lemons, the 30 elderflower heads and the dissolved sugar and citric acid. Stir and cover, leaving lots of space for the mixture to breath.

Stir every day for 10 days then add ½ Camden tablet to kill off rogue yeasts and strain and bottle. Keep until needed in many recipes.

Ice Cream

250ml (9 fl oz) elderflower syrup

2 egg whites

250ml (9 fl oz) double cream

125ml (4 fl oz) full fat milk

Elderflower petals or lemon balm leaves for decoration

1. Whisk the egg whites lightly. Heat the syrup in a pan until nearly but not quite boiling and pour onto the egg whites, whisking all the time. Leave to cool.

2. When very cold add the double cream and milk and stir thoroughly.
   Pour the mixture into an ice cream machine and freeze/churn or place in the freezer and beat well every half hour until frozen.

3. Serve with a sprinkling of elderflower petals in spring or lemon balm leaves.

All quantities can be adjusted to suit individual tastes.

Strawberries and Cream in Layers of Puff Pastry with Pavlova Ice cream

by Shaun Mitchell
at Plas Bodegroes

This recipe is great for dinner parties as it can be prepared beforehand, but you must work quickly at the end or your ice cream will melt.

450g (1lb) strawberries

10 eggs, separated

caster sugar

425ml (15 fl oz) milk

1 vanilla pod

75g (3oz) caster sugar

225g (8oz) mixed fruit puree (mostly strawberries)

350g (12oz) puff pastry

egg wash – egg yolk beaten with a little milk

150ml (5fl oz) chilled double cream

1. First make your pavlova. Weigh the egg

whites and then prepare 1½ times the weight in sugar (ie 10 oz white needs 15 oz caster sugar). Whisk the egg whites till very stiff then add ⅓ of sugar, continue whisking and five minutes later another ⅓ and then after 5 more minutes the last ⅓. Keep whisking till you can turn the bowl upside down and it looks very glossy. Spread on to greaseproof paper and bake at 100c, Gas ¼, 200f for 2-3 hours with the door slightly ajar.

2. To make the custard, scald the milk with the vanilla pod. Whisk the yolk and sugar until almost white then pour on the warm milk, return to the pan and heat slowly until it thickens enough to coat the back of a spoon. Strain into a cold bowl and stir until it is cool.

3. Now mix in ¾ of the fruit puree and transfer to an ice cream machine. When well churned add ½ of the pavlova, broken up, and put in the freezer.

4. Heat oven to 220c, Gas 7, 425f. Roll out puff pastry to ¼" thick, cut out using a heart-shaped or round cutter. Brush with egg wash and bake in the oven till golden.

To Serve

1. Slice the strawberries and whisk the cream. In a large bowl mix them together with the rest of the pavlova and the ice cream.

2. Slice the pastry discs into 3 horizontally and layer some of the filling into between each slice.

3. Serve with some of the remaining red fruit puree.

Gooseberry and Elderflower Cream Tartlet

by Lynda Kettle,
Ty'n Rhos,
Caernarfon

I find that this recipe works best with individual tartlets rather than one large one since the filling is very fragile, making it difficult to cut and serve.

175g (6oz) plain flour

75g (3oz) butter

scant tablespoon water

450g (1lb) gooseberries, topped and tailed

100g (4oz) sugar (adjust according to tartness of gooseberries)

50ml (2 fl oz) water

6 heads of elderflowers or 2 tablespoons elderflower cordial

125ml (4 fl oz) double cream

1 tablespoon sugar

1. Make the pastry in the usual way using a minimum of water and allow to rest at room temperature for ½ hour.

2. Grease tartlet tins and line with the pastry, which may need to be patched as it is very short. Chill for ½ hour, then bake blind in a hot oven at 230c, Gas 8, 450f for about 10 minutes.

3. Meanwhile in a wide pan dissolve the sugar in the water, add the elderflower heads or cordial and poach the gooseberries until tender, but still retaining their shape. Drain off the syrup and let it cool, before whisking into the cream with the sugar.

4. Fill the tartlets with the gooseberries and spoon over the whipped cream.

5. Bake at 180c, Gas 4, 350f for about 20 minutes. Serve just warm with home-made ice cream.

Honey Bara Brith

by Mariana Cooper, from New Quay Honey Farm.

The quality of the honey used greatly affects the flavour of the bara brith. We use our own pure Welsh honey, which I don't believe can be beaten for flavour.

350g (12oz) self-raising flour

350g (12oz) dried mixed fruit

1 tablespoon water

200g (7 oz) honey

200ml (7fl oz) cold tea

1 egg

1 teaspoon mixed spice

honey to glaze

1. Soak the fruit in the cold tea, preferably overnight.

2. Add the rest of the ingredients and mix well.

3. Tip the mixture into a greased and floured 1 k (2lb 4oz) loaf tin and bake for 1 to 1¼ hours at 180c, Gas 4, 350f.

4. Brush with honey to glaze while still hot.

Rhubarb and Ginger Mock Brulee

by Lyn Jenkins,
Cyfie Farm,
Llanfyllin.

I find this is a most popular dessert with visitors. During the summer I use different fruit for the base, and gooseberries or greengages are particular good.

675g (1½lb) rhubarb, chopped

175-225g (6-8oz) granulated sugar

1½ teaspoons ground ginger

small amount of red food colouring

450g (1 lb) Greek-style yoghurt (Rachel's Dairy)

250 ml (9 fl oz) double cream

½ tablespoon caster sugar

½ tablespoon demerara sugar.

1. Cook the rhubarb with the ground ginger and sugar until tender. Stir in the colouring, and leave to cool, then chill well in the fridge.

2. Whisk the cream until thick. Fold in the yoghurt and caster sugar.

3. Spoon the cooled rhubarb into the wine glasses until ²/₃ full. Spoon the yogurt and cream mixture on top so that is is well heaped. Sprinkle brown sugar on top.

4. Place in the fridge for a further 15 minutes until the sugar has a caramelised appearance.

Tidbits

We asked the winners of the 1996 Taste of Wales Awards what inspired them to achieve their goals

Lynda Kettle, Ty'n Rhos, winner of the Best Restaurant award

"That was a wonderful meal!" Those words, often heard over the last 26 years, still send a ripple of absolute pleasure down my spine.

Wales, our adopted home, has provided the backdrop and ingredients for my love affair with good food, good eating and the good friends I have made through this common passion.

During the early years at Ty'n Rhos it was sheer joy to see the healthy bloom on the young cattle as they grazed the lush spring grass, to see and smell the almost custard-like milk from our Jersey cows and to taste the rich cream simply served with home-grown strawberries. Inspiration would be drawn from the evocative smell of elderflowers on a dewy morning and later, in the kitchen, combining a freshly-picked head or two with gooseberries – a true marriage in heaven. Working days were long but no matter the exhaustion, enthusiasm to cook would be refreshed by the sight of wonderful spring lamb, well-hung beef, freshly-caught fish and tasty farmhouse cheese.

I am now indebted to a young team in the kitchen who have brought their own identity to many of the dishes yet share my enthusiasm and philosophy on food. I am also deeply grateful to my local suppliers who put up with my finicky ways and endeavour to supply the best.

Awards and accolades are always a thrill to receive, but for me the greatest reward is to see the look of total satisfaction on the face of a contented diner.

Andrew Hetherrington, Fairyhill, winner of the Best Hotel award

'The philosophy of Fairyhill is simple: genuine hospitality, to make everybody feel that they are the most important customer, and to make every guest wish to return.

A very famous international grouping of independent hotels and restaurants trades by offering the Five Cs: courtesy, calm, comfort, character, cuisine . . . by adding Croeso, this becomes a very useful listing to remind us of our objectives.

Working in such an idyllic location, we naturally wish to connect the region with the food we serve. The cooking at Fairyhill aims to achieve clarity and we believe that the central ingredient provides the defining flavour; the sauce and garnishes should add to this, not detract from it. The Gower Peninsula provides us with excellent produce such as world-famous Penclawdd cockles and laverbread, excellent fish and meat, vegetables and herbs that are grown both in our own gardens and by a local enthusiast. Samphire in season comes from the local marshes, and from further afield, excellent Welsh cheese and dairy produce.

With such an abundance of good ingredients the thought most often in our minds is not what shall we cook, but how shall we cook it.

Nesta Thomas, Lower Haythog Farm, winner of the the Farmhouse award.

I have been welcoming visitors to our home for many years. They travel from far and near, returning year after year, to enjoy the natural beauty of our country as well as the warmth of the welcome and the variety of cooking we offer.

Local produce plays a major part in my menu planning. Home-produced Welsh lamb, Welsh Black beef and pork are readily available, with fish, honey and cheeses, plus various dairy products close to hand; I am also able to offer home-grown vegetables, freshly picked, served within hours to the visitors. Preserves and chutneys are all home-made. I am always keen to promote the wonderful choice of locally-grown products which assist me in making interesting and creative menus. During the quieter winter months I work on new ideas for menus which will combine well with the ambience and house-party atmosphere of our business. It certainly seems to work, for our visitors just keep coming back!

Robert Allen, winner of the Best Bistro award.

I have long tried to follow the maxim of "think globally, trade locally". Fortunately I have in my a wife a like-minded partner who is the innovative genius behind our culinary efforts. Local produce gives most flavour and greatest freshness especially when linked into the known strengths of the area you are trading in – Gower cockles, Carmarthen cheeses, Pembroke dairy products etc. Wales has many fine foods coming from producers who often follow the same maxim and many of our clients support our business for the same reason.

Also

When a business becomes successful and you are keeping up with the daily demands of looking after today's customers, you can lose sight of those who have contributed to that success. We keep a register of regulars and even though the reservation book is full for the next few weeks, there will always be a few seats kept free to the very last moment, just in case our most loyal customers want to pop in. Of course, the list can also be used to promote special events during the year.

Margaret Smyth, winner of the Radio 4 Food Programme Best Farmhouse award

I grow organically nearly all of my vegetables and salad stuffs throughout the year along with much of my fruit. My baby carrots crop very well in window boxes . . .

I am happy to serve my guests breakfast at any time (in exceptional circumstances I have produced it at 4am and 7pm), but I do like to know approximately when they want dinner. It is annoying if they go off for the day without giving me a time as, you see, I have to go out and collect the vegetables and herbs and salad things an hour before they are prepared."

A French visitor from Paris

"I shall come back to Wales, if only for the cheeses" –
overhead by Fred Whowell at Goetre Isaf, Bangor

The Gastronomic Desert
From one who survived!

In 1981 when I opened my little restaurant in Harlech there were puzzlingly few establishments in North and Mid Wales offering good cooking of really fresh ingredients. This was especially evident in the use of fish. I was full of enthusiasm and bravado: I thought that I could do better. But I was to have a rude awakening!

Consistent quality in meat seemed impossible to find – the produce was there but not the required hanging. I was reduced to ordering beef from Scotland, sent by post. Good fresh fruit and vegetables were not available. I was forced to drive 30 odd miles to Bangor to obtain goods of tolerable quality. Cheese (the Welsh ones were still in their infancy) came by post from Paxton, Whitfield in London or from Patrick Rance in Berkshire. During my first year I had to drive to a car park in Dolgellau to meet a delivery of wine from a distinguished Shropshire supplier who declined to come any nearer to Harlech.

Fish was frozen. I was close to despair until one day a rather battered old man wearing a worn Guernsey, brine-soaked trousers and muddy shoes strolled into my kitchen, sat down and lit a cigarette. He smelt so strongly and deliciously of fish that I forgot to rebuke him for smoking and offered him a drink. He had the first of hundreds of large Pernods. He brought fish just an hour or so from the sea. He lifted my spirits and occasionally aroused my ire. I never knew when he would arrive or with what. He brought brill, sole, turbot, salmon, sea trout, bass, squid, langoustines, occasionally John Dory or halibut, lobsters and crab. He taught me how to deal with sacks of king scallops fat as fishy tangerines, and the succulent little queenies. The man was Frank Mills; now a much missed friend drinking Pernods and telling fishy stories in heaven, I have no doubt.

A little later a local man started collecting lobsters in Cardigan Bay, bringing them to me daily when the weather permitted, and I would look forward to the annual visits of the licensed netters who, during the runs, arrived early each morning with local salmon and sea trout.

Poultry effectively did not exist. Here the great Abergavenny firm of Vin Sullivan came to the rescue and also supplemented Frank's erratic fish supply. The goods came overnight by rail to Bangor and then to Harlech by taxi!

Over the next few years other restaurants joined me in my search. The demand did create a supply, tentative at first but stronger as the years went by. A delivery service of reliable fruit and vegetables began from Bangor. A local butcher hung meat specially for us. Fish and smoked products were delivered from Llandudno and a good friend, Tony Hallet, brought wonderful Welsh cheeses, farmhouse butter, thick cream from Anglesey and even hand-made chocolates.

Those of us who find joy in food are bound to share that pleasure with others, and progress will continue to be made. In this book you can see how far we have come in Wales, and I firmly believe that *The Red Book* – our own Welsh guide to eating well in Wales – can be a great force for maintaining and raising standards here.

Ken Goody

"A Chief Inspector's Cry"

By Martin Greaves

Had I been asked ten years ago to review the best places to eat in Wales, I would most probably have declined the offer!

However, like so much of Britain, Wales has seen a growing improvement in culinary terms over the past decade, but it was with a sense of some surprise that earlier this year I came into contact with so many providers of really worthy good food.

At the beginning, preparation for The Red Book began quite gently, but by mid-May I urgently needed help with the influx of entries. A team of experts now began to exchange ideas and I received reports of great perception and wit about so many new jewels in Wales's crown. We were in contact with the cooks and hotel keepers who enthused about the raw ingredients which they grew or sourced locally and put to the best use in their cooking. The quality of locally-grown organic produce, the best meats from native Welsh herds, the ever-growing range of local cheese and fish from wherever it was caught – all these ingredients inspired our chefs. They showed a new found self-confidence in the high quality of Welsh produce available today and in their own ability to cook it well.

It was not all easy going, though. As individuals, and also as a team, we have anguished over uninventive menus, unschooled service and uninspired food, often in surroundings we felt were unacceptable to discerning eaters-out. It is heart-rending for us to judge that a minimum standard of competence hasn't been attained in such instances and we must, if challenged, be prepared to back this up with a consultation based on the inspector's summary. Our desire is for proprietors to take our findings to heart, and follow them up with improvements so marked as to make it imperative that we review them again.

As a team we have not set out to criticise where usefully we can encourage, nor to carp where we would rather be constructive, nor have we wilfully sat in judgment on our peers. Our mutual ambition is to see good food in Wales become excellent, and the less good to become better.

Snippets gathered by the team...

- We quickly discovered that the chef here had much in common with our inspector – they both write a good deal better than they can cook!
- Were management to spend as much time managing as they do in organising their own time off, this would surely be a better run hotel.
- Home-made fudge could not take away the taste of the coffee so foul that I just had to order it again at breakfast. It was worse, and I've retired to my room for report-writing and N**c*fe.
- The menu's a bit pretentiously wordy, don't you think? "What are deep-fried string potatoes?" we asked. "Chips", she replied.
- A "specially-made sauce" actually came from a cheap bottle and was so acidic it ruined not only the few decent bits of avocado and prawns, but my half bottle of Fleurie and the rest of the meal as well.
- This is not a case of an establishment that serves bad food wittingly or unwittingly; it's simply that "my clients wouldn't know what to do with a sauce boat if you gave them one".....

Janets Cake Studio

Celebration Cake Specialist
4a/b Heol-y-Deri, Rhiwbina, Cardiff, CF4 6HA
Tel: 01222 616556

Unique and beautiful cakes with many designs to choose from.
Personal attention given to all our customers.
We also specialise in hand-made chocolates under the name of

Glamorgan Chocolates

Why not pay us a visit

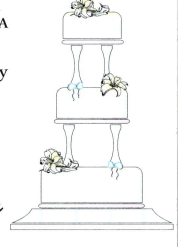

THE WELSH BAKERY

Suppliers of Fresh Traditional Bakery Products

....

Crusty Bread, Cakes and Pies

....

Celebration Cakes made to order

....

Extensive Range of Takeaway Rolls & Sandwiches

....

Open 6 days; 8.30am - 6pm

45 Old Bridge	16 Priory Street
Haverfordwest	Milford Haven
Tel: 01437 762981	Tel: 01646 695183

Unit 2,
Pencader Road,
Llandysul,
Ceredigion, SA44 4AE
Tel/Fax: 01559 363468
Partners:
Kees Huysmans
and
Ans Brouwer

Popty Bach

meaning
Little Bakehouse in the Countryside

For cakes and bread made the traditional way, down on the farm.

Tel:- 01559 362335

Or why not visit our Tea Room at The National Trust's Newton House, Llandeilo

Experience the true taste of fresh bread

Photograph courtesy of Wales Tourist Board

With the hustle and bustle of life today, very few of us have time to bake, but that doesn't mean we have to miss out on the true taste of freshly baked breads and pastries.

Flavours that cannot be matched, in this pre packed world.

At Fedwen Bakery we are busy six days a week from 7.30am to 5pm baking a wide range of delicious breads and pastries.

For the health conscious we have a selection of brown, rye, granary and wholemeal breads.

For those who like to indulge themselves our selection of pastries taste every bit as good as they look.

Daily deliveries to the catering industry.

Fedwen Bakery
49 King Street, Carmarthen
Tel & Fax: 01267 236578

The World's Finest Foods
G.COSTA & COMPANY LIMITED

Long established importer and manufacturer of speciality fine foods. Brands included in a wide selection of products are Blue Dragon, Zest Foods, Pogen Krisprolls, Skippy Peanut Butter, Celestial Herbal Teas, Conimex, Casa Fiesta, Curry Club, Lensi Pasta.

Prince of Wales Industrial Estate, Abercarn, Gwent. NP1 5AR.
Tel: 01495 244721
Fax: 01495 244626

PENCARREG
Soft creamy, Brie-style cheese
PENCARREG BLUE
Delicious, full fat, blue-veined cheese
Available nationally or direct from the company
WELSH ORGANIC FOODS,
LAMPETER, CEREDIGION
Telephone: 01570 422772

The Pumpkin Shed

For the best *Organic Vegetables, Fresh Herbs & Fruit in box scheme*

Small bag £6 per week.
Fruit bag only £6 per week.
Large bag £10 per week.

Cartref, Rhodiad - y - Brenin, St David's

Tel: - 01437 721949

Farm House Cheese Makers

Using milk from our own cows, we make the finest farmhouse Cheddar and Caerffili cheeses, which are suitable for vegetarians, available from our farm shop and specialist shops. Organic box schemes.

Caerfai Farm,
St Davids,
Haverfordwest,
Pembrokeshire

Telephone
01437 720548

GREENMEADOW MUSHROOMS

Bush Lane, Temple Bar Road, Kilgetty

01834 813190

FRESH PICKED MUSHROOMS DAILY & MUSHROOM COMPOST

GREAT TYRMYNACH FARM PYO

Pick Your Own and Ready Picked Fruit From June - August

orders for Asparagus Approx mid April

Great Tyrmynach Farm
Raglan NP5 2JP   Tel: 01291 690470

The Original Welsh Pantry Company

A Tradition of Quality

Welsh Pantry has over 20 years experience in supplying the retail trade with the finest range of gifts from Wales for holiday makers to enjoy here and at home including mouth-watering honeys, liqueur preserves, confectionery, biscuits, rock and novelties.

From the evocative Welsh scenes on the packaging to the sweet taste of the contents we know you will be delighted with what we can offer you.

**Marian Mawr,
Dolellau, Gwynedd,
Wales. LL40 1UU**

**Telephone:
(01341) 423962**

**Facsimile:
(01341) 422198**

B.H.C.
(Honey Suppliers) Ltd.

For a wide selection of honey.
Honey with various nuts
and dried fruits.
Spreads and mustards.

**Also introducing our award
winning Summerfruits
with honey.**

Telephone
01874 622335

or write to **Anne Preece**
at Unit 3, Ffrwdgrech Industrial Estate,
Brecon LD3 8LA

Welsh Lady

*Finest
Quality
Preserves
for the
connoisseur.*

*Exciting and unusual
varieties available throughout Wales
as a gift or to treat yourself*

Welsh Lady specialises in the Contract
Packing of Preserves, Jellies,
Chutneys, Mustards and Curds.

Contact Dio Jones by

Tel: 01766 810496

or Fax: 01766 810067
at Bryn, Y Ffôr, PWLLHELI,
Gwynedd, LL53 6RL.

Colin Davies

7 The Precinct. Killay.
Tel: 01792 290114

Welsh Lamb, Beef and Pork.
Cooked Meats our Speciality
Try our own dry cured bacon

Retail Butcher of the Year 1991
Meatex Meatmaster 1992
Welsh Lamb Display Champion 1992/95

Quality is not expensive it's priceless

PEPPERCORN
COOKWARE SPECIALISTS
5 KING STREET, LLANDEILO,
DYFED SA19 6BA.
Telephone: 01558 822410. Fax: 01558 824228

Cook Well - Eat Well

Top Quality Kitchen Equipment

Gadgets Galore

Catering for the Basic Cook or The Hotel Chef

CHRISTOPHER and
GLORIA VAUGHAN-ROBERTS

GRAIG FARM
AWARD-WINNING
FREE-RANGE
ORGANIC MEATS

From the heart of mid-Wales, we offer probably the widest range of organic and additive-free meats in the country, all grown to the highest welfare standards & without additives. All the usual meats, plus our specialities such as Welsh mountain mutton, dry-cured bacon & ham, fish from the un-polluted waters of St Helena in the south Atlantic, hand-made pies and pastries, etc.

Available from our farm shop, selected retail outlets or mail order.

**Graig Farm, Dolau,
Llandrindod Wells, Powys LD1 5TL
Tel: 01597 851655 Fax: 01597 851991
e-mail : sales@graigfarm.co.uk
http://www.graigfarm.co.uk**

The Welsh Venison Centre

Purveyors of quality fine Welsh meats, farm raised Venison - Beef - Lamb - Pork - Poultry & Game

Quality, tenderness and taste. Our Venison is the hallmark of top quality.

This Venison is guaranteed to be consistently tasty, tender and easy to cook.

Our Venison is full of natural goodness, No artificial means or growth promoters are used in the feed of the animals, it is a naturally farmed product.

Suppliers to hotels, restaurants, pubs and private trade catered for.

Mail order available

Haunch Roast

Venison

Please contact:
David Morgan or Lyndon Gerrish
Tel: (01874) 730929
Fax: (01874) 730566
WELSH VENISON CENTRE,
Middlewood Farm, Bwlch, Brecon,
Powys, LD3 7HQ

WELSH BROS.

(Butchers) Ltd.

We offer a quality personal service to Hotels, Pubs, Restaurants, Schools and Colleges etc.

We are a family business established over 30 years.
Welsh Lamb our speciality

Refrigerated deliveries of meat & poulty

Tel: (01633) 27 33 44 Fax: (01633) 27 88 44
Unit 31 Queensway Meadows, Newport, South Wales NP9 0SQ

caldey island

A range of delicious products from Caldey Island.

- Chocolate • Shortbread • Clotted Cream
- Yoghurt • Dairy Ice Cream • Cheese

Also available from Caldey Island Shop, Quay Hill, Tenby. Tel 01834 842296

Visits to Caldey Island:
BOATS FROM TENBY HARBOUR
Easter to early October. Mon-Fri from 10am.
Also
Saturdays in June, July & August.
Phone: 01834 844453/842879/842296

Established 1800

○ **FISHMONGERS**
○ **POULTERERS**
○ **GAME DEALERS**

Specialist Suppliers to the Catering Trade

Tel: 01222 229201
Fax: 01222 383303

Central Market, Cardiff, CF1 2AU

 # Oneida Fish
David Moore

For all your quality shellfish ask for Oneidia!

Our fish are held live in vivier tanks and are available all year round

❖ Lobsters
❖ Brown Crab
❖ Spiders ❖ Velvet Crabs
❖ Crawfish etc

For further information
Tel:- 01646 600220
Fax:- 01646 602240
**Oneida Viviers Brunel Quay,
Neyland, Pembrokeshire SA73 1PY**

TOP DRAWER
two
A joy for all food lovers.

We make our own pasta, salads, pattisserie, and specialise in Welsh farmhouse cheeses; a variety of breads are baked daily.
Plus of course there is lots more.

30 High Street Brecon.
Tel Brecon 622601

WENDY BRANDON
Handmade Preserves

Voted Best Jam & Preserve maker 1996/97
Over 100 different preserves made by hand at our restored 18th century mill.
Open all year - *visitors welcome*
Weekdays - 9am - 5pm ❖ Saturday 9am - 1pm
all other times by arrangement

Felin Wen, Boncath, Pembrokeshire
Tel 01239 841568

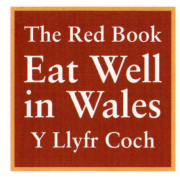

Entry Application for the 1999 Millennium Edition

Apply to: *The Red Book*, Glebe Farm, St Andrews Major, Cardiff, CF64 4HD

Establishment ....
(block capitals please)

Address: ....

....

....Post Code: ....

Tel: ....Fax: ....

Name: ....Position: ....

Please enter the above as an applicant for entry into *The Red Book*, Millennium Edition, in the following category (tick one only!)

    A Hotel / Restaurant / Inn with accommodation ❏
    B Restaurant / Inn / Pub without accommodation ❏
    C Guest House / Farmhouse with accommodation ❏
    D Bistro / Cafe / Tearoom ❏

(Establishments with an existing entry need not re-apply)

All entrants will be mailed a questionnaire requesting further details of accommodation, room rates, meal prices and opening hours in due course.

The Red Book will continue to highlight quality cooking using fresh local ingredients, and all entries to the guide will be by inspection only.

Please return your application form no later than St David's Day, 1st March 1998. Mark your diary now!

We want 1999 to hear from you

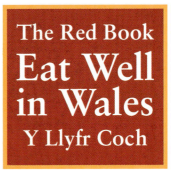

**The Red Book
Eat Well
in Wales
Y Llyfr Coch**

Comments on establishments listed and your recommendations for new entries for The Red Book, Millennium Edition, will be welcomed.

Send to: *The Red Book*, Glebe Farm, St Andrews Major, Cardiff, CF64 4HD

Name of Establishment(s) ....

Comments/Recommendations ....

....

....

....

....

....

....

....

....

....

Please Complete

Name: ....

Address: ....

....

....Postcode: ....

Date: .... Signature: ....

Order Form

Please send _____ Copy/ies of *The Red Book*, Millennium Edition, at issue price of £10 incl P&P. (for addresses in Europe add £1.50, North America £2.50)

I enclose cheque/postal order for £_____   (Cheques payable to Gilli Davies Ltd)

John Tudor & Son

Contract & Catering Butcher

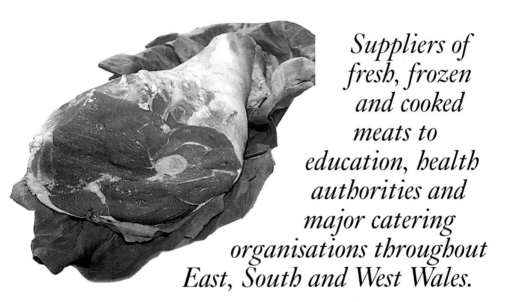

Suppliers of fresh, frozen and cooked meats to education, health authorities and major catering organisations throughout East, South and West Wales.

A member of the Federation of Fresh Meat Wholesalers.

Tel 01656 665127
Fax 01656 652780

15 Ogmore Crescent Industrial Estate, Bridgend, CF31 3TE

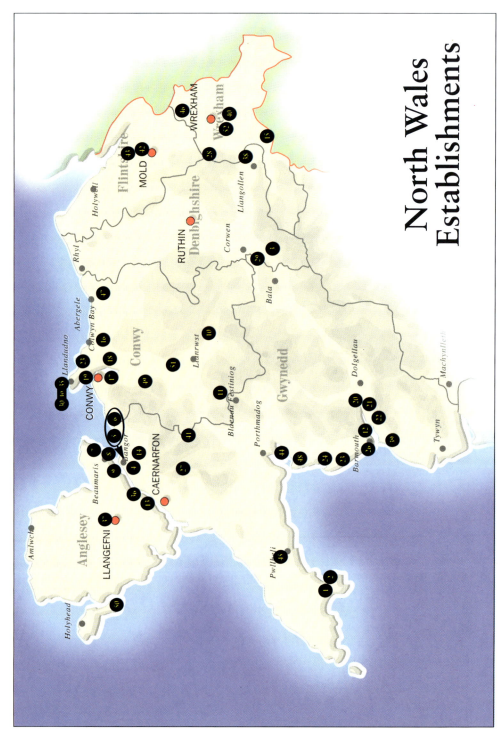

North Wales Establishments

Mid Wales Establishments

The numbers in circles 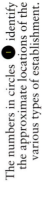 identify the approximate locations of the various types of establishment.

Whilst these maps are designed to guide you along your gastronomic tour of Wales, we respectfully advise you to check the exact whereabouts of the individual establishments, using a road atlas as guidance.

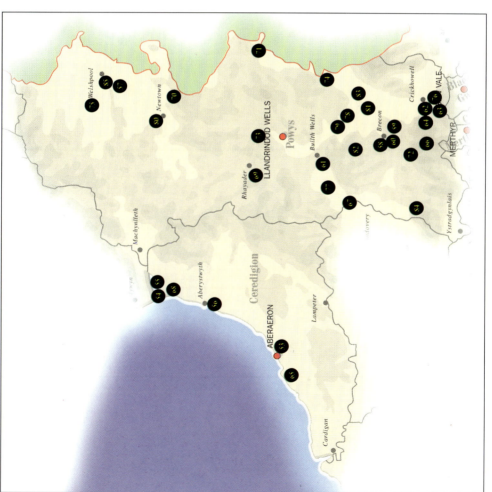

South & West Wales Establishments

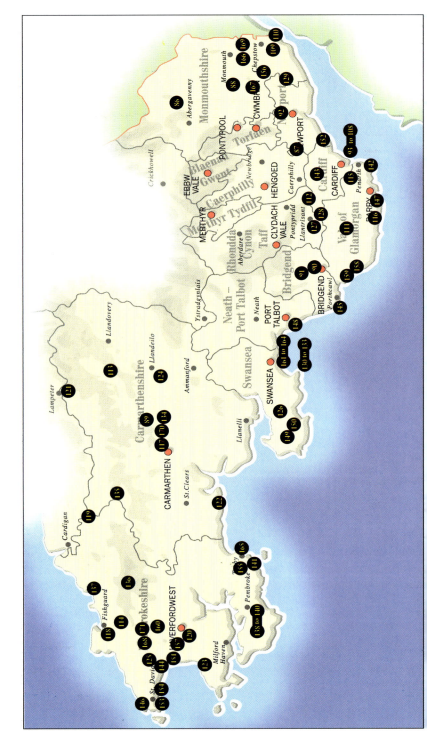

Index of Establisments

Name	Page
Aberavon Beach Hotel, Port Talbot	141
Allt-y-Golau Farmhouse, Felingwm Uchaf	122
Angel Hotel, Cardiff	107
Anglesey Sea Zoo, Brynsiencyn	55
Armless Dragon, Cardiff	108
Atlantic Hotel, Porthcawl	139
Beacons Guest House, Brecon	84
Bear Hotel, Crickhowell	87
Beaufort Hotel, Chepstow	117
Belle Vue Royal Hotel, Aberystwyth	83
Benedicto's, Cardiff	108
Berthlwyd Hall, Conwy	57
Black Bear Inn, Bettws Newydd	104
Blue Anchor Inn, East Aberthaw	121
Bodidris Hall, Llandegla	64
Bodysgallen Hall, Llandudno	66
Bontddu Hall, Bontddu	54
Borth Youth Hostel	157/8
Bramley's Tea Room, St Florence	146
La Braseria, Swansea	149
La Brasserie, Cardiff	109
Brecon Beacons Mountain Centre, Libanus	93
Broad Haven Youth Hostel	157/8
Bryn Gwynant Youth Hostel	157/8
Bryn Howel Hotel, Llangollen	71
Bryngarw House, Brynmenin	106
Buffs Restuarant, Cardiff	109
Bulkeley Hotel, Beaumaris	51
Bush House of Usk, Usk	153
Caer Beris Manor, Builth Wells	86
Caesar's Arms, Creigiau	119
Cafe Nicoise, Colwyn Bay	56
Canadian Muffin Company, Cardiff	110
Caprice, Penarth	137
Cardiff Bay Hotel, Cardiff	111
Carlton House, Llanwrtyd Wells	97
Le Cassoulet, Cardiff	111
Castle Coaching Inn, Trecastle	101
Castle Cottage, Harlech	62
Castle of Brecon Hotel, Brecon	85
Celtic Cauldron, Cardiff	112
Champers, Cardiff	113
Chandlers, Trefriw	79
Chirk Castle Tearoom, Chirk	56
Churtons, Rossett	76
Cilthriew, Kerry	92
Cnapan, Newport, Pembrokeshire	134
Copthorne Hotel, Cardiff	113
Cors, Laugharne	125
Cross Lanes Country Hotel, Marchwiel	72
Crown at Whitebrook, Whitebrook	155
Cyfie Farm, Llanfyllin	95
De Courcey's, Pentyrch	138
Dolmelynllyn Hall, Dolgellau	59
Dremddu Fawr, Lampeter	124
Dylanwad Da, Dolgellau	60
Egerton Grey, Porthkerry	141
Elan Valley Hotel, Elan Valley	91
Elm Tree, St Brides Wentloog	144
Emlyn Arms, Newcastle Emlyn	133
Empire Hotel, Llandudno	66
Epperstone Hotel, Llandudno	67
Erddig Restaurant, Wrexham	80
Fairyhill, Reynoldston	142
Fanny's, Llandeilo	126
Four Seasons Restaurant, Nantgaredig	132
Flolics, Southerndown	147
George's Cafe Bar & Restaurant, Haverfordwest	124
Gilby's Restaurant, Cardiff	114
Gio's Restaurants, Cardiff	114
Glanrannell Park Hotel, Crugybar	119
Glasfryn Guest House, Brechfa	104
Gliffaes Country House Hotel, Crickhowell	87
Goetre Isaf Farmhouse, Bangor	49
Griffin Inn, Llyswen	97
Guidfa House, Llandrindod Wells	94
Harbour Lights, Porthgain	140
Harry Ramsden's, Cardiff	115
Henry's Coffee Shop, Pembroke	135
Herbs Cookshop, Bangor	49
High Tide Cafe, Mumbles	130
Hilcrest House Hotel, Mumbles	131
Hilton Court Garden Tearoom, Roch	143
Hive on the Quay, Aberaeron	81
Huntsman, Dinas Powys	121
Junction 28, Bassaleg	103

King Arthur Hotel, Reynoldston	143
Kinmel Arms, St George	77
Left Bank, Pembroke	136
Lion Hotel, Berriew	83
Llanberis Youth Hostel	157/8
Llanerchyndda Farm, Cynghordy	90
Llangoed Hall, Llyswen	98
Llangollen Youth Hostel	157/8
Llwyn-y-Celin Youth Hostel	157/8
Llwyndu Farmhouse, Llanaber	63
Lochmeyler Farm, Llandeloy	127
Lodge, Tal-y-Bont	78
Lower Haythog, Spittal	149
Maes-y-Neuadd Hotel, Talsarnau	77
Manorbier Youth Hostel	157/8
Martin's Restaurant, Llandudno	68
Martin's Bistro, Bridgend	105
Milebrook House, Knighton	93
Miners Arms, Blaenau Ffestiniog	53
Le Monde, Cardiff	116
Morgan's Brasserie, St Davids	144
Museum of Welsh Life, Cardiff	116
Nant Ddu Lodge Hotel, Cwm Taff	89
Nantyffin Cider Mill, Crickhowell	88
New Quay Honey Farm, Cross Inn	89
Norton House Hotel, Mumbles	131
Number One, Swansea	151
Off the Beeton Track, Cowbridge	118
Old Rectory, Conwy	58
Old Stable Tea Shop, Southerndown	148
PA's Wine Bar, Mumbles	132
Pale Hall, Llandderfel, Bala	48
Pantgwyn Farm, Whitemill	155
Paysanne Restaurant, Deganwy	58
Pen-y-Gwryd Hotel, Nant Gwynant	73
Penally Abbey, Penally	137
Penbontbren Farm Hotel, Glynarthen	123
Penhelig Arms Hotel, Aberdovey	81
Penmaenuchaf Hall, Dolgellau	60
Penrhyn Castle Tearoom, Bangor	50
Pentre Bach, Llwyngwril	72
Penycwm Youth Hostel	157/8
Plantagenet House, Tenby	152
Plas Bodegroes, Pwllheli	76
Plas Cafe & Restaurant, Harlech	62
Plas Cichle, Beaumaris	51
Plas Newydd Tearoom, Llanfairpwll	70
Plas Penhelig Country House, Aberdovey	82
Porth Tocyn Hotel, Abersoch	47
Portmeirion Hotel, Portmeirion	75
Powis Castle Restaurant, Welshpool	102
Priory Hotel, Caerleon	106
Queen's Head Inn, Glanwydden	61
Ramsey House, St Davids	145
Red Lion Inn, Llanfihangel-nant-Melan	95
Richard's Bistro, Llandudno	68
Riverside Hotel, Abersoch	47
Seland Newydd, Pwllgloyw	100
Snowdon Ranger Youth Hostel	157/8
Soughton Hall, Northop	74
St Tudno Hotel, Llandudno	69
Stables Restaurant, Northop	74
Stone Hall, Welsh Hook	154
Tan-y-Foel Country House, Betws-y-Coed	53
Tates at Tafarn Newydd, New Inn	134
Three Cocks Hotel, Three Cocks	101
Three Main Street, Fishguard	122
La Trattoria, Llantrisant	128
Tre Ysgawen Hall, Llangefni	70
Trearddur Bay Hotel, Trearddur Bay	79
Tredegar Arms, Shirenewton	146
Tregynon Farmhouse Hotel, Cwm Gwaun	120
Ty Croeso Hotel, Llangattock	96
Ty Llen Restaurant, Swansea	150
Ty'n Rhos Country House, Caernarfon	55
Tyddyn Llan, Llandrillo	65
Upper Trewalkin Farm, Pengenffordd	99
Victorian Conservatory, Simpson's Cross	147
Village Green, Trellech	153
Walnut Tree Inn, Abergavenny	103
Waterfront Cafe & Bistro, Brecon	85
Welcome To Town Bistro & Tavern, Llanrhidian	128
Whitegates, Little Haven	126
Whitehouse, Penycwm	139
Windsor Lodge Hotel, Swansea	151
Wolfscastle Hotel, Wolfscastle	156
Woodhouse Restaurant, Pembroke	136
Woodland Tavern, Llanvair Discoed	129
Woods Bistro, Llantrisant	129
Wye Knot Restaurant, Chepstow	118
Y Bistro, Llanberis	64
Ye Olde Bull's Head Inn, Beaumaris	52
Yesterday's, Newtown	99
Ynyshir Hall, Eglwysfach	91